ESTATE PLANNING

How to Preserve Your Estate
for Your Loved Ones

A Practising Law Institute Guide

ESTATE PLANNING

How to Preserve Your Estate for Your Loved Ones

JEROME A. MANNING

Second Printing

Practising Law Institute

NEW YORK

Library of Congress Catalog Card Number: 92-062053
ISBN: 0-87224-046-0

Contents

Contents

This Book Is About . . .

This book is about living. Oh, yes, we'll talk a lot about death, but death is a part of life. So, this book is addressed to you, assuming you are a living person.

I expect that dying will be a new experience for you, an experience different from any other that you have confronted. The experience of dying is inevitable, and unlikely to be repeated. You will get only one chance at the experience. That brings me to the central point. You can approach the inevitable experience free-form, without any planning. That approach will allow your loved ones to fend for themselves. They will be challenged to make the best of what you will leave behind. Those leavings may be an utter shambles, and that would be a big challenge to your family and dear friends.

Another approach is to plan ahead, and prepare the way as best you can. But be forewarned. Planning for your death is not as easy as you may think. It takes time and energy, and it costs money. But beyond that, there are bumps ahead for you to get over. I am not referring to taxes, although they are very bumpy. I am referring to your feelings and judgments about the people closest to you. What do you want to do for them, and how do you want to do it?

Those questions will make you face issues that you may find very touchy. For example, how do you really feel about your husband or wife? Has it been a happy marriage? When you celebrate an anniversary, is it a duty or is it an event that you approach with gratitude and happiness? Your inner feelings will shape the estate plans you make for your spouse.

How about those kids of yours? Do they really care about you? Are family gatherings fun or misery? Does one child bring you joy while another brings nothing but heartache? Would you really like to divorce the lot of them? Well, you'll have to face those feelings when you're into your planning.

There are other delicate issues that you must wrestle with. You may have living parents. What part do they deserve in your plans? How about intimate friends, of whatever sex? And there may be others to consider, such as devoted colleagues and charitable organizations that have brought you satisfaction.

Facing up to all of that is why planning is not a happy ride around the block. You must confront deep feelings about your life, and some of those feelings will be provoking. There is only one way that planning can be done: take yourself by the hand and go to it. Otherwise, your passing on will end up as a real happening for family and friends whom you leave behind. Their adventure that stems from your lack of planning may be traumatic, costly, and deeply hurtful.

Would you like it if someone you had counted on left you to face an adventure like that?

Getting Acquainted

Estate planning concerns death and taxes, as you would expect. It won't be any surprise to you that both seem unavoidable, although there are major opportunities to postpone and alleviate the tax burden. We'll explore those opportunities. But estate planning is primarily about a larger subject, and that is people.

People Are Involved

The primary task in estate planning is not outwitting the government. Let there be no mistake about my point of view. Avoiding or reducing taxes is a major challenge, and deserving of time and effort. We'll devote both to that subject. The major task, however, is to create a plan that suits the people involved, with their particular problems, goals, personalities, biases, and characteristics. The Will maker (a Will is so important that estate planners capitalize the word almost without thinking) must be satisfied that his or her plan of gifts and inheritances seems right. (Incidentally, I am using the term "Will maker" rather than testator to escape the level of abstraction that sometimes creeps into the Latinate world of legalese.) The would-be beneficiaries will want empathy, fair treatment, and freedom from conflicts and manipulation. The task is large, because each person is unique, and requires patient understanding.

In the thirty-five years that I have been practicing as an estate planner and teaching law students, I have come across an endless parade of humans. I have been struck by how varied they and their wives, husbands, and children are. Some are warm, caring, sensible, and considerate. Some are artless and at peace; equanimity is their hallmark. But there are others aplenty: crass, flinty, stubborn, cold, bitchy, totally self-concerned. Some are afflicted by drugs and alcohol, or weighed down by family members who are. Some have guilty feelings about what they have done, including parking parents in nursing homes or mistreating children.

Some have painful secrets. There may be a retarded child, an abusive spouse, or a grandchild doing jail time. Some are downright nasty to those around them, and the reasons are well hidden.

And how extraordinarily angry some men and women are. If anger were a commodity, it would keep an army of traders busy. And some of those riled people want to punish family members for hurts, real or imagined.

There are individuals who are calculating master manipulators and expect to manipulate their families from the hereafter. Some revel in their ability to show their control of spouses and children. An elderly male client always was accompanied to my office by his wife, and whenever she sought to raise a question or make a comment, he told her to "shut up." And she did. But men don't monopolize the overt putdown. A woman who played with a string quartet and traveled to fascinating places was a classic scold, and more. She kept her husband in line by pointedly reminding him over and over that he had sold his prized real estate investment "too soon." Other manipulators are subtle and pull the strings coiled around their fingers while mouthing innocent banalities. I attended more than one family session with a great-grandmother who had needlepoint settees, served sherry, and moved her daughters and sons-in-law up and back like chess pieces.

With some people, their wires appear to be crossed, as if the combination of their characteristics was created in error. Conflicting aspects are presented by a personable, gregarious, charming individual who is stingy, mean-spirited, and self-promoting. One just like that, with whom I had worked, died recently. Those who eulogized him for his well-publicized community benefactions were unaware of his private skinflint nature. I knew his true self from years of exposure to it. I long had urged him, very unsuccessfully, to be generous with his millions toward children, grandchildren, and devoted business associates. In his mind a box of chocolates was sufficient to express his generosity. Whatever gifts he did bestow were prompted not by the heart, but totally by the tax opportunities that were explained to him. Depriving the government of revenue was a game he rejoiced at. A Scrooge indeed, but one who never met the ghosts.

In estate matters individuals reveal themselves at two stages. When preparing an estate plan, they demonstrate their true feelings about crucial issues. One is their own mortality. Dealing with that subject is a huge order for some perfectly rational folks. After leaping over that hurdle, individuals must confront how they truly feel for those who should be dear to them; spouses, children, grandchildren, and faithful friends. The circle of concern is sometimes wider. There are instances of Will makers who had received crucial help at earlier times from devoted cousins or other relatives, or from dedicated teachers. In their Will plan, some individuals show extraordinary generosity, and express graphically how deeply they were touched by those who gave them understanding and support. A client who was known in his industry to be demanding and difficult for any person who was a business associate proved by his Will that his reputation was misleading. He tangibly remembered those who had served him, even the lowliest of employees, and sedulously made certain that no one was overlooked.

Other individuals are forgetful, pretending to believe that they were entirely self-made. A few even have a touch of megalomania. In their calculation, nothing is owed to anyone. Any heir, even a spouse or child, is a beneficiary only because the bestower was unable to carry his or her goods along to the final resting place. I have watched men and women provide for those around them by default, and without feelings of true generosity. Sometimes the bestower's spirit is so mean that the inheritance is deliberately weighed down with inappropriate conditions and terms, simply in order to lessen its enjoyment.

The second manner in which human beings reveal themselves in the estate context occurs when they are heirs, or had expected to be. What amazing characters many of them have. And how shamelessly they exhibit their raw and dark aspirations.

I have learned how overwhelming and corrupting greed can be. In some folks it is an insatiable craving. A widow of senior years particularly comes to mind. She inherited a fortune of more than $40 million, made up of cash, works of art, marketable securities, and opulent homes, and it was not enough. The lady begrudged what had been left to others, including children of her husband's prior marriage. Another lady campaigned tirelessly for a huge inheritance, even leaving her elderly and ill husband at home while she traveled about, so that he would miss her company and his dependency would increase. Sad to say, her tactics succeeded, and her inheritance dwarfed the bequests for his children of an earlier marriage. One cannot help but surmise that these marriages were hardly made in heaven. I hasten to say that an avaricious nature is not exclusively a trait of women. I have observed the same sickness in the male animal.

Among heirs, other powerful feelings often run riot. Jealousy and rivalry abound, and won't be contained. In my experience, a standout in this was a pair of brothers, twins to boot, who had inherited a real estate fortune from their father. But their rivalry was so intense that they fought over it in court for three years, each incurring staggering legal fees, and hurling abominable abuse at each other and at each other's family. Each one, of course, told a heartrending story to his lawyer of mistreatment and lack of consideration. Sad to say, the lawyers tried, but could not persuade their clients to mend their disagreements without public warfare.

That willingness to fight in court is a sign of the current times. When I began to practice law, right after the Korean War, families were loath to scrub their laundry in full view. Disappointments and frustrations were often swallowed, particularly by inheriting children, who deferred to their parents' wishes and decisions. Will contests were rare. Often accommodations were made within families to keep matters seemly. Today, everything and everyone is fair game. Accommodations have become rare. If the world is watching, so what! Will contests abound. So do challenges brought against relatives who were serving as executors and trustees, concerning their management of estates and trusts. What spectacles do we see regularly! A mother and her own children tearing at each other over an enormous inheritance, and in full public view. Siblings scrapping over managerial decisions in the handling of a parent's estate. In one memorable estate, brother and sister, who were co-executors, were so enraged at each other that they argued over whose signature on an estate check should be the top signature. Their lawyers had to patiently evolve a signing procedure that the hate-filled siblings reluctantly subscribed to (in what order, I wasn't told).

Where does all this greed and hostility come from? I confess that it perplexes me. Oh, I am sure that among siblings, the seeds of rivalry and bitter feelings go well back to some earlier time. Maybe they threw sand at each other on a beach forty years ago, and that started it. Rivalries are occasionally due to specific events, or are intensified by them. I represented a young man who was at war with his family, and mighty displeased with the provisions for him in his late father's Will. He was particularly hostile to an older brother, and as the case moved along I discovered why. A dozen years before, when my distressed client had been a college student, he was rolling right along with good grades and a girl friend. His older brother came to the campus for a visit, was introduced to the young woman, and, lo and behold, the brother courted and married her. The loss of the lady — and her continuing presence in my client's life — were far more than he could bear.

I can only report that those base human emotions frequently spill over when inheritances are at stake. Maybe sibling rivalries should be anticipated. All of us have heard of them back to psychology 101, and we have experienced them personally or in the families of friends. But greed! How widespread and unbounded it is. How potent and controlling it can be. What prisoners it takes! Avarice suffuses many of our fellows, and maybe most.

I have observed wise parents and grandparents who understood. They made shrewd choices because of their concern for the vulnerability of their offspring. Those perceptive Will makers declined to heap more wealth on their children and grandchildren, who already were well educated and quite comfortable. Instead, the fortune was left for universities and museums and research, to enrich the lives of those in the community, and to open the doors of opportunity to the less fortunate. Ironically, the wisdom of the choice was demonstrated in some instances by the despairing cry of children who felt deprived, despite their Ferraris, fine houses, luxurious vacations, extensive wardrobes, and high living. For them, charity always began at home, no matter what.

Some would-be heirs did not understand while their forebears were alive, and will similarly fail to understand when those parents and grandparents pass on. Unhappy with their portion, they have destined themselves to be dissatisfied no matter how blessed they may appear to a bystander. As one exasperated and very wise mother observed about an older son, who was affluent and well past forty — he'd be unhappy if his inheritance were multiplied ten times over.

My view, upon which I'll expand, is that family advisers play an important part in estate planning. They may be lawyers, accountants, investment advisers, or simply avuncular types. The role of the family adviser is to listen carefully to the human facts that are told, to observe constantly, to perceive actual and potential conflicts between people, to understand the assets that are involved, to be very well informed about tax issues, and to provide guidance. The job is weighty and very big. There are no magic wands that will vanquish human foibles, no incredible solutions to reduce taxes to a sop for the government, no mighty ways to create an abundance of assets that will satisfy the needs and wishes of each family member. But much can be done.

With an adviser available for later consultation, let us begin. Bear in mind that our discussion will cover problems experienced by people at many economic levels. Estate planning is not solely for the affluent.

Will Basics

A Will passes on the assets that a person has at death. What assets? Everything that that person owns. But be careful here. Some things that you may believe you own, you do not.

Example

> Friends of yours own their home like this: "Fiona Martin and Buford Martin as joint tenants with right of survivorship." That is the way the deed reads; the same deed they received fifteen years ago when they bought the place. When Buford died, he and Fiona were separated, but still married. Buford made a Will leaving the house to their daughter, Kristin. Fiona will inherit the house because the deed gave her that right. Buford was powerless to leave the place to anyone else.

If you have been putting money aside for your son Chadwick under the Uniform Gifts to Minors Act (UGMA), or the more recently designed Uniform Transfers to Minors Act (UTMA), and you are the custodian of the fund that has been building, that money belongs to Chadwick, not to you. You cannot dispose of it at your death.

Some people have funny ideas about making a Will. They think it means that soon a drastic event will occur, even death. Forget it. I have been writing Wills for clients for more than thirty-five years. That drastic event never happened to them. They died later, when their time was up. Indeed, I have had a client or two who rewrote his or her Will at least twice each year, and they're still around. Among clients I worked for, I remember three who made it past one hundred, and currently several are at ninety or more, all having written Wills a few times.

Is a Will really needed? If you don't make one, the law steps in. You would die intestate, meaning without a Will, and the state legislature will have decided who inherits from you.

Example

> If a single person who lives in New York dies intestate, without ever having children, the parents would inherit

everything. It makes no difference that the deceased wanted six dear friends to inherit. The parents are entitled because New York law says so in that situation, when there's no Will.

Some people are fearful that making a Will plays into the hands of lawyers or of probate judges or that it attracts extra taxes. Many believe that significant amounts will be saved by creating a "living trust." As to taxes, that's pure baloney! As to the rest, we'll go over the possibilities in the chapter on Avoiding Probate (starting at page 223).

Q: When I make a Will, should I list my assets?

A: Definitely not. There's no need. Anyway, they're bound to change by the time you die, so your list wouldn't be accurate.

Q: But suppose I want to leave my car to my son.

A: Do it, but don't specify a particular car if you intend him to inherit any car you may own at your death. For example, if your will specifies the 1990 Toyota and before you died you traded it in for a Volvo, your son will get neither. Simply say in your Will: "I bequeath any car that I may own at my death to my son Keith, if he survives me."

Q: What do I do when I have very specific things that are to go to certain people, if I still have those things when I die?

A: Those you specifically list.

Example

"I bequeath my engagement ring to my daughter Kristy, if she survives me."

Example

> "I bequeath my collection of chess sets to my nephews Carter and Nolan, if both survive me, to be divided as they may agree, and if only one of those nephews survives me, I bequeath the collection to him."

Q: What happens if they disagree?

A: You make choices when you write the Will. Either let the beneficiaries figure it out, come what may, or specify that if they disagree, some third person, for example, your executor, makes the division between them.

Example

> "I bequeath my 1939 Packard to my son Carlton, if he survives me, and all other cars that I may own at my death to my daughter Sharon, if she survives me."

Example

> "I bequeath my Persian rug that is customarily kept in my living room, to my sister Leah, if she survives me."

Q: What if I give the rug to Leah next year as a present? I'm tired of it and I am thinking of buying a different Persian rug for my living room.

A: If you don't change your Will, Leah would also get the new one when you die, unless you identify the first rug in your Will more particularly, by color or design or where or when you bought it. If you make the more detailed identification, then Leah would not get the new one under your Will, but of course she'd have the first one.

Q: Suppose I want my son to have my General Electric stock? Shouldn't I specify that?

A: Let's not get carried away. That stock is not unique. Why compose your son's bequest that way? Maybe because you believe General Electric to be a good investment. But once he inherits, he wouldn't be obliged to keep it. He could sell it and go on a spree or make a down payment on a Porsche, or even give the stock to his girl friend Glenda, whom you dislike, and she could sell it. Also, you may surprise yourself and sell the General Electric during your lifetime because you fall out of love with it. Then your son would inherit zero.

Q: What's better?

A: Decide on how much you want your son to have. If that's a rather moderate part of everything you own, like $25,000, leave that particular amount for him in your Will. If the bequest for him is to be a healthy part of your estate, like one-third, then leave him that percentage.

Q: You mentioned his girl friend Glenda. I have this feeling that they will marry. Would she inherit from me if something happens to Keith before me?

A: I presume you really mean "if Keith dies before I do." Should that happen, Glenda would not inherit from you, because you didn't include her in your Will. But if Keith survives you, what he inherits outright from you he can do with as he pleases, even give it to Glenda at any time. And if Keith dies after you die, he could let Glenda inherit everything he has, including what you left to him.

Q: Can't I stop her from getting what I want Keith to have?

A: Only by not leaving Keith's inheritance to him outright. You could leave it for Keith's lifetime use, and specify who will inherit after him. But that cuts down the inheritance you are leaving Keith; it's not completely his to use. You have to choose: either Keith gets full control, or you refuse that to him in order to deprive Glenda. Which is more important to you?

After your Will disposes of specific things and leaves cash bequests, it disposes of the balance. That is commonly called the residuary estate. It comprises whatever is left after other individuals receive their inheritance of specific items or particular cash amounts, and after the expenses, debts, and taxes are paid. The residuary can be greater than you now expect if your holdings increase in value before you die. And the residuary could go the other way if your assets shrink before you die.

Example

You now own assets worth $750,000, counting everything. You make a Will that says: (1) your home, worth $250,000, to your son; (2) your jewelry, worth $15,000, to your three granddaughters to divide; (3) the sum of $5,000 to your favorite sister, Kate; (4) the residuary estate minus all estate taxes to your daughter, Nola. Nola gets what's left. Her inheritance bears all estate expenses, and any bills that come in after you die. If those bills are large, if the expenses are heavier than expected, she gets less. If you pay a hefty income tax in six months, Nola gets less. If the estate taxes are larger than expected, she gets less. But, if that stock you bought five years ago finally takes off, Nola gets more. If your aunt dies and leaves you $50,000, Nola gets more. If you are involved in a lawsuit over a business deal and collect, Nola gets more. Her inheritance is the most flexible one.

Q: Suppose I want to be sure that she gets at least $250,000, like her brother who is getting the house?

A: Then say in your Will that Nola is to receive a bequest that is equal to the value of the house when you die. Also say that Nola's bequest is to be paid before your sister or grandchildren are entitled to their inheritance. In other words, give her a priority ahead of them. In this plan, notice the critical point concerning the value of the house; that will govern the priority bequest to Nola. It should be determined in a neutral way. You could not predict it now, because market prices swing back and forth. Your Will could call for the executor to obtain an independent appraisal. An alternative is to use the figure that the tax authorities come up with in valuing the house for death tax purposes.

The executor's job must be filled. The executor manages the estate. The job usually lasts about three years. The executor's duties are described in the chapter on Trusts and Trustees (starting on page 111), in which the work of an executor and a trustee is compared. Your Will could name one or more executors. Whoever is chosen should be scrupulously honest, be willing to spend time, and be acceptable to your beneficiary. Family members deserve first consideration. Individuals and banks are likely to be considered if family members won't suffice. When more than one executor is selected, it is customary to choose at least one family member, for example, your spouse or child, to serve as one of them. But be careful. If you have two children and choose one of them, the other may feel slighted.

Feelings run high when death visits a family. A child can be easily bruised by being discriminated against when the executor is selected. In a recent estate I worked on, the deceased person named his son as executor, and directed that if the son was not serving as executor for any reason, the daughter would be executor. The Will was written in another city and I had not been consulted about the Will. I would have urged the father to name both children as executors, but my suggestion might have fallen flat. When her father died and his direction became known, the daughter was furious. She felt that although her father probably cared for her as much as for her brother, the father was nothing less than a male chauvinist, and that disturbed her greatly.

Death and Gift Taxes

Yes, Virginia, there are taxes to deal with when death occurs. They are in addition to the income taxes that you paid during your lifetime. This is not a one-tax society. Although we are taxed on our income as we earn it, we are also taxed when we spend it. The federal and local governments impose sales taxes, property taxes, excise taxes, and user fees. And we are also taxed when we transfer our accumulated income at death to our heirs.

Throughout most of this century, the federal government has levied an estate tax. States also have death taxes, sometimes called estate taxes or inheritance taxes. In fact, the federal government motivated the states to adopt those taxes. The federal Internal Revenue Code allows a credit after the federal estate tax is computed for state death taxes actually paid. That credit, therefore, cuts down what is paid to the IRS. The amount of the credit varies with the size of the taxable estate, but the point is that there is no credit if no state tax is paid.

Rather than see the feds keep all the money, all the states have adopted death taxes that are at least equal to the credit in the Internal Revenue Code. Boosters of some states — I mean you, Florida — have been known to say estates there are free of state death tax. Not! Each state collects at least the federal credit amount. Some states, for example, New York and Massachusetts, have their own ways of computing death tax, which result in state death taxes larger than the federal credit amount.

In a moment we'll look at the basics of the federal estate tax. But let's not overlook other taxes that can affect planning. There is income tax to consider, of course. One issue is, if I transfer some income-producing assets to my children, who pays the tax on the income that comes in later? Generally, the recipient of that income will. There are exceptions, which we'll discuss in the chapters on Children (starting on page 67) and on Trusts and Trustees (page 111).

There is also a gift tax. The federal government has one, and it has been in place for sixty years. In rates and many other aspects it mirrors the federal estate tax. A few states, among them Connecticut and New York, have their own gift tax. The federal government does not offer any credit against its gift tax for a similar tax that is paid to a state.

Finally, there is a tax on gifts and inheritances for grandchildren (and other beneficiaries who are young enough to be the grandchildren of the person who confers the gifts and bequests). This is the generation-skipping tax. We discuss it in the chapter on Grandchildren (starting at page 87).

The federal tax scheme is not beyond understanding. Let's first look at the gift tax.

Federal Gift Tax

A transfer of cash or property during your lifetime to someone else, or to a trust for his or her benefit, is a candidate for the gift tax. The crucial point is whether the person making the transfer has given up "dominion and control" over the property.

Example

Hubert gives his daughter $25,000 outright. That's an easy one. The gift tax applies. But maybe no tax will actually be due because there are exclusions and a very important exemption. We'll review them in chapter 1 on Tax Opportunities.

Example

Gina puts $50,000 in a trust for her five-year-old granddaughter. Gina names herself trustee. The trust document says that as things go along, the trustee may pay to the granddaughter as much of the trust fund's money and investments as the trustee decides. As Gina is the trustee, she controls the purse strings. Even though she cannot pay any trust money to herself, she has not gone far enough so that a gift has occurred for federal gift tax purposes. But save your cheers; that is not a happy resolution. Every time Gina pays any trust money for her grandchild, she has given up that much control, and a gift then occurs for gift tax purposes. The worst will come when Gina dies or resigns as trustee. That is the point when she has lost dominion and control. The entire trust fund will be in Gina's estate for estate tax purposes. If it has grown larger, the tax will be more than would have been paid at the outset if Gina had put aside the initial gift of $50,000 for her granddaughter in a trust and named someone else to be trustee.

In addition to exclusions and a major exemption from gift tax, there are important deductions. If you give $1,000, or any other amount, to charity, that is completely deductible for gift tax purposes. The same deduction is available if you give a thing to a charity, such as a painting to the local museum or a religious article to your church or synagogue.

Then there is the marital deduction, which pertains to gifts to your spouse, or in trust for your spouse's lifetime benefit. These gifts are fully deductible.

Example

Lance buys an elegant necklace for his wife SuAnn, worth $25,000. The marital deduction protects it from federal gift tax because they are married. Note that if Lance gave that to SuAnn and they were just good friends, it would be a taxable gift. There is the same unhappy result if SuAnn were Lance's daughter and the gift was occasioned by Su-Ann's birthday or marriage.

Example

Sean starts a trust for his wife Lida and puts $100,000 into the trust, naming the Security Bank as trustee. Lida will receive throughout her lifetime all the dividends, interest, and other income that the trust earns. Because they are married, the gift is completely deductible by Sean for gift tax purposes. Before you conclude that this plan presents a neat way to get around the tax, note the tax law's mighty hand. Someday, when Lida dies, the trust will be counted as part of her estate for federal estate tax purposes. The government has thought of all the angles.

Take note that the gift tax marital deduction is not at all available under these or any other examples if the wives (here, Su-Ann and Lida) were not U.S. citizens when the gifts were made. It makes no difference that they were and continue to be U.S. *residents*.

When such gifts are made, a gift tax return may have to be filed, even though an exclusion or exemption or deduction may save you from actually paying any tax. The due date for the return is April 15 of the next year. If tax is payable, it is due then.

We'll review the tax rates in chapter 1. If the tax is not paid on time, the government charges interest and might insist on a penalty. The government does not have to accept your return as you filed it. It has three years to challenge it or raise questions.

Federal Estate Tax

The federal estate tax struts on center stage when an individual dies. The entire process, from preparing the return through dealing with IRS representatives, is a happening many tax advisers, no less the general public, have had little experience with. We'll save the contest with the government for the chapter on Paying Taxes (starting on page 199). At this juncture, let's look at the makeup of the taxable estate upon which the estate tax is figured.

The starting point is to add up the entire estate before deductions are taken. That total is the gross estate for federal estate tax purposes. It includes all items that the individual owned in his or her name and would be disposed of by the deceased person's Will. So, there could be cash, stocks, bonds, real estate holdings, business interests, money owing from any source, patents, copyrights, and mineral interests. The gross estate also includes items that are easily forgotten, such as cars, boats, furniture, jewelry, china, antiques, works of art, collections of stamps and guns and porcelains, and what not. If any of these holdings are community property (discussed on pages 32–33 and 43–44), when death comes only one-half of the value of the assets is in the gross estate.

Then there are other parts of the gross estate that you may not readily think of. Some of these would not be disposed of by the person's Will, because the decedent did not own them in his or her name.

Example

> Holding property in joint names with someone else will not deter the government. I am talking about cash or securities or real estate in the name of the deceased and someone else, with that someone else inheriting the entire property under the deed or via bank or brokerage listing as the surviving joint owner. If the other person who outlasts the deceased is his or her spouse, who is a citizen, one-half of the value is included in the gross estate. If that someone else is a different party, say, a child, or if the someone else is a noncitizen spouse, the entire value of the jointly owned property is in the decedent's gross estate except for any portion that the survivor (here the child or noncitizen spouse) can prove was acquired with funds that the survivor contributed.

Example

> Any cash or property traceable back to gifts that the deceased person had put in an account under the UGMA or UTMA when the decedent was serving at the time of death as the manager (custodian) of the account will be pulled into the decedent's gross estate.

Example

> If the decedent had created a trust for someone, and at the time of death is serving as the trustee with discretionary control of the flow of benefits from the trust, all the trust assets will be catapulted into the decedent's gross estate for estate tax purposes.

Example

> If the deceased person had been a trustee or custodian of an UGMA or UTMA account, which we just described,

and resigned the position within three years before dying, the resignation would have come too late. The assets in the trust or UGMA or UTMA account won't escape the gross estate.

Example

Any bank account or U.S. savings bond in the name of the decedent that was, by the terms of the account or bond, payable on death to someone else, is part of the decedent's gross estate. Any bank account in the name of the deceased that is in trust for someone else and becomes payable on death to that someone (a Totten trust) is also part of the gross estate.

Example

If the decedent was a participant in his or her company's pension plan, the death benefit is part of the decedent's gross estate. I'll say more about this in the chapter on Insurance and Retirement Benefits (starting on page 151).

Example

Any insurance on the decedent's life is included in his or her gross estate unless steps were taken to avoid that result. Those steps are reviewed in the chapter on Insurance and Retirement Benefits (page 151).

Example

If an individual creates a trust for his or her own lifetime benefit, whether called a living trust or by any other name, it will be completely swept into the gross estate. It makes no difference who the trustee is. The same estate tax rules will prevail as if the living trust had never been created. Surprised? You ought to know that the government can't be outflanked so easily. We'll revisit this business in the chapter on Avoiding Probate (page 223).

Once the gross estate is computed, some deductions are possible. Anything left to charity, in any amount, is fully deductible. Funeral expenses and debts of the decedent are deductible. Costs of managing the estate, including the compensation of the executor and the fees of the lawyer whom the executor uses, are deductible.

A crucial deduction concerns an inheritance left to the surviving spouse. This is the marital deduction.

Example

Marlin leaves his wife Kerry all household possessions, life insurance, and $200,000. It's all fully deductible. There would be the same answer if the cash amount were $2 trillion for Kerry. There is no dollar limit on the marital deduction.

Example

Jason leaves $100,000 in trust for his wife Michelle, who will receive all the dividends and interest and other income earned by the trust for her entire life. It's fully deductible under the estate tax marital deduction. There would be the same result if the trust were $1 billion. But if Michelle had lived with Jason and was not his wife, even if their relationship had been going on for twenty years, and even if they had children, nothing would be deductible. The marital deduction is only available to folks who were legally married to each other when death intervened.

Example

Megan and Harland live in California and everything they have is community property, including condo, cash, investments, and sailboat. Megan dies and her Will leaves everything she owns to Harland. One-half of the value of the community property is included in Megan's gross estate for estate tax purposes. As that half is left to Harland, it is fully deductible under the marital deduction. The other half of the community property was Harland's and is not involved in computing the estate tax for Megan's estate.

Example

Jointly owned assets, pension benefits, and life insurance, as well as works of art and all sorts of jewelry, pass outright at Claudine's death to her husband Wayne. All of it, no matter how valuable, would be eligible at Claudine's death for the estate tax marital deduction.

An exception to these marital deduction results would occur if the surviving spouse were not a U.S. citizen at the time of death. All is not hopeless, however. With a bit of creativity in planning, which involves a special brand of trust, the estate tax marital deduction could be obtained. That is in contrast to the gift tax marital deduction, which never can be obtained if the recipient spouse is not a U.S. citizen.

Before you conclude that the ancient institution of marriage may not be so bad as some folks say, let's look further down the road. Any inheritance that is good for the marital deduction will be part of the surviving spouse's gross estate for estate tax purposes when he or she later dies if those assets, or anything they were transformed into, are on hand when that subsequent death occurs. So the marital deduction works a deferral of estate tax until the surviving spouse dies. There is no free ride here.

The government could be frustrated in selected situations. Assume that the marital deduction was obtained when wife Isabelle died, for an inheritance of $2 million that she left to her husband Judson. After the funeral, Judson burned up the whole $2 million, and more, at the track and fancy restaurants and expensive boutiques, having a good time and seeking to impress a bevy of damsels. There would be nothing left to be taxed at Judson's passing. The government would be disinherited. But if Judson made gifts to any of his female admirers, whether in cash or by buying baubles for them, he'd be confronted by the gift tax that we looked at a few pages back. If he married one of those damsels, gifts to her after the ceremony would escape gift tax via the marital deduction.

In the case of a decedent, when all the deductions are subtracted from the gross estate, the taxable estate is known. The estate tax is then computed. The rates, and available offsets to the tax, will be explored in the next chapter.

The deadline for filing the estate tax return is nine months after the date of death. The estate tax is also due then, unless tax attributable to certain business interests is involved. That exception will be explored later in this book. If the tax is not paid at the deadline, interest will be due and penalties might be imposed.

As with the gift tax return, the government is free to question the entries in the estate tax return. The time for raising questions is three years from the due date of the return. How the government and the estate's lawyer handle the situation will be looked at in the chapter on Tax Payments (starting on page 199). There are other subjects to explore before we concern ourselves with the tax process.

CHAPTER

1

Tax Opportunities

Federal gift and estate taxes are a bugbear. Many well-informed people would be harsher, and would assert that those taxes are excessive, destructive, and horrendous. The point is, they are with us. In this era of large federal budget deficits and spiraling costs, those taxes are not likely to be swept aside or moderated, even though they do not produce impressive revenue.

I feel strongly that taxes are only part of our planning concerns. The major concerns are how best to arrange one's affairs and provide suitably for family and others who merit attention. But taxes are a cost of doing that, and therefore they deserve part of the spotlight.

The federal rates on taxable gifts and estates are rugged. I emphasize *taxable* because there are paths to nontaxable gifts and inheritances. We'll review them soon. For now, let us look at the stress created by those rates.

The following table shows the amount of tax the federal government wants when a taxable gift or estate reaches a particular size. The amount shown is what is given or left by an individual *before* using any exemptions or credits or exclusions that the individual may have. Those available offsets, and how they will be used, are the major story of this chapter.

Transfer Tax Rates

Taxable Amount of Gift or Estate	Federal Tax
$ 250,000	$70,800 plus 34% on the excess over $250,000
500,000	$155,800 plus 37% on the excess over $500,000
750,000	$248,300 plus 39% on the excess over $750,000
1,000,000	$345,800 plus 41% on the excess over $1,000,000
1,250,000	$448,300 plus 43% on the excess over $1,250,000
1,500,000	$555,800 plus 45% on the excess over $1,500,000
2,000,000	$780,800 plus 49% on the excess over $2,000,000
2,500,000	$1,025,800 plus 53% on the excess over $2,500,000
3,000,000	$1,290,800 plus 55% on the excess over $3,000,000

The upper rates of 53 percent and 55 percent are scheduled to fall back to 50 percent in 1993. Don't put money on the prospect. The reduction has been deferred twice before and is a sure bet to be postponed again.

The tax law applies those rates cumulatively. For example, if you make a taxable gift of $250,000 in 1992, the tax on that is computed under the table to be $70,800. If you make a later taxable gift in 1993 of $100,000, the tax is determined after counting the first gift. So your place in the tax table is in the slot between transfers of $250,000 and $350,000. The gift tax rate on that second gift of $100,000 will be 34 percent. If the next thing you do is die, and your taxable estate is $650,000, the estate tax is computed after taking account of the two earlier gifts. The estate's place in the tax table is in the slot between $350,000 (the sum of the two lifetime gifts) and $1 million, which is the total of all taxable transfers you made during life and at death. The estate tax would be $241,000. That is the tax on $1 million ($345,800) minus the gift taxes previously incurred on the $350,000 of gifts ($70,800 + $34,000 = $104,800).

But don't lose hope. Those taxes will be reduced by a credit that is a major help.

For the very affluent, the tax costs are more severe. For them, the gradual incline in rates is phased out if their taxable transfers by gift or inheritance are greater than $10 million. The phase-out is complete when more than about $21 million of taxable transfers have been made. Those extremely wealthy individuals face a flat federal tax of 55 percent on their taxable gifts and inheritances.

Defusing the Taxes

If someone aimed only at foiling the federal government and paying not one red cent in gift or estate taxes, the remedy is at hand. Simply leave everything to charities. The tax law dealing with lifetime gifts and inheritances has no ceiling on the deduction for charitable gifts and bequests. That contrasts with the income tax, where there is a percentage limit on the charitable deduction for income tax purposes.

In their estate planning, most people would find no solace in the available deduction for charitable giving. So we'll proceed and review how the tax toll can be alleviated while making plans for family members and others.

To begin with, the federal tax that is produced by the preceding table is levied on the transfers that the bestower makes. For lifetime gifts, the bestower is responsible for the tax. (I am using the term "bestower" for the person who bestows the assets; more narrowly, gifts have donors, trusts have grantors, and estates have testators.) For inheritances, the bestower has the opportunity to allocate the tax among the beneficiaries of the estate or have it paid off the top of the estate. We'll discuss that further in chapter 10 (page 268–71). Let's think of it for now as the burden of the bestower's estate to pay the tax.

Every person has a credit to offset some of the potential tax on gifts and inheritances that he or she would bestow. The official name for it is the unified credit. It amounts to $192,800, which blots out that much tax. The full unified credit offsets the federal tax on $600,000 of gifts or bequests. The credit first can be offset against the tax on lifetime gifts; if it is not exhausted in that use, what remains is usable against the estate tax. So, in the illustration I used of:

1992 taxable gift	$ 250,000
1993 taxable gift	100,000
Taxable estate	650,000
Total taxable transfers	$ 1,000,000

if the unified credit had never been used before 1992, it would be available to soak up the taxes to the level of $192,800. The usual way of looking at it is to measure the workings of the credit by the exemption from tax that it creates, which is on the first $600,000 of gifts and bequests. The result is that no federal gift tax has to be paid on the 1992 or 1993 taxable gifts, which aggregated $350,000. That leaves $250,000 of exemption available from the estate tax.

When the total exemption of $600,000 has been claimed in the three steps (gift of $250,000 plus gift of $100,000 plus estate of $250,000), what remains is a taxable estate of $400,000. The tax that has to be paid on that is $153,000, as follows:

Taxable Transfer	Tax	Minus Credit	Balance to IRS
$ 250,000	$ 70,800	($ 70,800)	0
$ 100,000	34,000	(34,000)	0
650,000	241,000	(88,000)	$ 153,000
$ 1,000,000	$ 345,800	($192,800)	$ 153,000

The unified credit is very important. It slashes the tax on transfers amounting to $1 million from the starting point of $345,800 to the bottom line of $153,000. As every person is entitled to the unified credit, which exempts $600,000 from tax, moderate estates are protected from serious tax erosion. More is involved. As each spouse has such a credit, the spouses together can make taxable gifts and bequests aggregating $1.2 million. That amount of exemption is meaningful.

Maximizing the Exemption

An important point that we'll explore is how best to claim the unified credit and get the most out of the exemption from tax that the credit makes possible.

In order to understand the maximum use of the unified credit, we have to take a detour and look at the marital deduction. The tax law contains a major bias in favor of marriages. Transfers between spouses, whether they be lifetime gifts or bequests in Wills, can be set up so as to be free of tax when they are created. There is no quantitative limit on this opportunity.

Q: You mean that I could give my spouse a million dollars without tax.

A: Sure. You can do it now via gift or at your death. It could be any amount, even a billion dollars if you are so fortunate.

Q: What's the catch? There has to be a catch!

A: When your spouse dies later, whatever is left of the marital gift or bequest will be subject to estate tax. The marital deduction is a deferral. No tax need be paid when the first spouse dies or when a spouse makes a gift of anything to the other spouse. But the government gets its due when your spouse dies later, or if your spouse makes taxable gifts during his or her lifetime.

Q: Suppose my spouse remarries after I'm gone?

A: If your spouse is in control of the inheritance that you left and he or she remarries, then your spouse may pass those assets on at death to the new spouse without tax, just as you had passed your assets to your spouse. Another marital deduction would apply, protecting the assets from federal estate tax. So, the deferral of estate tax

6

would continue. Of course, that move would disinherit your kids, and your accumulated assets would be channeled to someone you wouldn't have provided for. If your spouse made gifts to the new bride or groom, the marital deduction would prevent gift tax. Once again, your kids would be cut off. Keeping the government away from your assets isn't the only point that matters. If you wouldn't want your spouse to be able to endow a new husband or wife with your estate, you could use a trust to hold the inheritance that you leave for your spouse. That arrangement would deny your spouse the ability to channel your assets to someone like a new spouse. Meanwhile, you would have deferred the payment of estate tax until your spouse's death. We'll address that subject in chapter 2 (starting on page 31).

Many people who have solid marriages, or would wish to protect their spouses as fully as they can, would ordinarily be tempted to leave everything to their spouse under the marital deduction so that he or she may enjoy a tax-free inheritance. That could be done very simply, even if the bestower has an enormous estate. A two-sentence Will would suffice to gain the promised objective:

> "I, Clark Jones, declare this to be my Will, revoking all prior Wills and Codicils. I devise and bequeath all of the property that I may own at my death, real and personal and wherever it may be situated, to my wife Hillary, and I name her to be my executor, without bond."

But doing that can be a blunder. Here are reasons.

The $600,000 exemption that is created by the unified credit has not been used. You might be puzzled because the marital deduction will assure a tax-free inheritance. But remember the eventual reckoning involved in using the marital deduction: no tax when the bestowing spouse transfers the gift or bequest, but exposure to tax for the beneficiary spouse later on. That tax catch-up need not be present to the extent that the exemption is used. Here are examples.

Example

Leave the exempt amount, which is $600,000 if none of it was previously used, in trust for the surviving spouse's benefit. All the income would go to him or her, and the trustees can be authorized to use principal for the spouse for good reason. At the spouse's later death, the trust belongs to the children, or continues for their benefit.

Example

Use the trust, but provide that during the surviving spouse's life income not only can be used for him or her, but also can be used for the children and grandchildren. The trustees could be authorized to use principal for them.

Example

Leave the surviving spouse out completely in arranging the exempt amount and devote it totally to others, such as children. Their inheritance could be outright or in trust.

Under any of these alternatives, there is no federal gift or estate tax when the bestowing spouse makes the gift or bequest, and there is none either during the surviving spouse's lifetime or at his or her death. That holds true even if a trust is used as the exemption vehicle during the surviving spouse's life and by the time he or she dies the trust assets have grown in value so that they exceed the original amount of $600,000. Full protection from tax will prevail.

The person who wants the most favorable tax results for the two spousal estates should not fail to exploit the exemption. Even if the trust that the first spouse creates does not appreciate at all by the time of the second spousal death, a substantial tax saving can be realized. If we assume that the rate of tax that otherwise would apply to that $600,000 at the second spouse's death would be 40 percent, the family will save tax of $240,000 by exploiting the exemption. Just think how hard it can be to amass that much money!

Sometimes the people involved are not sure if they want to make the effort to use the exemption.

Example

> The couple is childless. When one dies, all the assets are to be devoted to the other. Neither wants to impose a trust on the spouse who turns out to be the survivor. An outright inheritance is favored. Eventually, when both spouses have died, their accumulated assets will go to nephews and nieces, or various friends. At the first spousal death, the marital deduction would protect the inheritance in full. Saving the estate tax at the second spousal death is not a real priority, as would be the case if the couple had children or grandchildren. Or, the assets that the spouses have aggregate about $600,000 at today's values. As the surviving spouse also has a unified credit available that would shelter that much capital from tax, the surviving spouse's exemption should suffice, and the exemption of the first spouse who dies would be surplus protection.

Here is an opportunity to use a device known as a disclaimer, which is synonymous with renunciation. Starting with the notion that a beneficiary cannot be forced to accept a legacy, the tax law allows anyone to turn his or her back on an inheritance without tax cost to him or her. The legacy will then be de-

9

toured to someone else, either by terms of the Will or because the state law will do the detouring. The point is that no gift tax will be imposed on the person who turned away from the legacy, if he or she acts within nine months of the death of the party who left the legacy. Timely action merely means signing the appropriate papers. So, a would-be beneficiary can actually decide within nine months whether to accept a legacy or allow it to be detoured to someone else, and no gift tax is charged to the disclaimant. If the detour would end at the front door of a person who is favored by the disclaimant, such as a child or a sibling, the journey may have a happy ending. A disclaimer can be made of some or all of a legacy, so the would-be beneficiary can choose to accept part of an inheritance and allow the rest to be detoured away.

The disclaimer law especially favors a spouse. He or she can do a written disclaimer within nine months even though the result called for by the Will is that the spouse will have financial benefits from the disclaimed legacy. For example, the Will could leave an outright legacy to a spouse and go on to say that if the spouse disclaims all or part of the legacy within nine months the disclaimed legacy will be detoured to a trust for the personal benefit of the same spouse. No other beneficiary can make a disclaimer that is free of gift tax if that same person will have any personal financial benefits from the disclaimer of the legacy.

Putting the disclaimer to work in our planning, we see that an option can be provided by the first spouse in his or her Will. The option is that the surviving spouse can, via a disclaimer, elect not to accept all of an outright inheritance, but instead allow the amount that could be exempt from estate tax to go into a trust for his or her lifetime benefit, and at the surviving spouse's later death, the trust's assets will spill over to the favored beneficiaries, who are relatives and friends. But remember that the surviving spouse must act in timely fashion by signing papers for the disclaimer within nine months of the death of the bestowing spouse. And the Will of the bestowing spouse must have prepared the way by providing that if the disclaimer is made, the disclaimed assets are to go into a trust for the surviving spouse's benefit. That trust is activated by the surviving spouse's disclaimer. If there isn't any disclaimer, the trust never happens and the outright inheritance remains in full force. The decision as to whether to save the estate tax at the second spousal death is made, therefore, by the surviving spouse.

Beyond the Exemption

Let's move away from the $600,000 exemption and discuss whether the rest of the estate ought to be devoted to the surviving spouse under the friendly wing of the marital deduction. Assume that there are offspring, either of the current marriage or of the Will maker's earlier marriage. If the first spouse who dies focuses on minimizing estate tax, then at his or her death the most that would be left for the children to inherit would be the exempt amount of $600,000. Everything else would be packed into the marital deduction inheritance, which cannot provide any benefits whatever for the children during the life of the surviving spouse. So the children must wait until the surviving spouse's death before they will be entitled to inherit anything more than the $600,000 exemption.

If the surviving spouse is a parent of the children, they might be delighted to know that their remaining parent is secure and well provided for. Their affectionate regard for that parent may be the total sum of their feelings. Having to wait to inherit may not concern them one whit. And then, that may not be the way they feel. One look at mom or dad enjoying life, cavorting, traveling with a companion of the opposite sex, spending money

If the surviving spouse wishes, he or she can make significant lifetime gifts to the children. If the spouse has the unified credit intact, he or she could make transfers up to $600,000. Further, the widow or widower can make individual annual $10,000 gifts to any number of recipients. If those gifts from the surviving spouse are on top of an inheritance for the children of $600,000 from the parent who dies, the children will be doing well, all without any payment yet of federal gift or estate tax. The same results can be had if the marital deduction inheritance is via a classic trust, which specifically permits the beneficiary spouse to make lifetime gifts to the children. The waiting game can thereby be significantly shortened, but the widow or widower's cooperation is crucial. Without lifetime gifts that he or she initiates, the wait will go on.

Notice the dynamics of this program to provide an inheritance early and generously for children. The spouse who dies first creates the plan that involves using the exemption each spouse has to swing substantial assets to the children. The plan is touched off by the death of the first spouse, when his or her unified credit is exploited for the children's benefit. But the second part of the plan depends on the assent and action of the surviving spouse. He or she decides whether to move forward with the gifts that use up that individual's unified credit and will add another $600,000 to the children's assets. In second-marriage situations, or where relationships between the children and surviving spouse are frayed, the second part of the plan cannot be counted on. Even when those negative aspects are absent, the full plan may not be implemented. More than one widow or widower has decided that the children are insufficiently attentive, or that providing them with another $600,000 may incline them to be too independent of their widowed mom or dad.

Annual Gifts

Another opportunity for tax-free transfers is available annually during each person's lifetime. This opportunity is in addition to the $600,000 exemption that is created by the unified credit.

The annual opportunity is to hand out up to $10,000 to anyone. Yes, if the mood strikes, you can walk down Main Street, or drive to the local mall, and give out $10,000 to each person you meet. It doesn't matter if you don't know their names, or never saw them before. And after you have done it in favor of every man, woman, and child who comes by, you can plan on returning in order to do it again next year, and the year after, and so on, until you expire or your supply of funds runs out.

This opportunity for giving is called the annual gift tax exclusion. Its scale is smaller than the unified credit opportunity ($10,000 compared to $600,000).

Q: How many times can I give my daughter $10,000?

A: Each and every year, without limit.

Q: In addition to using my $600,000 exemption?

A: Yes, or without using the $600,000 exemption.

Q: So I can give $10,000 to each child annually. Can I give the exemption of $600,000 to each child at least once?

A: No. The exemption of $600,000 is your personal lifetime total amount, whether you have one recipient or five dozen. The annual exclusion limit is $10,000 per person, year after year, no matter what the grand total may be. Notice that any unused part of the $600,000 exemption can be invoked against the tax at death on your estate. There is no such opportunity with the $10,000 annual exclusion.

Here is a pleasant surprise. The annual exclusion can be doubled if the giver is married and his or her spouse consents to the use of that person's privilege to make annual gifts of $10,000. If you wish to give the maximum annual amount to any person, your spouse can accommodate you by consenting, and the limit for that year is increased to $20,000. The spouse's consent does not require that any of the gift money come from your spouse. All of it can come from you.

Your spouse's consent should be shown on a gift tax return that he or she files. But that alone does not mean that any tax has to be paid.

Q: If I want to give $20,000 to my daughter, and my spouse will consent, can I give only $10,000 to my son?

A: Yes. You can give any amount to your son up to $20,000 and, if you wish, you can give him nothing.

Q: If my spouse wants to give $15,000 to someone I don't like, such as my sister-in-law Melanie, do I have to consent?

A: No, with a but. If you want to make your own gifts this year of $20,000, there must be mutual consent to any gifts for the year by either spouse. Consent is an all-or-nothing business. So, you have to consent to what your spouse does, and vice versa, in the same year, or there is no consent for any gift that year. Remember that if you consent to the $15,000 gift to Melanie none of the money need come from you.

Q: If I consent this year to my spouse's gifts, do I have to consent again next year?

A: Each year is separate.

The annual exclusion of $10,000/$20,000 can be used even if the gift is larger. The exclusion blots out the gift up to its available maximum. The exclusion is available whether the gift is made in cash or stocks or real estate or anything else.

Example

Your son Cory wants to buy a house and your spouse and you wish to help. You will give him $100,000. You may decide to give him some sixty-day U.S. Treasury bills that you own instead of cash. With your spouse's consent, $20,000 of the gift is absorbed by the annual exclusions that your spouse and you have.

Q: What happens with the balance of $80,000?

A: That balance is a taxable gift. As your spouse is consenting to the gift, half ($40,000) is treated as coming from him or her and the rest from you.

Q: Do we pay tax?

A: If each of you has enough unified credit remaining to cover that person's gift of $40,000, the credit offsets the tax. If you previously exhausted your credit by earlier gifts to which your spouse did not consent, but your spouse never used his or her own credit, you pay gift tax on $40,000, but your spouse will not pay anything due to his or her credit.

Q: My spouse died two years ago, and I am not married now. What is my limit under the annual exclusion now?

A: $10,000. If your spouse did not use up his or her unified credit during life or with an estate, that credit is not available to you. The available exemption under your unified credit would be $600,000 reduced by any use that you previously made of your credit.

When you make gifts in something other than cash or marketable securities, attention must be given to the question of value. Assume that you decide to give your daughter the interest you have in a corporation that owns a local retail business. You invested in this enterprise ten years ago, and you own 15 percent of the stock. You and your business partners feel that a reasonable value for your interest is $20,000. Your spouse will consent to the gift. Returns are filed showing the gift, with each spouse claiming the $10,000 annual exclusion on that person's return. So far so good. But the IRS may come back and assert that the gift of the 15 percent business interest to your daughter is worth $35,000. If the IRS prevails, the annual exclusions won't suffice to blot out the gift tax. Instead they do part of the job by absorbing $20,000 of the $35,000 gift. Now your spouse and you have a balance of $7,500 beyond the reach of the annual gift tax exclusion. If each spouse has enough unified credit left, they will offset the gift tax on the balance.

Remember that the annual gift opportunities may only be used once for a beneficiary in a particular year. If you are single and give your daughter Diane $10,000 for her birthday on March 12, you cannot do any more for her in the same year under the umbrella of the annual exclusion.

Tuition and Medical Expenses

During an individual's lifetime, he or she may make payments of someone else's tuition or medical expenses, and they are not regarded as taxable gifts.

Tax-free tuition payments cannot be stretched to include room, board, books, or other education-related items. Tuition can be at any recognized institution, whether it is a local nursery school or the Sorbonne.

If grandma wants to "do something" for little Kate, grandma can pay Kate's tuition and give Kate $10,000/20,000, and neither is a taxable gift.

To come under the tuition umbrella, the payment must be made to the educational institution directly. If dad creates a trust that pays tuition expense for his children, that is not within the tuition safe harbor. But if grandma creates a trust that pays a grandchild's tuition, that payment does escape the tentacles of the generation-skipping tax, which we'll review very shortly.

Similarly, medical expenses must be paid directly to the facility or person who provides the service: hospital, nursing home, doctor, nurse, or issuer of a medical policy. Again, creating a trust for these purposes is not good enough to earn the special status. But payment from a trust for a grandchild's medical expense escapes the generation-skipping tax.

A payment of tuition or medical expense enjoys freedom from gift tax no matter who the beneficiary may be: friend, relative, lover, total stranger, it matters not.

Generation-Skipping Exemption

In the chapter on "Grandchildren" (starting on page 87), the reader encounters the mysteries of the generation-skipping tax. This levy on gifts and inheritances for grandchildren is surely a jolt to many citizens. But be not disheartened. Each person has an exemption of $1 million from the wicked tax. A married pair can provide $2 million between them for their children's darlings.

For lifetime gifts, one spouse can make the entire transfer of funds or property up to a total of $2 million at one moment or over time, and the other spouse's exemption can be brought to the fore by his or her consent.

So, as with the unified credit and the annual gift tax, the exemption from generation-skipping tax attributable to a non-giving spouse can be made available for use when the bestowing spouse makes transfers.

For those who are fortunate enough to have funds or property to spare of that magnitude, lifetime gifts for grandchildren that are shielded by the combined exemptions of $2 million are a good tax plan.

The exemption is usable whether the beneficiary is your grandchild, your spouse's grandchild via another marriage, the offspring of a second cousin, or a stranger to your blood who is youthful enough to be your grandchild were you related. More will be said about this identification of grandchild-like beneficiaries in the chapter on "Grandchildren" (page 90).

As to Income Tax

Our discussion of exemptions, the annual exclusion of $10,000/20,000 from gift tax, and payments of tuition and medical expense has no relation to income tax. If you make a gift that is eligible for the $10,000/20,000 annual exclusion, that is nontaxable only for gift tax purposes. You cannot "exclude" that amount from your income tax.

If a payment is made for tuition or medical expense that is sheltered from gift tax or generation-skipping tax, that eligibility does not also bring you income tax relief. Tuition you pay for someone else is not deductible for income tax purposes. Medical expense paid for a dependent may be deductible for income tax purposes. To be a dependent, an individual must not only be within a family group, like a child, grandchild, parent, sibling, nephew, niece, or in-law, but additionally the individual must receive more than half of his or her support from the benefactor.

Bear in mind that income tax is a separate world.

Forms of Transfer

Lifetime gifts and bequests under Wills can be made in different forms. Outright to the recipient means no controlling strings are attached by the bestower. That can be very nice for the recipient.

An outright transfer by gift or bequest can be used in conjunction with the federal unified credit of $192,800, which erases gift and estate tax on $600,000 of property. An outright transfer by gift or bequest also can be used in conjunction with the $1 million exemption from the generation-skipping tax. With rare exceptions, the annual gift tax exclusion of $10,000/20,000 and an outright gift are compatible. So far, so good. Now let us focus on those tax opportunities and the use of trusts.

There are all manner of trusts. Examples of how they can be designed, how they can operate and for what ends, are explored in the chapter on "Trusts and Trustees" (starting on page 111). At this juncture we want to see what species of trusts are acceptable to grab the tax opportunities we have been inspecting.

There is no problem in using trusts and invoking the $600,000 exemption from gift and estate tax or the $1 million exemption from generation-skipping tax, either for gifts or bequests. The way is not so simple when the objective is to be eligible for the annual gift tax exclusion of $10,000/20,000. Obviously, that haven is available only for lifetime gifts, so our attention will center on lifetime transfers, and bequests won't be involved.

If you wish to put $10,000/20,000 in a trust this year, and maybe repeat the gift in the future, with each transfer eligible for the gift tax exclusion, a particular form of trust is necessary.

The tax law offers two primary alternatives from which you may choose. In one alternative, the trust terminates automatically when the beneficiary attains twenty-one years, come what may. If that form of trust is selected when the beneficiary is only a tyke, say age four, and over the ensuing years the trust grows through fortuitous investments while the beneficiary grows erratically, woe may be ahead. When the tyke blows out twenty-one birthday candles, the trust assets belong to him or her. If the individual is immature or has dropped out, does drugs, or runs with a wild bunch, the assets may be thoroughly dissipated.

If that ruinous end can be forecast when the young person is still under twenty-one, there may be no cure. The trust cannot be changed. Its finale at age twenty-one was required by the tax law. One possibility exists, if the rambunctious youth will go along. When the beneficiary reaches the age of majority, which is eighteen in many states, or at any time after that, he or she can agree in writing that at age twenty-one the assets in the trust are to be rolled over to another trust that will keep on going for his or her benefit.

The other alternative offered by the tax law runs along a parallel path. Here the trust can be written to go past age twenty-one, to any later time, even for the beneficiary's entire life. But the beneficiary must have the right for a brief time at age twenty-one to halt the trust and take the assets. If the beneficiary decides to terminate the trust, it ends. If the beneficiary who is informed about the trust fails to act within the period of decision, say sixty days, the trust continues and he or she cannot later reverse course and demand to take over the trust's holdings. This alternative offers the promise of operating more effectively than the trust that would end completely at twenty-one. Enlisting the beneficiary's active cooperation is unnecessary. What is needed is the beneficiary's refraining from action, and the trust will stay in place.

A similar manner of obtaining the $10,000/20,000 annual gift tax exclusion is to put the gift, and future additions, into a custodianship under the Uniform Gifts to Minors Act (UGMA) or the newer Uniform Transfers to Minors Act (UTMA). This vehicle, which bears resemblance to a trust, has a characteristic that may discourage a would-be bestower. It automatically ends at age twenty-one, and, for UGMA accounts, in some states at eighteen, and thereupon the assets belong to the young person. If persuaded to, the young person could agree at the termination date that the assets should be placed in a trust for his or her benefit.

Our discussion underlines the dangers of pursuing too avidly the annual gift tax exclusion of $10,000/20,000. It is very inviting to make an annual gift each and every year. The fund will build via the yearly addition to the trust or UGMA or UTMA account, plus dividends and interest, plus appreciation. Many thousands of dollars may be in the trust or UGMA or UTMA account when the child nears the termination date. We hope he or she is sound in every way, and the nest egg will be earmarked for constructive use. But a gift program that is started when the beneficiary is very young takes off in the dark, for the youngster's future development is only a guess. If the child becomes an undesirable character, the bestower's plan may turn extremely sour.

Sometimes anxiety sets in because the fund has grown large and seems too rich to turn over to a young person, even though he or she is not obstreperous. A way to bring the size of the nest egg down is to spend some of it on the beneficiary. Vacations or summer camp or such extras as tennis lessons and skiing instruction might be worthy ideas. Such spending may not be frivolous. Not only may the average child benefit, but the superathlete may find directions for a worthwhile and rewarding life. Observing what Monica, Ivan, Gabriela, and Andre earn via tennis makes one wonder. In the old days, a child who played hooky to work on his jump shot or curve ball was in for a sound parental paddling. Today, Michael and Larry and Bret and Cecil have brought new ideas to parents. Some soundly encourage talented youngsters and tap trusts and UGMA or UTMA accounts for help. Unfortunately, others eye their kids as potential meal tickets.

When the youngster's fund has enjoyed super growth, it may be much too robust to feel any significant dents from expenditures for luxuries. Spending for education might be the right number under those circumstances.

The annual gift certainly has a place in planning. If daughter Jennifer needs $35,000 to buy a car and furnish a new apartment, the annual exclusion would greatly reduce the taxable part of her parents' gift to her. And if mom and dad spread the gift over two years (say November 1992 and January 1993), none of it is taxable, so the unified credit need not be resorted to in order to avoid paying gift tax. Another way of reaching the same tax-free result is to make the entire transfer in one year, but give Jennifer $20,000 and give $15,000 to her husband.

Good sense is called for in weighing the worth of the exclusion. The giver should not let the annual exclusion trample his or her judgment. If a one-time transfer will be made for the benefit of Ronald, who is twelve going on six, it would be foolhardy to use a trust that must end at age twenty-one. Making $10,000/20,000 of the one-time gift eligible for the annual exclusion is a poor reward for the risk involved. A trust until an older age than twenty-one seems superior for Ronald's gift. Let the giver create the longer-term trust and tap his or her unified credit to avoid paying a smidgin of gift tax. But in other circumstances to turn away from the annual exclusion may be a bit much.

Example

Grandpa and Grandma Simmons have eight grandchildren, all darling and exceedingly brilliant. Their ages range from three to seven. G-ma and G-pa have decided to create trusts and give each adorable moppet $20,000 now and the same amount each year for the next four years. By shaping the gifts within the tax shelter of the annual exclusion, tax-free gifts are made over the entire five-year period aggregating $800,000 ($20,000 x 8 = $160,000 x 5 = $800,000). Not a single call has to be made on the grandparents' unified credits to shelter the gifts from gift tax. Further, with the right form of trust, the older folks' exemptions from generation-skipping tax do not have to be tapped. Shaping the trusts that are the medium for their gifts saves a bundle for the senior Simmonses because substantial transfers are made, yet their $600,000 and $1 million exemptions will remain intact for future use.

That example brings us to the point of inspecting the kind of trust that must be used to be a nontaxable gift for generation-skipping purposes. We'll note in a moment that for gift tax purposes other trusts can be used and entitle the giver to use the annual gift tax exclusion. But the generation-skipping tax has exclusive requirements. To meet its requirements there can be only one current beneficiary of the trust, and if the trust is to halt at a particular time, say when the beneficiary reaches age twenty-five, the trust assets must go to him or her. Additionally, if the beneficiary dies before the planned ending of the trust at age twenty-five, the beneficiary's rights must be such that the trust assets would be included in his or her gross estate for estate tax purposes.

Unlike the strictness of the generation-skipping tax, the gift tax offers other trust opportunities for annual nontaxable gifts.

One is a trust that continues past age twenty-one, but requires that the income, such as dividends, interest, and rents, be paid currently to the beneficiary. In other words, retaining income inside the trust cannot be sanctioned. In this type of trust, the annual gift tax exclusion is available for the beneficiary's right to income, which is measured by the government's actuarial tables.

Those tables assign a value to an individual's benefits, depending on the terms and facts surrounding those benefits. For example, if two people, one twenty and one seventy, were given the right to receive $1,000 a year apiece for life, the twenty-year-old has the more valuable opportunity because of the longer period of enjoyment that lies ahead. In addition to assigning relative weights to each person's financial opportunity, the actuarial tables tell us what is the value today of a benefit. Let's say the twenty-year-old has a life expectancy of sixty years. At the rate of $1,000 a year for those sixty years, our young recipient will collect $60,000. But would you pay him or her that amount in cash now to take over the right to collect those annual payments, even if they were guaranteed by every bank in the country? Certainly not! Having payments spread out over time is not so valuable to the recipient as collecting the full sum now. The actuarial tables place a present value on a person's right to be paid over a lifetime, or to receive payment of a sum in the future after another person has died.

All of this plays an important role in determining the value of someone's right to receive payments from a trust. A typical situation is a trust that says that income, in the form of dividends and interest, will be paid to a beneficiary for life. If the tables indicate that the present value for a person of that beneficiary's age to receive income payments, starting now, is, say, .700000, that factor is applied against the principal amount placed in trust from which the income payments will come. The resulting amount is the present value of the beneficiary's right to income.

For example, if $50,000 is placed in trust for that beneficiary, the value of his or her right to receive income is $35,000 ($50,000 x .700000). As that right to income is at least equal to the $10,000/20,000 annual exclusion, the gift to the trust is excluded from taxable gifts up to the full exclusion of $10,000/ 20,000. The balance of the $50,000 gift above the exclusion can be protected from gift tax by the $600,000 exemption. If the $10,000 exclusion were used, that balance would be $40,000; if the $20,000 exclusion were used, the balance would be $30,000.

Notice that the tables tell us whether the present value of the right to receive income from a trust is at least equal to the amount in the annual exclusion. If only $10,000 is placed in trust, then the value of the right to receive the income payments will fall below the allowable annual gift tax exclusion of $10,000/20,000. The exclusion would not be used to its fullest.

In designing a gift plan, the giver will ordinarily want to put enough in the trust to enable the flow of income to be meaningful from the start. Let's assume that objective to be in the mind of Damian, who wants to get going with a fund for his bright and aspiring son Mark, and that Damian also wants to help his widowed sister Amy.

Example

Trust is created for Mark, who is sixteen, to last until he is thirty, when the trust assets will be turned over to him. All the income must be paid to Mark, starting now.

Example

Trust is created for widowed sister Amy, who is fifty-seven, to last until she dies. The trust assets will then go to her children. All the income must be paid to Amy, starting now.

Each trust is funded now with $100,000. As the right to income of Mark and Amy, respectively, is worth more than $10,000/20,000 under the actuarial tables, the annual gift tax exclusion will soak up that much of the gift. If the giver makes the gift in each case with his or her spouse's consent, two annual gift tax exclusions can be claimed. Note that the exclusion can be claimed only in the year of the gift. So when $100,000 is given in one bunch, an excess above the exclusion is inevitable. The balance of each transfer needs coverage from the unified credit to avoid gift tax cost.

If Damian wishes, he can add to either or both trusts next year and in any later year. Let's assume he wants to continue to exploit his $10,000/20,000 annual exclusion from gift tax. A gift each time of $100,000 isn't necessary. But the amount given by Damian should be large enough that, using present values, the right to additional income from the new gift that Mark and Amy will have in their trusts will be worth at least $10,000/20,000.

In that arrangement, a special requirement is necessary to appease the government. The trust must actually produce income in order for the giver to claim the $10,000/20,000 gift tax exclusion. No flow of income, no exclusion. That is in sharp contrast to the trust that will end at age twenty-one, with the assets then becoming the young beneficiary's property. Not only may that brand of trust withhold its income from the beneficiary in order to build the trust, or because the youthful beneficiary has no need for income, but the trust need not have any flow of income at all. So, for example, stock of dad's business can be used for this trust to age twenty-one, even though the corporation has never paid a dividend going back to 1921 when great-grandpa founded the enterprise. But if that stock were used for the trust that runs past twenty-one and requires that income be paid currently, the government will rise up in opposition to the claim of the annual exclusion.

Another scheme to use the annual exclusion centers on the beneficiary's right to withdraw principal from the trust. This is the famous *Crummey* power (named after a party to the lawsuit that established the power), more fully discussed in the chapter on "Life Insurance and Retirement Benefits" (starting at page 151). Without stealing that chapter's thunder, we can say now that the power of withdrawal is a device to permit the annual exclusion to be used. The withdrawal power can be embroidered on any trust. The trust could have any terms governing income and the disposition of principal, as long as the leading beneficiary can make the withdrawal. Two unvarnished words of truth about the arrangement:

1. The beneficiary is expected to refrain from invoking the power.

2. The government does not have friendly feelings for the *Crummey* power.

CHAPTER

2

Husbands And Wives

W hether or not you put your spouse on a pedestal, the law does. When you plan you must be mindful of your spouse's special status.

Inheritance Rights

The law permits you to snub your children at your death, as well as your grandchildren, parents, friends, and assorted others. A scorned child might attack your Will as the product of your incompetency or of improper influence that diverted you from leaving that child an inheritance. But if the Will was properly prepared and the estate lawyer plays his defenses well, the Will would withstand the attack.

Q: Isn't my spouse in the same position?

A: Your spouse will be a beneficiary of your estate whether you like it or not. Even if you have been victimized in your marriage, the state's law, with very rare exceptions, compels you to leave some inheritance to your surviving spouse.

States approach the subject in different ways. But all of them apply their rules whether your marriage was made in heaven or has been a miserable adventure.

In a few states, the prevailing principle is community property. The foundation for this was Spanish law, with a special French touch. The idea is that husband and wife are economic partners. They own together what they acquire during marriage. An exception to this rule is an inheritance or gift that is given to one of the spouses by someone else, say a parent. That legacy or gift belongs exclusively to the recipient as separate property. But that exception aside, co-ownership is the theme of community property. Louisiana (where the French touch is), Texas, New Mexico, Arizona, California, Washington State, Idaho, and Nevada observe community property rules. In some ways, Wisconsin has adopted them.

The great majority of states emulated English law. Even though Elizabeth I and Victoria were storied monarchs, England was a male-dominated society. Husbands ruled, even to the extent of having the right to manage any property their wives had owned when the marriage began. Wives were relegated to supervising the kitchen and the nursery; they had no say about any assets that either spouse owned during the marriage. The husband took full ownership of property that he acquired through his investments and work, and he could do with it as he pleased. At his death, he could disinherit his wife, except that if he owned any land, the widow was entitled to lifetime benefits for her remaining years from one-third of that land. It could be hoped that there were rental payments to sustain her. But, as land receded from being the dominant source of wealth in England, and manufacturing and other businesses grew, so that men made money in many different ways, widows could easily be disinherited by well-to-do husbands. A woman had protection against such callous treatment only if she had property of her own, usually due to an inheritance from her parents. If she were wealthy enough, so that she was a financially fetching creature, her rights could be augmented by a property settlement agreement made with her would-be husband on the eve of marriage. But few women were so favored in England. If the widow was left high and dry by her husband, and had no inheritance from her own parents, she could find herself in a deplorable state. Even if you never attended law school, you were exposed to such slanted notions of spousal relationships by reading Trollope and Galsworthy, who depicted husbands flexing their property muscles, and perhaps you saw such exercises dramatized on Masterpiece Theatre.

In forming their early law on this continent, most American states borrowed from English law. Those states are known as the common-law states, which distinguishes them from the eight community property states. The common-law states are as diverse as Vermont, North Carolina, Kansas, Alaska, Ohio, and Montana. Many of the forty-two common-law states have liberalized the Olde English approach, giving women rights their ancestors never had. In almost all the common-law states today, the surviving widow is entitled to inherit a share of her late husband's holdings. In parallel fashion, a widower has similar inheritance rights should his wife predecease him. The size of that compulsory inheritance (sometimes called the forced share) varies from state to state.

Another variation is whether the decedent's holdings include property that is not squarely in his or her name, such as life insurance that is payable to someone else, accounts in the joint names of the decedent and someone else, and assets that were put in a trust by the deceased spouse who enjoyed benefits from that trust during his or her lifetime. In many states, such maneuvering can succeed. A plotting spouse can channel property to third persons at death and frustrate the inheritance claims of the surviving widow or widower to a share of everything that the decedent had controlled. State laws that tolerate such plots operate in a neutral manner. That is, maneuverings are permitted whether the third person who is rewarded is a needy child or a money-grubbing girl friend or boy friend.

In applying its forced-share rule for widows and widowers, each state has its own prescription.

Example

In Florida, the surviving widow or widower can claim 30 percent of the decedent's holdings, but would have little chance of getting to assets that were not squarely in the decedent's name.

In New York, the surviving spouse can reach out to many assets that the decedent tried to maneuver with and did not hold squarely in his or her name. But New York has permitted a deceased spouse to minimize considerably the compulsory inheritance of the widow or widower. While the minimal inheritance share consists of one-third of the estate, the decedent's Will may leave that share in trust with the surviving spouse entitled only to income, such as dividends and interest, and without any access to the capital. A change in New York's law is under consideration, but a liberalization would not be to everyone's amusement.

In many states, the couple's home is treated specially and the surviving spouse cannot be deprived of its use. Sometimes the law of the state gives the widow or widower a right to claim other assets from the estate, no matter what the Will says, such as a car or furniture or a specific amount of cash.

Precluding an Inheritance

The rules dealing with how little can be left as an inheritance for a widow or widower will entice some folks. They are the ones who laugh sympathetically when Henny Youngman pleads, "Take my wife . . . please." Or they may not be laughing because they are gritting their teeth so firmly. They may even be so depressed by their marital state that they want to know if they can leave absolutely nothing to their surviving spouse.

Q: Is a zero inheritance for a spouse possible?

A: Yes, if that spouse has signed away his or her rights of inheritance. That may have been done in an agreement that was made just before marriage, or even after the wedding.

Q: Are those agreements solid?

A: They can be, if properly put together. If an agreement like that is challenged after the funeral by the regretful widow or widower, a court could rule that the spouse who surrendered inheritance rights can repudiate the agreement if at the time of signing he or she was not given a fair disclosure of the assets and income of the other person, or if the acquiescing spouse did not have advice from a lawyer concerned with his or her rights. Some courts will concern themselves about whether the agreement works out to be conscionable when the marriage ends.

Very often a man or woman who is about to embark on a second or third marriage wants such an agreement in order to protect assets that he or she wishes to leave to children from an earlier marriage. But sometimes a well-to-do person who never was married or is without children nevertheless seeks such an agreement as part of the arrangement for the forthcoming marriage.

Most married people do not focus on how little they can provide for their wives and husbands. Even a spouse who had obtained a surrender of inheritance rights in a premarital agreement (also called an antenuptial agreement) sometimes has a change of heart. Sharing a bedroom can lead to amazing things. After many years of some sort of bliss, an individual who had insisted years ago that a premarital agreement must precede the wedding, may conclude that his spouse deserves to be a major beneficiary of the estate, even the primary heir. But not every marriage takes on a happy glow. In many situations, the spouse who had insisted on the antenuptial agreement continues to adhere to it and declines to be more generous to his or her spouse. I vividly recall one husband whose attitude swung back and forth. He and his bride made a premarital agreement that severely clipped her inheritance rights. He decided after a few years of marriage to provide more liberally in his Will for his wife than the agreement required. But one momentous day he discovered to his consternation that his wife had an artificial eye. In great anger, and without an ounce of sympathy for his wife, he instructed me to revise his Will and reduce her inheritance to the minimum amount he had committed to in their premarital agreement. In his view, he had been deceived and that merited retribution. I was unable to dissuade him from his decision.

Tax Advantages of Marital Status

The federal tax law encourages generosity to the spouse. We'll see that between spouses, assets can be transferred by lifetime gifts or bequests at death without federal gift or estate tax. No other individual, no matter how devoted, faithful, caring, or deserving, ever stands in as favorable a tax position as an individual's spouse. This status is a deliberate congressional policy. It should not be overlooked by men and women who live together without benefit of a marriage ceremony. While tax opportunities certainly should not be the motivating reason to take marital vows, couples who act as if they are married and are committed to each other should not deprive themselves of their federal government's blessings. Since this tax policy dates back to 1948, and has been reinforced in recent years when the opportunities were enlarged, the risks of marrying and then seeing the tax blessings evaporate is very slender.

The Gift Tax with Spouses

The first opportunity to save gift taxes starts when the couple joins hands in matrimony. In their lifetimes, husband and wife may give each other cash, stocks, bonds, real estate, jewelry, paintings, antiques, cars — all sorts of property and things — without federal gift tax. They can do it over and over, back and forth, any time of day or night, and without any limit on quantity or amount, just so long as they are married and are U.S. citizens. They don't even have to file a federal gift tax return to report what they are doing, with one exception when a certain kind of trust is used as the vehicle for the gift. Even then, the return is for procedural reasons and does not require that a tax be paid.

If the recipient spouse is not a U.S. citizen, the opportunity for such tax-free gifts is limited to an aggregate value of $100,000 annually for everything given in the particular year. The $100,000 opportunity can be availed of each year. If the giving spouse is not a U.S. citizen, but the receiving spouse is, the usual rule allowing unlimited tax-free gifts governs.

If a couple should split and divorce, assets can be transferred between them to settle each other's rights with full protection from federal gift tax.

Q: Aside from being nice or fair to my spouse, do those gifts between us serve any tax purpose in our planning?

A: Yes, each spouse should have some property in that person's sole name in order to have the benefit of certain tax exemptions that are available. Chapter 1 on Tax Opportunities discussed the $600,000 exemption and also the $1 million exemption relating to grandchildren.

Only the spouse is so favored for a tax-free gift. No other individual, not your loving children, adorable grandchildren, doting parents, faithful friends, or dependable neighbors, stands in such a divine position for federal gift tax purposes.

Q: Can't I give my kids anything without paying gift tax?

A: Sure you can, but only up to a certain limit. We discussed the annual $10,000/20,000 exclusion in chapter 1 on Tax Opportunities (pages 14–18).

Q: How about charities?

A: Our discussion is about individuals. You may give anything you want, even the shirt off your back, to any charity that the IRS recognizes without federal gift tax.

Q: Well, if my spouse and I have a strong marriage, shouldn't the older one put everything in the younger spouse's name in order to exploit the favorable gift tax opportunity and avoid future inheritance taxes?

A: You're going too fast. If you read on, you will discover that federal death tax won't be a problem for inheritances between spouses. Any amount of cash and property can be inherited by the surviving spouse free of federal estate tax. If the surviving spouse is not a U.S. citizen, the result is harder to reach, but it is achievable. If you remain unconvinced, be aware that another tax looms ahead, which is the tax on capital gains. Its existence may persuade you not to put everything in your life partner's name.

Gifts between spouses can take many forms. Outright is simplest. But trusts also can be used and so can joint ownership. Let's take a reading.

If husband gives cash or securities or anything else to his wife, that property is now hers, to have and to hold as she pleases. He may have some influence with her, and if he is displeased by her handling of the gift he may abort any ideas of doing it again. But she can invest in Magical Widgets, Inc., if she pleases, or spend her money at Tiffany's, bet it at a roulette table, or give it away to the first homeless person she stumbles across. Truth be known, almost surely she'll do none of those. She is likely to watch her nest egg very closely, and invest her funds with care. Oh, she might buy a bangle, try a slot machine, or slip a bill to an appealing street person, but not with the bulk of her gift. That money, those securities, that property, they spell economic independence, at least to a degree. She's come a long way, baby, and she's too smart to squander independence!

A spouse who wants to make a gift, but shuns the idea of handing over a chunk to his or her beloved, can use a trust. The kind of trust and the fallout from employing it will be surveyed when we review how inheritances can be set up for the surviving spouse. At this point we can summarize that review by confirming that the trust need only provide income to the beneficiary spouse without giving him or her a modicum of control over the trust principal or the investment policy for the trust.

Some assets lend themselves to joint ownership. Leading examples are cash, stocks, bonds, and the family residence. Handling assets that way is very common, and sometimes is done reflexively after advice from a bank teller or broker. Putting assets in both names may serve some psychic purpose, but an important point should be digested. For federal tax purposes, nothing is saved by doing it. Not one penny.

Q: Is anything lost?

A: Yes, joint ownership can deprive a surviving spouse of a chance to reduce capital gains.

The Role of Cost Basis

We need to look at capital gains and the thing called basis. If I buy shares of AT&T at 40, that cost is my basis for tax purposes. ("Basis" is an easy concept: it's the figure you use as the cost when you're figuring a gain or a loss on a sale. As you will learn, the basis need not actually be the cost.) When I later sell those shares, I measure the selling price against my basis. If I sell at 45, I have a gain for tax purposes of 5. If I sell those AT&T shares at 36, I have a loss of 4. My gains or losses have to be reported on my federal income tax return. I'll be charged tax on the gains, unless I have incurred losses that I can use as an offset. If I only have losses in a particular year, or an excess of losses over my gains, I'll be able to deduct those losses to a certain extent against my other income and offset the unused part of my losses in future years against new gains I obtain or against other income.

Basis and potential capital gains have a bearing on spousal planning. If a husband buys the AT&T shares at 40 and gives them to his wife, she takes over that tax cost of 40, even if the AT&T shares are then selling at 50. When she later sells those shares, even if that occurs many years from now after the husband has died, her cost basis is the same 40. If the market price of those shares had climbed to 70 when they are sold, there would be a large capital gain of 30 points.

In contrast, if the husband who bought those shares at 40 had retained them in his name and at his death his wife inherited them, the cost basis would be transformed by the passage of the stock through the husband's estate. His wife's basis for the inherited stock would be equal to the value of the shares for estate tax purposes. That value is usually determined as of the date of the husband's death, although under the rules (to be reviewed later) the date for valuation could be up to six months after his death. Let's suppose the estate valuation for the AT&T shares at the husband's death is 60. That becomes the wife's cost. If she sells the shares later at 70, her gain is 10. All the gain between the husband's purchase (at 40) and the value of the stock in the husband's estate (60) vanishes for tax purposes.

Q: But if the husband had the stock when he died, how about the estate tax?

A: On inheritances between spouses, the estate tax will be zero. Even if the widow or widower is not a U.S. citizen, that result is attainable. The change in basis at death is a free ride for the surviving spouse. The potential capital gain from the time of purchase is wiped out up to the date of the deceased spouse's death without an estate tax cost.

Q: How about this scenario: he buys the stock at 40 and gives it to her. Should he fall seriously ill, she'll give the stock back to him and inherit it from his estate when he dies. What is the tax situation?

A: No gift tax at any point, and no estate tax on that stock when he dies. The cost basis for the stock will go up, as we indicated, unless the husband dies within one year after the stock was returned to him. In that event, the law won't give the widow a wipeout of the potential capital gain up to the time of death. Instead, the original cost basis of 40 would continue and be the starting point for measuring the gain if the widow sells the inherited stock. But the cost basis would go up if the husband left the stock to a beneficiary other than the widow.

The cost-basis rules are in between the extremes if the asset is held in joint names when a spouse dies. For example, assume that the husband bought 100 shares of AT&T at 40 and put them in his and his wife's names as joint tenants with right of survivorship, either at the time of purchase or later. Both spouses are U.S. citizens. The joint registration, whenever it occurs, is free of gift tax and there is no change in the tax basis. When the husband later dies, the wife automatically inherits the stock outright, no matter what the husband's Will may provide. That is the result under state law due to the registration of the shares in joint names with right of survivorship.

For federal estate tax purposes, property owned jointly is treated specially when the surviving spouse is a U.S. citizen. In our illustration, one-half of the value of the stock will be included in the husband's gross estate. If the AT&T shares were then worth 60, a total of $3,000 for 50 shares would be part of his gross estate. Because the surviving widow inherits the shares and is a U.S. citizen, that inclusion does not lead to estate tax (due to the marital deduction). For cost-basis purposes, the widow will be entitled to a change in basis for those 50 shares to $3,000. But her basis for the other 50 shares, which were not included in the husband's gross estate, will continue unchanged at 40 ($2,000). When she later sells the entire holding of 100 shares at 70 for $7,000, her basis will be $5,000 and her gain will be $2,000.

That result is poorer than if all the shares had been in the husband's name and inherited by the widow. Her basis, fully transformed at his death, would have been $6,000 (100 x 60) and upon a sale at 70 after the husband's death (for proceeds of $7,000), there would be a gain of $1,000 due to postdeath appreciation. But having the AT&T shares in joint names affords her a better basis position than if the husband, during his lifetime, had transferred all 100 shares to her as a gift. In that case, her basis immediately after the gift would have been $4,000 (100 x 40) and would not have changed at her husband's death. On a sale at 70 for $7,000, her gain would be $3,000.

Things are vastly different, however, for community property when one spouse dies. That form of ownership is the prevailing law for assets acquired during marriage, except via gift or inheritance, in eight states: Louisiana, Texas, New Mexico, Arizona, California, Washington, Idaho, and Nevada. For all purposes in those states, property so acquired is looked upon as held in a marital partnership even if it is registered in the name of only one spouse. Some other states, with Wisconsin as a leader, have edged toward a similar system, particularly for division upon divorce of property that was so acquired during the marriage. But for inheritance purposes, those eight states stand apart in recognizing that assets acquired by the couple, other than by gift or inheritance, form a community of property.

Each spouse may generally dispose of his or her share of the community at death as that person pleases. At death, only the deceased spouse's half of the community, whether it be a home or any other asset, is included in his or her gross estate for estate tax purposes. There is no estate tax if the surviving spouse inherits the decedent's share of the property, due to the marital deduction. But because of a special provision in the tax law that traces many years back, the tax basis is transformed at death for the entire community property asset. The basis change to the value at the time of death is not limited to the half that went through the deceased spouse's estate. The basis changes to the same degree for the share of the property that belonged all along to the spouse who survives, just as if it had been inherited.

Whatever form of ownership was involved, the transformation of basis at the time of death is often referred to as the basis step-up. That reference assumes an upward change from original cost to the higher time-of-death value, because we are so accustomed to valuation increases, whether due to inflation or other forces. But if assets declined in value between the date of acquisition and the time of death, the same transformation in the cost basis that we have reviewed will occur. This time, however, the basis will slide downward to the time-of-death value.

The Spousal Residence

It is worth focusing on the family residence, whether it be a house, condominium, or cooperative apartment. The family residence is a popular asset for registration in both spouses' names, for example, as joint tenants with right of survivorship. Unlike community property, which envelops spouses by the act of marriage, joint tenancy doesn't just happen to people. Instead, they choose it by electing to register ownership of an asset in that manner. They become owners together, but usually each has the right to undo the togetherness and obtain his or her half of the property or the value of half in dollars. In a few states there is another alternative: tenants by the entirety, which usually exists only for houses and other real property. That form of ownership is strictly for husbands and wives, who are joined in a togetherness so thorough that neither, acting alone, can undo the binding ties to the property that they elected when they took on that form of ownership. In some states, simply putting ownership in the names of the spouses and describing them in the ownership document as husband and wife will be equivalent to specifying one of those alternative forms of ownership.

A key characteristic of each form of joint ownership is that one spouse acting alone cannot transfer ownership of the property to a third person or mortgage the property. Both spouses must join in the transfer or mortgage transaction. Another key characteristic of the joint ownership forms is that the surviving spouse inherits automatically at death under either form of registration, no matter what the deceased spouse's Will may say. The tax results that we have described apply to both of those alternatives.

Q: What about tenants in common?

A: That is a 50-50 arrangement without automatic inheritance at death. Each spouse owns a one-half interest and can dispose of it as he or she pleases. At the first spousal death, one-half of the property is in the decedent's estate for all purposes. The surviving spouse does not inherit the deceased spouse's half automatically. Instead, inheritance of the decedent's half occurs via a provision in the Will in favor of the surviving spouse. The basis rules will parallel the rules that govern joint tenants with right of survivorship.

Q: What if the residence is community property?

A: At the first spousal death, one-half of the residence is in the late spouse's estate for all purposes. The surviving spouse inherits the missing half via a provision in the Will in his or her favor. Even though the surviving spouse's half is not included in the decedent's estate for estate tax purposes, the spouse's death triggers a change of basis for the entire residence as a community property asset. You may wonder why the basis rules work that way. Chalk it up to horse-trading long ago when that part of the tax law was designed.

When one spouse dies, the significance of whether there is a favorable basis change for the residence depends on what happens next. If the surviving spouse stays in the residence until he or she eventually dies, the tax basis will be irrelevant. Without a sale of the place, no gain or loss occurs.

If the surviving spouse sells the residence, there are two possibilities for relief even if the sale price is higher than that individual's basis. Both opportunities depend on the home's being the surviving spouse's principal residence. (Therefore, a vacation home won't be similarly blessed, and a sale of that home at a price higher than the cost basis will produce the usual gain, just as would occur with a sale of shares of stock.)

One opportunity for tax relief occurs if all of the proceeds from the sale of the principal residence are used to buy another principal residence. This rollover allows any potential gain to be put aside or suspended. If a new principal residence is acquired, but at a price less than the proceeds of the sale of the old residence, a partial gain results.

Example

Marilu and Quincy acquired their home as joint tenants in 1970 for $50,000. Quincy died in 1991 when the principal residence was worth $400,000. Marilu automatically inherits. One-half the value of the residence (or $200,000) is part of Quincy's gross estate. There is no estate tax due because of the marital deduction. Marilu sold the place last month for $400,000 and yesterday used $280,000 to buy a condominium apartment, which is her new principal residence. Marilu has $120,000 from the sale that was not reinvested in her new home. Income tax has to be confronted. Marilu has a gain for income tax purposes that results from comparing her cost basis with the sale price of $400,000. Marilu's cost basis is $225,000, composed of two pieces: (1) $200,000 for the half of the old residence that was included in Quincy's gross estate and (2) $25,000 from Marilu's half of the residence that was not so included (that was the amount paid for that half in 1970; nothing has taken place since to change that segment of the basis). The full gain is $175,000 (proceeds of $400,000 − basis of $225,000). The gain would not be taxed if she had invested all $400,000 of the proceeds in the condo. With $120,000 of the proceeds not reinvested, a gain of that amount is taxed now for income tax purposes. The rest of the gain ($55,000) is looked upon as having been put in the condo, and that much of the gain is suspended. If Marilu later sells the condo and becomes a renter, the suspended gain would be taxed.

Rollovers of proceeds from sales of principal residences can be used over and over, without limit, by any taxpayer. Another relief provision may be used only once in a lifetime, and then only if the seller is fifty-five or over and the house had been the principal residence for at least three of the last five years. In that case, up to $125,000 of gain is wiped out, not just suspended. In our example, when the entire sales proceeds were not used for a new home, a surviving spouse who is fifty-five could invoke this wipeout provision for relief, together with the rollover opportunity.

Hence, a sale without a full basis change at death may not prove too hurtful to the surviving spouse. That knowledge may help a couple decide on whether they should own their house in his name or her name or both names.

The Estate Tax Between Spouses

I have referred in abbreviated fashion to the estate tax results when one spouse dies. It's time to look closely at that situation.

When a spouse dies, an inheritance of any size can be left for the widow or widower without federal estate tax. The tax-free inheritance can consist of anything: stocks, bonds, cash, priceless antiques, valuable art, boats, cars, other kinds of stuff, oil wells, patents, the home, real estate investments, businesses, life insurance, and (with a possible exception) pension and other retirement benefits. No matter what the composition and how valuable it may be, the inheritance can be preserved from federal tax at death, even for a surviving spouse who is not a U.S. citizen.

Once again, the spouse enjoys a special advantage. The tax law does not smile so benignly on inheritances for any other beneficiary except recognized charities. Whether or not the widow or widower be deserving, whether independently wealthy or in need, whether a faithful caring spouse or otherwise, whether the decedent's first or eighth spouse, the spousal inheritance can be clear of federal estate tax. The official moniker for that tax break is the marital deduction.

An important point to note is that in order to gain that blessed status, the inheritance must be left for the surviving spouse in such form that whatever has not been consumed or given away by the widow or widower before that worthy's death will be exposed to federal estate tax when the survivor subsequently dies. That is how the closing scene will play. The marital deduction is therefore really a deferral. There need not be any federal estate tax when the first spouse dies, but the government will get its due at the second spouse's death.

That rule of thumb indicates that the estate tax, like the gift tax, hits when assets are passed to the children's generation.

Let's look at a variety of spousal inheritances, which typically come via provisions in a Will. Incidentally, in ancient days in England, real property (land) was disposed of by a Will and personal property (such things as coin of the realm) was disposed of by a testament — hence the familiar phrase, "Last Will and Testament." Today, the word "Will" suffices.

An outright disposition by Will is eligible for the marital deduction, unless the inheriting spouse is not a U.S. citizen. Any kind of property can be left outright to the surviving spouse.

In the examples that follow, take note of the special language that lawyers use. When it comes to giving away cash or securities or objects like jewelry, the Will maker says, "I bequeath." All of those assets are classified as personal property, as distinguished from real property, which is land and such improvements on the land as buildings. The bequest is often called a legacy; the words are synonyms.

When it comes to giving away real estate, such as a house or condominium or forty-story building on Pine Street in lower Manhattan, the Will maker says, "I devise," and more often, "I devise and bequeath" (because personal property may be mixed in with the real estate).

After expenses and debts are paid and bequests of cash and particular assets and devises of particular real property are taken care of, the balance of the Will maker's property is called the residuary estate, or the residue. As that remaining pot of assets may consist of personal property and real property, the residue is given away in the Will with the words, "I devise and bequeath."

Example

"I bequeath $50,000 to my wife Chelsea, if she survives me."

Example

> "I bequeath all of my stock and interest in Magical Widgets, Inc., to my wife Fiona, if she survives me."

Example

> "I devise and bequeath to my husband Logan, if he survives me, all of my right, title, and interest in my real estate located on Tenth Street in Longview, Ohio."

Example

> "I devise and bequeath to my beloved wife Stacy, if she survives me, the residue of the property that I may own, whether it be real property or personal property, and wherever it be situated."

There are many attributes to an outright inheritance. The recipient is in complete control of the property. He or she may spend it rashly, consume it slowly, invest it wisely, squander it on friends and gold-diggers, preserve it for the children to enjoy, or shrewdly conserve it for a dark, rainy day.

Because of that absolute control, some wives fret about leaving inheritances outright to their husbands. Diana Marlin may be fearful that her prized necklace will adorn some honey who cuddles up to the bereaved Mr. Marlin right after the funeral. Diana may be further concerned about the other assets she owns; that when her husband later dies, he will feel it to be his duty to devote what he has, including his inheritance, to support Delilah, who became the second Mrs. Marlin, and may even have been a dear friend of Diana, the first Mrs. Marlin.

Husbands have their concerns, too. Their anxiety is that an outright legacy will be loaned to a despised brother-in-law, or invested foolishly, or used as a retirement fund by a new husband or "great good friend."

Q: Can't I specify that what I leave outright to my spouse has to be passed on later to my children?

A: No. If it is your ardent wish that the children will eventually inherit, an outright bequest to your spouse won't assure that. You should leave the assets in trust for your spouse's lifetime benefit and provide that at the spouse's death the trust assets go to the children.

Q: How do I know that if I use a trust, my children will really benefit when my spouse dies?

A: That is a major part of the trustee's responsibility. If the trustee fails in his or her duty, the trustee will be liable to your children. You must choose your trustee carefully.

Those worried spouses may decide to eschew an outright bequest for their spouses and select a trust as the vehicle for the inheritance. What prompts that conclusion? Usually more than devotion or concern or economics. In marriage, sex plays a role even after death does them part. Sexual attitudes have a lot to do with whether this husband or that wife will write a Will with a trust to hold the surviving spouse's inheritance. Leaving the inheritance outright is more than some Will makers can bear, precisely because of anxiety about who will be sharing the surviving spouse's bed. A long-time client agonized over the issue of how to leave his expensive home for his (second) wife's lifetime use because of his conviction that she would not be alone when all the lights were turned out at night. And more than one anxious wife has been in pain over the thought that her jewelry would eventually end up around the throat and fingers of a scheming siren.

When the Will maker dies, the surviving spouse may bridle at the means taken to discourage his or her enjoyment of the liaisons, meaning that the survivor did not gain the inheritance outright. There may be resentment that the decedent did not really have faith in his or her spouse. There will be initial annoyance, even hostility, toward the trustee, who is a constant reminder that faith was lacking. That attitude to the trustee may never change. As to the sexual politics that may have prompted the deceased spouse to use the trust to hold the inheritance, the surviving spouse's life will unfold as it will. If the surviving spouse wishes to cuddle with a new friend, or an old and all too familiar one, the trust won't be an inhibition. Who ever heard of a trust driving any breathing soul to a nunnery?

In one situation, a trust is required, sexual politics be what they may. If the surviving spouse is not a U.S. citizen, a trust will be necessary to assure a tax-free inheritance.

Some items don't meld neatly with trusts, such as the living room furniture. But there is no rule that forbids putting Great Aunt Helen's needlepoint settee in a trust. Of course, if state law enables the surviving spouse to reject the Will's provision and elect instead to take a piece of the estate outright, the idea of using a trust to manage the surviving spouse's inheritance will be frustrated.

There are particular tax results that flow from inheriting outright. The heir will be responsible for reporting dividends, interest, and gains from the inheritance on his or her individual income tax return. If a gift is made by the spouse, to children or anyone else, gift tax rules must be heeded by the spouse. When that heir dies later, what is left of the inheritance will be part of his or her estate for estate tax purposes.

Marital Deduction Trusts

Trusts offer a totally different arrangement. In chapter 5, some important aspects of trusts are covered, notably what is income and what is principal, and the differences between the point of view of the person who receives trust benefits now and the beneficiary who must wait for benefits to fall in. Trusts can be shaped in many different ways to deal with particular needs and goals. But for a spouse's inheritance, there are two basic choices of trust that will be eligible for the marital deduction. (A third choice, known as the estate remainder trust, is rarely used.)

One choice traces its pedigree back to 1948, when the marital deduction was developed by Congress. Because of its lineage, I call it the classic marital deduction trust. It has two requisites. First, the surviving spouse must be entitled to all the trust income for life, which would include dividends, interest, and rent from real estate. The spouse must report that income on his or her personal tax return. If any income is tax-exempt, the recipient spouse enjoys that income tax status. Sales of assets of the trust can generate capital gains. They are taxed like any other capital gains, but not to the surviving spouse. The reason is that the assets of the trust, and gains or losses relating to those assets, are principal and not part of the surviving spouse's entitlement. The tax on a capital gain would be paid from the trust principal by the trustee.

The widow or widower's right to income must continue until death intervenes. The tax law will not recognize the marital deduction for a trust if the Will directs that the flow of income can be interrupted by remarriage or a live-in relationship with someone of the same or opposite sex. And there can be no back-door interference with the spouse's income, such as a direction that expenses that state law would normally charge to principal are instead to be paid from income. An example of a maneuver that would be unacceptable would be directing the trustees to pay the trust's capital gains taxes from income — or even giving them the option to do so.

The second essential ingredient in the classic trust for the marital deduction is that the surviving spouse have the right to dispose of the trust assets in favor of anyone. When these trusts are written, the right of disposition is usually granted to the surviving spouse to exercise in his or her Will, instead of allowing it to take place while that spouse is still alive. The strategic reason for restricting the exercise of the right of disposition to the surviving spouse's Will is to achieve a more reasoned and temperate result. The idea is that making a Will is a solemn event, and the widow or widower may be more circumspect in directing how the trust assets will be disposed of after that spouse dies than if he or she had a free hand during lifetime. The right to dispose is called a power of appointment, and when the holder can exercise it in favor of anyone in the world, it is a general power of appointment. To gain the marital deduction the surviving spouse need not exercise the general power. It suffices that he or she may do so.

The Will of the spouse who died first would specify how the trust assets are to pass when the surviving spouse dies without exercising the power. That specification must not be neglected. Because the surviving spouse is not duty bound to exercise the power, it is critically important for the original Will maker to spell out what direction the assets are to go in when the surviving spouse eventually dies. If the surviving spouse does not exercise the power and the original Will maker did not do any spelling out, the law would step in and cart the assets away to beneficiaries selected ultimately by a bunch of politicians. Who those selected beneficiaries might be would turn on the particular facts, but the chances are that if the original Will maker were still around to observe, he or she would not be pleased.

The second ingredient for the classic marital deduction trust is really a message to the widow or widower: you have the right to dispose of the trust principal as you want, beginning with your death. If you refrain from doing anything, then I have specified what will happen when you're gone. If you don't object to my plan, then let it unfurl after your death.

That opportunity for the surviving spouse to exercise the power and thereby control the disposition of the trust assets proved very worrisome. With the sharp increase in the divorce rate, there was growing concern that in multiple-marriage situations the children of an earlier marriage would suffer from the whims of the widow or widower when that spouse eventually died. Congress stepped in and decided to allow a trust to be eligible for the marital deduction when only the first requirement was satisfied: that the surviving spouse be entitled to the trust income for his or her life. No control over the principal at any time need be given to the widow or widower. Another essential ingredient for this trust is that, when the deceased spouse's estate tax return is filed, the executor advises the IRS that the trust is believed to be qualified for deduction under the rules of the marital deduction.

This latter trust is widely known by the acronym QTIP, which stands for Qualified Terminable Interest Property. A reader may be forgiven for sneering at that blot on the language and ascribing the reference to hopeless legalese and excessive cuteness.

Since the second necessary element of the classic marital deduction trust, the right of disposition, may be omitted when the QTIP trust is chosen, the true difference between the trusts is sharply revealed. That difference is control over the final destiny of the trust assets. The creator of the QTIP may specify what will become of the trust assets when the surviving spouse later dies. The widow or widower need not be allowed to interfere one bit with that specification. The trust's creator may therefore endow his or her children, or any other selected beneficiary, with the trust assets when the surviving spouse dies.

When the surviving spouse is not a U.S. citizen, either the classic trust or the QTIP must be used for the widow or widower's entire inheritance, even to hold the house and its contents, in order to make use of the marital deduction. In addition, one of the trustees must be a U.S. citizen or a U.S. bank, and that trustee must be responsible for looking after the estate tax that is due from the spousal trust.

In addition to the required elements that the classic and QTIP trusts must have, there are optional ingredients that may be added if the creating spouse wishes.

One of these is access to principal. The trustees can be empowered to dip into principal for the surviving spouse. But the trustees cannot be authorized to use principal for anyone else, as that would divert trust benefits away from the widow or widower and decrease his or her right to all the income, in violation of the requirement for the marital deduction.

The trustees' power to pay out principal can be narrow or broad. Examples of a narrow power would be to use principal to attend to medical and nursing expenses. The power to pay out principal can be expanded beyond that, to the ultimate point of allowing the trustees to pay principal to the surviving spouse for any reason or purpose. But notice that whether the power is narrow or wide, or somewhere between, the trustees control it. (Interestingly enough, the jargon of the law encapsulates an attitude: trustees don't tap or gain access to principal, they "invade" it.)

Q: Can't the trustees be directed to use principal?

A: Sure. Examples: "If my wife's trust income in any year is less than $50,000, my Trustees shall pay principal to her to make up the deficit." Or, "If at any time my husband Brock incurs medical expenses in excess of $500 that are not covered by insurance, my Trustees shall pay them from principal."

All sorts of wrinkles and approaches can be woven into the situation. An inflation adjustment can be tacked onto the direction that if income falls below $50,000 (or any other desired amount) the deficit must come from principal. The medical expense possibility can be modified by a requirement that the procedure or treatment be prescribed by a physician as necessary or advisable.

Q: How about giving my spouse access to principal without having to go to the trustees?

A: That can be done by authorizing the spouse to make withdrawals of principal from the trust. If you make that too open-ended, the beneficiary spouse could decimate the trust. If you really want a trust for your spouse, you might put a ceiling on the amount of principal that the spouse can withdraw from the trust. That could be an annual maximum, say $10,000. Or it could be a lifetime maximum, say $75,000, or an amount equal to a percentage (say 10 percent) of the trust principal's original value.

Note that if a spouse who is not a U.S. citizen can take trust principal, or be given it by the trustees, for any reason beyond hardship, estate tax will fall due on any principal that actually is received by him or her.

An option that can be tacked onto the classic marital trust is authorizing the surviving spouse to make gifts from the trust during his or her lifetime. In order to preclude a distortion of that authorization, the right can be confined to gifts to particular people, such as children and grandchildren. That limitation may provide comfort to the spouse who created the trust. This option is forbidden for the QTIP trust.

But the QTIP trust does allow another option. The surviving spouse can be given a power of disposition at death over the QTIP trust assets. That would be a power of appointment that is exercisable by the surviving spouse's Will. The power can be limited in its scope so that, for example, it may only be exercised in favor of the children and other descendants of the spouse who had created the trust. This power can be very handy because it introduces flexibility into the trust. For example, assume that Susan and Michael have three children, who are age twenty, eighteen, and sixteen. Susan's Will creates a QTIP trust for Michael, because she is concerned that following her death he may be whisked to the altar by his pretty blonde secretary, or some other irresistible creature. But if Susan dies first, she would want Michael to review what would be an appropriate inheritance for their children from the trust, which would take place when Michael dies later. That may be twenty or more years from now, when the children will have developed further, or maybe failed to. The older son may never get his act together, so that he should have his inheritance in a trust. As to the younger son, he may have parlayed his electric guitar into recordings that bring him a handsome income. He may turn out to need nothing in the way of an inheritance from his parents. Maybe a token of their love and affection would be very fitting. The rest of the trust could be passed on to the daughter, who seems level-headed, but unlikely to pursue a career that generates much money. By giving Michael the limited right at his death to parcel the QTIP trust among the children and their offspring, Susan has made sure he'll have a chance to review the family picture up to his last breath and act appropriately. And if he did fall prey to that blonde hussy, he would be unable to divert the trust to her.

Making Choices

It is obvious that choices have to be made. In approaching decisions, some assets call for particular treatment.

Life insurance is special. Among all assets it is the only one that has a low value today (the cash value) and is absolutely certain to have a higher value when the insured dies. That swing in value lends itself to planning opportunities, which will be discussed in the chapter covering Life Insurance (starting at page 151). For the moment, it is predictable that many individuals will opt to put their life insurance in a trust to save estate taxes both at their death and later at the passing of the surviving spouse.

Retirement benefits from tax-qualified pension and profit-sharing plans are also special. The surviving spouse is once more placed on a pedestal by the tax law. The alternatives to be weighed for these benefits will be looked at in the chapter on Retirement Benefits (starting at page 151). In many cases, the decision will be that they are to be paid as an annuity for the surviving spouse.

The family home may already be owned in a way that inhibits further decisions. If title is currently held by the spouses as joint tenants with right of survivorship, or as tenants by the entirety, the surviving spouse will automatically inherit the home as sole outright owner, and will have a partial adjustment to the property's cost basis, as we discussed earlier in this chapter (at pages 44–47). Nothing can be said in the Will of the first spouse who dies to alter that result.

If the prospect of that inheritance disturbs one of the spouses, a change to full ownership of the home by one spouse is possible only with the cooperation of the other spouse. If such cooperation is forthcoming, a new deed signed by both spouses will be required to transfer the title to the one spouse who takes over the complete ownership. For example, if the decision is made that the husband will be the sole owner of the house with the plan that it will be left for the lifetime use of the wife, a deed changing the current ownership to him is necessary, together with a new Will for him that bequeaths the house at his death for her use.

A change of this magnitude is a serious matter. The spouse who is asked to give up a share of the ownership now is giving up a lot: the right to participate in present ownership, the right to say yes or no to any new mortgaging of the house, and the certainty of inheriting the place if the other spouse dies first. If the surrendering spouse were to consent, how would he or she know that the house will be available for lifetime use when death takes the spouse who is the complete owner? That person may make a new Will today that contains the appropriate provision, but Wills can be changed willy-nilly. Why alter the prevailing joint ownership? An ownership change for the house may promise rewards, for example, by putting title entirely in the name of the husband, who is older and in rocky health, in order to improve the basis position for the younger wife who is expected to be the survivor of the couple. To assure the younger spouse, confidence about the entire plan and its faithful observance is needed.

In many situations, ownership of the home ought to be left outright to the other spouse. Doing that will provide security to him or her and will avoid a pack of legal rules about houses that are left for lifetime use instead of outright. Further, if the principal residence is left outright to the surviving spouse, he or she clearly has the opportunity to invoke the two relief rules in the income tax (discussed at pages 46–47 above) should the house be sold. Neither the rollover-of-gain provision nor the one-time reduction of up to $125,000 of gain can be used if the surviving spouse is not the complete owner.

Because the residence is both a major family asset and the port in life's journey, decisions about it will have important financial as well as psychological consequences.

The contents of the home are usually left outright. In terms of dollar value, furniture, rugs, china, glassware, utensils, and equipment have modest worth for the great majority of families. Leaving those articles outright to the surviving spouse is appropriate. Now and then, there are valuable items or pieces that have sentimental aspects.

Q: I don't wish to leave my jewelry to my husband so he can delight a new wife with it. What should I do?

A: Leave it to your children. If there are valuable pieces, particularly items you no longer wear, you might start giving them to the children during your lifetime, or, if that would be rushing you, do that in your Will. You must be mindful of gift and estate tax. Everything you own is fair game for those taxes. The discussion of Tax Opportunities in chapter 1 offers ideas about avoiding those taxes if you wish to give the jewelry to the children soon.

Q: I have a dining room set that once was owned by my great-grandmother. I want my daughter to have it and then pass it on to her daughter, who is now seven years old.

A: You can leave it for your husband's lifetime use, then to your daughter outright or for her lifetime use. Or if your husband is not concerned about it, skip him. Unless the set has real economic value, the tax points are negligible.

Q: We have works of art that are pretty valuable. What do we do?

61

A: One choice is to leave them to the surviving spouse, which is easily done without federal estate tax. He or she can then decide on the next step. We'll discuss the choices at that stage in the chapter on Children (starting on page 67). But, as a forerunner of that, remember that when the surviving spouse dies, those works will attract estate tax, and it could be heavy. Will the children want to use up other estate assets, such as cash or marketable securities, in order to pay the tax on those works of art? If not, they may decide to dispose of most, or even all, of them.

Q: I own vintage cars that I have collected for years. I have some good ones, including a very handsome 1935 Rolls. My wife has no interest in them, but she knows I adore collecting. I don't think my kids want them, except for the money the cars would bring.

A: You should consider a direction in your Will that the cars are to be sold upon your death. That is particularly so if you can't imagine your wife ever going for a spin in one of them. If that would just not be her style, spare the dear lady anxiety. In other words, make the decision for your wife and relieve her of feeling guilty about disposing of things that you cared about. She may even take pride in learning how much money your craze for vintage cars translated into. The proceeds of sale can be invested for her benefit. Taxes will not be troublesome. The transformation of cost basis at your death wipes out the tax on any gain and the marital deduction silences the estate tax.

After making choices about those kind of assets, attention must be turned to what remains. It may be considerable, even worth a lot. Should it be left outright to your spouse, or in trust for his or her lifetime use? Lots of questions must be answered to make that decision. Among them are:

1. *Is your spouse well enough to manage an inheritance?* If not, a trust is a sensible protector.

2. *Does your spouse have managerial skill?* Investments need care. Expert guidance may make the difference for your spouse between living free of financial worries and experiencing economic misery. Making investment decisions by just hanging on to something you had invested in out of respect for you can be a serious mistake. Even if you were a shrewd and clever investor, those skills would go away with you; they do not create some bewitched aura around the investments themselves. The investment climate can change rapidly, and what you did may soon be out of favor. Also, you may have had special reason to keep certain assets. For example, you may have focused your investment strategy on common stocks because you had the stomach to ride out swings on Wall Street, but, although that strategy was rewarding, it would scare the bejabbers out of your surviving spouse. Or, to take a more precise example, you may have retained your holdings in IBM because you bought them years ago at very low prices when Big Blue was the darling growth stock of every investment adviser, and if you had sold your shares during your life the capital gain would have been awesome. With the transformation of basis at your death, that problem of gain vanishes and IBM shares, and other holdings, should be viewed afresh for investment purposes when you're gone.

3. *Is your spouse the parent of your children?* If not, a QTIP trust may be the right method of inheritance so that the

principal will be conserved for your children to inherit eventually.

4. *Even if your spouse is the parent of your children, does the prospect of his or her remarrying bother you?* Aside from that concern, are you troubled about your spouse's being a soft touch for everyone who asks for money, like your son-in-law or your widowed sister or your shiftless brother-in-law? If any of these anxieties besets you, use a trust for your spouse's inheritance. Your spouse can then truthfully say that all decisions about money matters are out of his or her hands.

5. *Does your spouse prefer not to be the responsible decision maker about investing the inheritance?* Some people believe that hiring an investment adviser would resolve all problems for the inheriting spouse. But meeting with prospects, hiring the adviser, reviewing his or her recommendations, analyzing the results, deciding whether to continue with the adviser or take on a new one — all are decisions. Money and investments need care. There are no short cuts or magical arrangements for providing the necessary care. The bestower's decision to use a trust, coupled with the selection of astute trustees, may prove to be a relief to the widow or widower.

In many cases, an outright inheritance is sensible. In other cases, that would be foolish, and a trust is a far wiser choice. Sometimes an appropriate stance to take is something outright and the rest in trust. When we discuss Grandchildren (starting at page 87), we'll see that a portion in trust may be a clever way of leaving a sizable inheritance down the line for grandchildren.

If a trust is decided upon, should it be the classic marital trust, in which the surviving spouse has the right of ultimate control over the assets, or the QTIP, in which that control need not be given? The issue of control deserves much attention. One other aspect should be given consideration, especially in single-marriage families in which the bestower has confidence in the good sense of the other spouse. The right to make lifetime gifts from the classic marital trust can be given to the surviving spouse. He or she could assist children in that fashion. The spouse's ability to give can be circumscribed, so that only a favored group, such as descendants, can receive anything. A right to make lifetime gifts from a marital trust cannot be given to a spouse in a QTIP trust.

Choices are inevitable when death does you part.

CHAPTER

3

Children

For many concerned parents, a financial base for their children is a dearly sought objective. How often we observe a proud parent who has sweated over the years to achieve that goal. And if the objective cannot be achieved through parental work and sacrifice, maybe it can be reached via the child's marriage. Who does not have a relative or friend who boasts of his or her child's success in marrying well.

After years of watching clients' dreams for their children reduced to rubble, I have reached certain convictions. Inheritances and gifts of wealth for children are grossly overrated. Yes, money is nice. It can provide a footing for a child starting out, a foundation for a fine career. Money buys houses and eases the way for young families. But money is not a sure anodyne for personal ailments. I recall a young man who had the extreme good fortune to have been born into a very affluent family. At an early age, a trust fund set up by his grandparents and great-grandparents was available. The youngster, sorely beset by temptations, dropped out of school and demanded that the trustees permit him to live on his inheritance. Work was not for him! Anyone who rose early enough to hold a 9:00 to 5:00 job was a

blithering fool. Efforts of his sorely disturbed parents, and by responsible trustees, to bring sanity to the situation were unavail-
ing for a prolonged period. Finally, therapy and patient parental
understanding brought improvement, but by no means did anything like normality ever take hold.

Many young people squander their good fortune or wreck
their prospects. Meanwhile, others, who were not financially
favored at all, take hold of opportunities, start their families, and
fly ahead in their careers. The story of many immigrant families
shows what can be done.

Why such varying outcomes? The psychiatric world would
know better than I. But observing the human parade during a
career prompts my conclusion that financial oomph from family
or via marriage is not always productive and can lead to disaster.

I don't suggest that some financial backing is all bad. Heav-
ens, no. On the contrary, money can play a marvelous role, up
to a point. I find other aid from parents to be just as vital, and
often more so. What aid? Encouragement and emotional support. Understanding and empathy. Interest and complete faith.
Showing the way as a role model. And then there is love, un-
conditional, abiding love. Many youngsters who have been
showered with expensive cars, fancy wardrobes, costly jewelry,
every imaginable technological gadget, and just plain money
would trade it all for a package of hugs, emotional backing, and
the certainty of love from parents who are "there" at all times.

When encouragement and loving attitudes are freely given by
parents, along with financial help, the combination can be sen-
sational. But financial aid can be too much, too soon. Children
can be swept off their feet by ill-timed or excessive funds. In-
centive, determination, and self-worth are precious ingredients
for a child. They are also perishable ingredients. Invaluable also
is encouragement to find one's way in a topsy-turvy, highly
competitive society in which distractions abound. A shower of

money can easily interrupt a child's serious approach to learning, or his or her resolve to undertake a career or leap at a challenging opportunity. Similarly, easy promotions in a family business can warp a child's attitude, as well as curdle the interest of key employees, all to the detriment of the company's prospects and, more important, of the child's promise of growth.

When offering financial support through gifts and in providing an inheritance, a parent should proceed cautiously. Doing less is apt to be better than doing more.

A major question is the age at which funds or investments should be provided to the child. A lot depends on the particular child. Some mature and take responsibility more rapidly than others. Age alone is not decisive. I have come across families in which the children are forty and more, with offspring of their own, and they are just as foolish about finances and responsibilities as spoiled teenagers.

Some guidelines about age are possible. In today's world, the age of majority, which is eighteen in many places, is almost certain to be too young, as is twenty-one. Drinking and voting at those ages may have been accepted by society, but handling money is a far different business for most young people. Children need to finish their education and have some idea of how hard it is to earn money before it is shoveled into their hands. How about twenty-five, if education is completed? Over and over parents have learned that they were far more responsible and experienced in economic realities at twenty-five than their children seem to be in today's society. But there is hope. Children seem to be ready by thirty, if they ever will be. By then most of them know what job searches are about, have had substantial work adventures and experience at dealing with people in varied situations, and even serious thoughts about the opposite sex. They also should have discovered that compensation does not grow on trees no matter how energetic and earnest they may be in their efforts.

If a child's financial windfall is to be substantial, breaking it up into installments can be wise: a bit at one age, maybe even twenty-five, a good dose at thirty and the balance at thirty-five or forty. Sometimes one-third or one-half at twenty-five and the rest at thirty does nicely. These approaches at financial sanity are achievable with trusts. Although the chapter on Trusts and Trustees (starting on page 111) covers the topic pretty fully, if I do say so myself, it is worth mentioning some points here.

Trusts are flexible financial vehicles. A wise trustee can be very helpful when authorized to release funds to a child for sound reasons, like education, getting a start in a career or business, and buying a home. If a child doesn't really need trust money right now, a trustee who has been armed with the right authority can withhold all or most of the funds, thereby keeping them in the trust where they will grow, until an opportune time is reached to release some or all of the funds to the child. If the trust was designed to last until the child reached forty and, to everyone's delight he or she has bloomed at twenty-seven, a trustee with the right authority can terminate the trust at that point and allow the child to take the money and flourish.

Making Gifts

There are tax advantages to starting a gift program early. As chapter 1 on Tax Opportunities indicates, a parent can make a tax-free gift to a child each year up to $10,000. Recall the points we made in that chapter: that figure can be doubled to $20,000 if the giver's spouse consents to the use of his or her parallel giving opportunity, and consent is available even if all the funds come from only one person. Further, the consenting spouse need not be the child's mother or father.

The gift need not be outright. It can consist of money or stocks and bonds, an interest in a business, or any other kind of investment or property. In order to avoid a child's squandering the gift or becoming spoiled, the gift can be via a trust, so that a trustee will invest and manage the funds and preserve them for the child until a suitable age is reached. Or the gift can be via a vehicle known as the Uniform Gifts to Minors Act (UGMA), which is a statutory imitation of a trust, or its more recent counterpart, the Uniform Transfers to Minors Act (UTMA). Instead of a trustee, the fund manager is a custodian. Under state law, the custodian typically can invest in a wide range of financial opportunities and use the fund for the child's benefit. But the UGMA or UTMA is different from a trust in a very key aspect. UGMAs only last until age eighteen or, in some states, twenty-one; UTMAs end at twenty-one. In contrast, a trust can be run beyond such tender ages. In addition, every state does not authorize its UGMA or UTMA custodians to hold every conceivable kind of property or investment.

The tax law recognizes a trust to be a separate taxpaying entity, but not so for the UGMA or UTMA. Any income or profits earned by a custodian acting under the UGMA or UTMA will be taxed to the child as if he or she were the owner. While the child is under fourteen, there is a special rule. The effective federal income tax rate will be the parent's, not the child's. This is known in the trade as the kiddie tax. It is something of a nightmare. It was invented by Congress to prevent exploiting the lower income tax brackets that young children have. It is a misguided idea, and creates lots of work for preparers of income tax returns.

The kiddie tax also applies to payments of income from a trust to a child who is under fourteen. In contrast, a trust that keeps its income is a taxpayer apart from the beneficiary. The trust pays income tax thereon, as well as on its gains. There is an alternative available for the spirited, so long as the creator of the trust remains alive. Assume that a parent creates a trust for a child, with the objective of building the trust during the child's formative years. By including certain management provisions in the trust, the creator can see to it that he or she is responsible for paying the tax on the income and gains of the trust. In essence, that is a tax-free gift to the trust, for the tax law requires that result during the creator's life when those management provisions are present. This aggressive plan allows the trust to retain its income and gains without tax cost to the trust, which is an extra growth factor. The results are surprisingly attractive. It should be noted that the creator is probably not taxed at any higher rate than the trust would be. Income tax rates for trusts are not low. The 28 percent rate is reached by a trust when taxable income exceeds $3,300 and the top rate of 31 percent applies when taxable income exceeds $9,900. So the creator can even be taxed at lower rates than the trust would have been. An additional benefit of artificially foisting the tax on the trust's creator is that the parent erodes his or her potential estate. It is even possible to put this arrangement in place so that if the creator of the trust decides to shed the burden of paying the trust's income tax and let the responsibility fall on the trust, that can be achieved.

If a parent can afford to make them, repetitive annual gifts of $10,000/$20,000 for a child can build handsomely. Further, an interest in a fledgling business or venture that is put aside now for a child may appreciate in value several times over during an ensuing decade or so. These growth opportunities and the miracle of compound interest can be stupendous. But bear in mind my caution of not overdoing it to the child's sorrow.

The program can be accelerated. If a parent decides to use the unified credit now to offset taxable gifts, instead of saving the credit to use against estate tax, gifts for a child can be greater. Remember that we noted in chapter 1 on Tax Opportunities (pages 4–5) that each person has a credit of $192,800 that can be used against federal gift tax or estate tax. That credit cancels the federal tax on gifts or inheritances totaling $600,000. A parent can put aside that amount now for a child without federal gift tax. More is possible. With the consent of the other spouse, his or her credit can be similarly exploited even if the consenting person does not contribute any property or money. So, $1.2 million can be given now, or in chunks over time. Watch that grow! Well invested, that fund can double in ten years. But be cautious. Design the plan sensibly so that the gift and the growth are healthy for the child.

Inheritances

Unlike gifts made during someone's lifetime, an inheritance is created precipitously or under sad or difficult circumstances. Sometimes it comes at an inopportune time in a child's life. That is all the more reason for the parent to be very thoughtful at the preparation of the Will in choosing a plan that won't be disruptive.

A Will must be written for today's circumstances, with the children as they now are. Although the parent is youthful and vigorous, death may take that person prematurely. So long as the parent continues to live, there is always time to revamp the Will and use different provisions when the child is older and has met some of life's challenges.

When the child is in an early phase of life, an appropriate means of handling his or her inheritance must be crafted. Most likely a trust should be provided in the Will. Suitable trust terms, including the right time for termination, must be selected. Of crucial significance will be the choice of trustee, and more than one might be wise.

What if the offspring are plural — there is more than one child? When the family assets available for the children are moderate, and the children are young, a single trust for all the children should be considered. For example, suppose there are four children under thirteen and the available inheritance for them is a grand total of $300,000. Here is a situation that needs creativity. The available inheritance for any of the children is not ample. These youngsters have a long way to go before education is complete and they can scramble to their feet. Large amounts may be required for each child. Further, their needs won't be identical. This child may require expensive orthodontia or assistance to overcome a learning disability. That daughter may have her heart set on being a physician, which means long and expensive schooling and training.

If their parents were living and continued to raise the children, they would spend their available money for the children according to the parents' goals and priorities. If the parents are not living, that kind of flexible spending should be emulated. A separate trust for each child won't do it, because it seems inadequate in this case. A trust of $75,000 per child is not a robust inheritance when one realistically appraises the costs of raising the child and education. The daughter with medical school dreams may need lots more, even if she wins scholarships or has student loans. And maybe the youngest child will have less expensive goals and be able to reach them by attending a community college or an institution with a work program.

The single-fund trust is a financial stand-in for what the parents would have done if death had not claimed them. They would spend money according to goals and needs. Equal spending for the children would not be the rule. Instead, raising and educating the children would be the objective, with money used according to priorities. After all, if the oldest had an appendectomy, the parents would not search around for ways to spend an equal amount on the other three children. The trustees' role would be to emulate the parents' financial approach.

Q: Doesn't that put a heavy responsibility on the trustees?

A: You bet it does. But the right people may be available to take on the responsibility. For example, the children may have an aunt who relates to them well and is very sensible. She could be an ideal trustee.

Q: But suppose she has no investment savvy?

A: Then another person with that savvy could be selected to handle that aspect of the trusteeship.

Q: But suppose the aunt interferes with the investment ideas that the savvy person has?

A: The Will can give each trustee a separate and exclusive role. We'll discuss this more in the chapter on Trusts and Trustees (starting on page 111).

Another illustration of the appropriateness of the single trust for all the children is when they are of widely different circumstances. For example, in the family there are three children, a daughter of nineteen and sons who are fourteen and eleven. The family assets are modest. The daughter is halfway through the state university. The younger son was in a serious accident three months ago and receives physical therapy regularly. What should be done if the parents die now? Equal spending on these children would be distorting. The daughter has had two years of college already paid for when the parents die and neither son has had any such benefit. They will need a larger portion of the available money to grow up and obtain their education. If $200 is spent monthly on physical therapy and special care for the younger son, why should an equal amount have to be spent on his siblings for something?

The single-fund trust aims at flexibility. It is designed to meet situations like the ones we have looked at, when the family funds are not robust. But if the funds are adequate, it is clearly better to have a separate trust for each son and daughter, each trust having enough clout to handle whatever the particular child may need. An important characteristic of separate trusts is that financial equality is the starting place for the children. Separateness diminishes the chance of one child's getting favorable treatment in allocating the family inheritance. That may help to suppress or diminish jealousies and misunderstanding among the children. In turn, that will ease the trustees' responsibility and headaches, as they are spared the necessity of determining priorities that may highlight one child's plan over the others.

I hasten to say that separate trusts do not assure domestic tranquility. When the daughter in our last illustration has had two years of college already paid for when the parents have died, a smaller burden will be borne by her trust for education than will be the burden on her brothers' trusts. When all of them have been educated, she may have more left over from her inheritance than her siblings. On the other hand, if she goes on to graduate or professional school and they do not, she may have a smaller amount left in her trust than her brothers have in theirs. Exactness is not possible with either the single trust for all children or separate trusts for them. Reality requires that the parents try to do what is best. They cannot be expected to achieve perfection. The parents must follow a priority. If they would like to avoid creating any cause for misunderstanding by the children and the available assets justify separate trusts, that should be the chosen path. If the parents are more concerned about being able to stretch their moderate assets to achieve rough justice among children who have varying needs, the single trust may be the inevitable choice.

If the single trust is used, an ending date needs to be selected. That usually would be when the youngest child should have reached the objectives that the parents had in mind. An example might be when the youngest child graduates from college or attains the age of twenty-two, whichever occurs first. The trust then ends and whatever assets are left would be divided equally among the children. It is likely that not very much will remain for them to share. Conceivably, though, there might be. If the parents are concerned that the youngest child may not yet have the acumen to handle what is left, more can be done. For example, if any child is under twenty-five and his or her share is $50,000 or more, that share could stay in trust for that child until he or she reaches twenty-five years of age.

When separate trusts are used, a design must be made for their operation. Usually one format is used for all the children. For example, while a child is under twenty-one (or twenty-five) the trustees would have authority to use the income for the child or retain it in the trust and reinvest it as part of the trust principal. Income used for the child is reported on the child's individual income tax return. When neither parent of the child is living, the kiddie tax does not apply. So normal income tax rules would apply even for a child under fourteen. Income retained in the trust is reported on the income tax return of that child's trust. It should be noted that retaining the income is usually done to increase the trust's size, or because the income should not be shoveled into a young child's hands. Retaining income in a trust is inadvisable in tax terms due to the compressed income tax rates that trusts operate under. In this sum-

mary of a trust's income tax rates, notice how quickly the top
bracket is reached.

Trust's Taxable Income	Applicable Tax
Up to $ 3,000	15% rate
Over $3,000 but not over $9,000	$495 plus 28% rate on excess over $3,000
Over $9,000	$2,343 plus 31% rate on excess over $9,000

As to trust principal, there are two aspects. One is the discretionary authority of the trustees to use principal for a child. It is
best not to restrict this authority to such narrow purposes as
medical expenses. Rather, make the authority broad and rely on
astute trustees to exercise that authority judiciously. That approach makes the child's inheritance available to cope with vicissitudes and unexpected happenings that so often erupt in a lifetime. The trustees are in control of this aspect of using trust
principal. Their word prevails, no matter how much the child
may implore them for money, unless their conduct is so severely
egregious that a court would intervene on the child's behalf.

The second aspect relating to trust principal is when the child
can get it regardless of what the trustees say. Some parents do
not want the child ever to be able to take the capital out of the
trust. Because of instability or illness or disability or persistent
bad judgment or a lousy marriage, or some other concern about
the child, the parents may feel it wise to have the principal retained in the trust throughout the child's lifetime. In a minority
of situations, the child appears sound and without any of the
characteristics that would unsettle the parents, but nevertheless
mother or father or both feel that a lifetime trust is preferable.

That may be the parental attitude particularly if the inheritance is quite substantial.

In some situations, a lifetime trust is selected for at least part of the child's inheritance because of tax advantages. In chapter 1 on Tax Opportunities (pages 19–20) we mentioned the generation-skipping tax that applies to gifts and inheritances for grandchildren and other young folks. The opportunity to exploit the $1 million exemption from that tax may motivate a parent to select a lifetime trust for some of a child's inheritance in order to obtain that exemption when the principal will descend to the child's offspring, even though the child is sound in every way and could very competently handle the inheritance personally. More will be said about this in the following chapter.

In most cases, the inheritance will be released to the child as one or more ages are attained. There is no particular format that is just right. Some like a program of releasing principal to children in equal segments at twenty-five, thirty, and thirty-five. Others prefer two stages, say thirty and thirty-five, or possibly twenty-five and thirty. Sometimes the first installment is one-third or one-fourth and the next installment is larger. Myriad combinations are conceivable. Some opt for a later age, at least for the final distribution. Every parent will have a point of view. I recall one anxious mother who thought that the appropriate age for turning over any principal to her college-educated son would be sixty.

Sometimes the chosen formula is to release principal at intervals that are tied to the last surviving parent's death, so that, for example, the first payment would be five years after that date, so long as the child was at least twenty-five years old.

Remember, these are mandatory provisions. When the child hits the magic age or point in time, he or she is entitled to have the payment, come what may. Some cautious and concerned parents prefer delaying one or more installments until the child is at a riper age, when he or she ought to have matured. In the meanwhile, the trustees have their discretionary authority to use principal for the child, which can embrace such purposes as education, travel, acquiring a home, starting a family, investing in an attractive business, and coping with the expenses of a reasonable living standard.

In some cases where the trust would continue with at least some principal until the child should be responsible, say forty, the trustees are empowered to accelerate handing over the principal to the child if he or she exhibits to the trustees' satisfaction a maturity and sense of responsibility that deserve such an earlier ending of the trust. There is hardly any set of factors, accelerations, slowings, or barriers that cannot be woven into the fabric of the trusts. Bear in mind, however, that the design of the vehicle is one thing. Choice of wise and attentive trustees is quite another. I'll have more to say about that in the chapter on Trusts and Trustees (starting on page 111).

All the children do not have to be treated alike. If parents wish to be more liberal or trusting for one child and more cautious with another, different plans can be designed. But caution must be the byword. Missteps can reverberate for an entire generation, and beyond. Children interpret gifts and Will provisions as signs of parental love. While distinctions between children might be acceptable cerebrally, they may fail to convince at heart. When a Will or a gift reveals discriminatory results, a child can be pardoned for not understanding what mom or dad did.

A parent who is intent on making distinctions between children, and is not concerned about the impact on the filial relationship, should reflect further. How about the relationship between the children, not just now, but in the future? If Laurie is to have her full inheritance at thirty, but Jodi is not to have hers until forty, war may erupt between them. Resentments from old scores can be reignited by such treatment. Even if the children are sweet darlings toward each other today, different treatment can cause serious hurt. Parents ought not to discriminate in arranging inheritances except for compelling reasons, such as disability or illness.

That principle ought to be doubly observed. First, do not create inheritances that are unequal in size for children, if possible. That could cause a storm. And a disappointed child could feel the ache for years and years. The goal of fairness should be borne in mind throughout the plan. For example, if mom's sapphire ring, worth $10,000, is to be left to Samantha, an equalizer, even cash, should be left to Scott, so that he feels that he was given a fair shake. Even if one child is financially better off than another, via career or a fortunate marriage, there should be a bias for even-handed treatment. Only in the severest cases would unequal treatment be appropriate and understood. And then an explanation ought to be given in the Will or, preferably, in a private letter that is to be opened after the parent dies. If one child made a very advantageous marriage, that may be a poor reason. In our free-wheeling social maelstrom, marriages are easy come and easy go. A long-time married couple is not immune from possibilities of a breakup.

Second, when the shares are equal, the terms of the inheritances should be parallel, unless compelling circumstances convince the parents otherwise. In the old days, some parents mechanically left inheritances outright to sons, either immediately or at an age like thirty, while shares for daughters stayed in trust for their lifetimes. That is an intolerable notion and, truth to tell, it always was. Such disparagement of a child may lead to a lifetime of psychiatric treatment, and could earn the parents a cold and nasty remembrance.

Guardians

A serious topic concerns the selection of a guardian for children. The guardian I have in mind does not manage money. That task falls to trustees under our program. By all means, avoid having to use guardians as financial managers. The reasons are compelling. First, guardianship of money ends at the age of majority, which commonly is eighteen. That is too early for almost any child to come into serious money. Second, guardians are governed by a raft of strict rules relating to safekeeping of funds, constant court supervision, limits on permissible investment, and restrictions on spending for the child. The rules were developed with the aim of protecting against the wicked or foolish guardian, and they succeed in hampering the honest and attentive guardian and his or her ward. The situation is fraught with strictness, bureaucracy, and expense. In contrast, a trustee has the authority to spend and invest what the parent decided on, which is spelled out in the Will. The trustee is fully accountable in court for his or her decisions and performance, but is not perpetually supervised like a misbehaving juvenile, as a guardian is. A trustee may use trust assets for a child's growth and development, while a guardian in many places cannot pay for music lessons for a gifted child without court approval. While an observer might feel that obtaining the judge's approval might not be a problem, the initiated know that time and expense are involved in seeking that approval. All the expense would come from the child's funds that the guardian has charge of.

Q: If a guardian is not to handle my child's inheritance, what is the guardian's job?

A: The guardian has the role of substitute parent when the biological parents have died.

Q: What does the guardian decide?

A: Lots of everyday things that parents normally handle. Some are major questions, such as with whom the child will live, what school the child will attend, what religious training the child is to have, whether the child can marry at seventeen.

Q: What happens if I die and my child's other parent is living?

A: The surviving parent raises the child, not a guardian. Unless a court finds the surviving parent to be unfit, which is rare, the guardian you had in mind won't have a role. The guardian will come in only when neither parent is alive and the child is still a minor.

Q: Who chooses the guardian?

A: That is the prerogative of the child's last surviving parent, subject to court confirmation.

Q: Suppose my spouse and I are divorced. Our child lives with me. Can't I name a guardian to bring the child up if I die?

A: The surviving parent has the right to do the parenting, unless he or she is found to be unfit.

Q: But what if I had remarried and the child has lived very happily with my second spouse for more than ten years?

A: Your newer spouse has to take a back seat. Your first spouse has the right to raise his or her child and to make all parental decisions. In fact, he or she could effectively block your second spouse from contact with the child.

Q: Even if my first spouse lives far away, has a new family, and just barely maintains contact with my child?

A: Even then. The law favors the surviving biological parent.

The personal guardian or the surviving parent does not manage the child's inheritance, for that is the trustee's role. If you are concerned that your former husband or wife will be able to plunder your child's inheritance, that is extremely unlikely if you make careful preparations and use a trust for the child. The trustee controls the purse strings. Your reassurance comes from careful trust provisions and wise selection of the trustee. But anything spent by the trustee for the child, whether it be for clothing, vacations, or education, relieves the surviving parent or the guardian of the expense. So indirect and incidental benefits are gained by your former spouse, if he or she raises the child after your death. In addition, there is an interplay between the trustee and the guardian or surviving parent. If the guardian or surviving parent wants to enroll a child in an Ivy League school, or send the child to an enriched language program abroad for the summer, but the trustee won't pay for that large expense, the child and parent or guardian may have to revamp their plans.

One last point, which may or may not be soothing: the role of the guardian, if there is one, ends when the child reaches majority. The surviving parent has the parental connection role for life. The trustee is on the scene as long as the trust continues.

The Family Business

A crucial family goal may be involving the children in a family business and paving the way for them to assume leadership of the enterprise. An important component of the goal may be that mom or dad would have to learn to share control of the business, or even to play a subordinate role.

In order to transfer ownership interests to the children, early and sustained action may be essential, in hope of attaining the goal without hurtful tax cost. The keys are nurturing the children's interest in the business, recognizing the opportunity for action, and (on the part of the older generation) being willing to get out of the way. We'll discover once again that taxes are only part of the problem in this delicate subject. Our focus will be on this intriguing topic in the chapter that discusses the Family Business (starting on page 185).

CHAPTER

4

Grandchildren

Who can resist grandchildren, especially the little ones. Their irrepressible smiles and giggles, their sweet arms thrown around your neck, their untiring energy for games, their guileful innocence — it's all a lot to deal with. When little Rachel says in a telephone conversation, "Grandpa, I wish I could crawl through the telephone wires and give you a big kiss," all is lost. Even a cynical, know-it-all, crusty captain of industry would melt.

Grandchildren seem to be like springtime. They promise hope, renewal, and better times. Some people are sufficiently senior to be witnessing these blessings again through great-grandchildren. That achievement may even produce some wry and ironic observations. As explained to me in San Francisco by one silver-haired lady who boasted of twelve grandchildren and four great-grandchildren: "I don't mind having great-grandchildren, but it bothers me to be the parent of a grandmother."

People often put much of their planning faith in grandchildren. One reason is that those tykes cannot be denied. The joy of grandchildren is a deep motivation in numerous cases. Sometimes that joy permeates the client, but he or she nevertheless will not include the grandchildren in any of the major plans due

The Generation-Skipping Tax

The tax landscape for grandchildren shows one major difference: the generation-skipping tax (known to regular users as the GST, but we'll try to ignore that shortcut). This separate tax must be confronted whenever a gift or bequest is made for a grandchild, or someone of a grandchild's generation. That someone could pop up in different ways. As a rule of thumb, it would be someone who is two or more generations younger than you are, or would be if the two of you were related. Examples aside from your own grandsons and granddaughters would include your spouse's grandchildren via another marriage and the offspring of your nephews and nieces.

As for unrelated people, some simple arithmetic will identify a beneficiary who is two or more generations younger than you are. A generation is twenty-five years, and you are in the middle of that span, with twelve and one-half years on either side. The next slot is between twelve and one-half years and thirty-seven and one-half years younger than you. That is the children's generation. Anyone younger than you by more than thirty-seven and one-half years is in the grandchild's generation, or even below. Here are examples:

Example

You were born in 1940. Your friend Amy was born in 1962. She is in the slot reserved for children.

Example

Amy was married for a time, and has a daughter who was born in 1985. Vis-à-vis you, that daughter is in the slot of grandchildren.

Any gift or bequest you may provide for Amy is free of the generation-skipping tax because in relation to you she is in the children's generation. But any gift or bequest for Amy's child would get tangled up in the generation-skipping tax.

One more point may be important. Assume that your brother Paul is sixty-five and a widower. He's been smitten by a curvaceous delight who can't be more than twenty-six. There is a span of thirty-nine years between them. If Paul gives her $25,000, he must contend with the generation-skipping tax. But if Paul marries the curvaceous lady before writing that check, that tax is aborted because she is Paul's spouse. Any spouse of Paul is automatically put in his generation, no matter how many years are spread between them.

When confronting the generation-skipping tax, it is essential to make peace with an important fact. That tax is not a substitute for other taxes. Instead, it is in addition to other taxes. So, if Paul does not marry the lady, but they are dear friends, and when he dies she inherits $500,000 from him, two taxes are involved: the regular estate tax and the generation-skipping tax.

How did this double-barreled tax setup come about? Well, the first barrel is the regular gift and estate tax. That has been in place for more than half a century. You are looking down the second barrel because of clever work done over many years by advisers who guided their clients very shrewdly.

Here is an illustration of what used to be done in the old days. George, a wealthy guy, created a $500,000 trust for his daughter Alice in 1940 and paid the regular gift or estate tax. The trust contained these terms:

(1) All the income would go to Alice throughout her life.

(2) The trustees could pay principal to Alice for any reason.

(3) Alice could draw 5 percent of the trust principal each year willy-nilly without any reason. She also could withdraw principal at any time for her support, maintenance, health, and education.

(4) Alice is a trustee and no investments can be made without her approval. The only restriction against her is that she cannot participate in the trustees' authority to pay principal to her under item 2, so only the other trustees can do that; but that restriction does not apply when she makes withdrawals under item 3.

(5) When Alice dies she can direct in her Will how the trust assets are to be disposed of in favor of any persons she selects.

(6) If Alice dies without making any direction in her Will, the trust assets are divided up for her children.

It happens that Alice died in 1965. The trust was then worth $5 million. Her Will exercised Alice's right to dispose of the trust assets in favor of her children Cindy and David, both of whom were toddlers when Grandpa George died in 1940. Alice's Will put the inheritance in trusts for Cindy and David that are replicas of the trust that Alice had. Our crystal ball tells us that Cindy will live until the year 2027, when she will be ninety-one, and she will leave three children. The same crystal ball reveals that David will live until the year 2028, when he will be eighty-nine, and he will leave four children.

By the time each dies, *each* will leave trust assets of $20 million. In other words, the trust assets will have grown from $500,000 to $40 million over the years since 1940. That is a restrained estimate of growth. If the assets had been invested in a successfully aggressive manner, the sky could be the limit. George's seven great-grandchildren will inherit that fortune. Similar trusts to continue on for their lives are not possible, because the law puts limits on having trusts for beneficiaries who were not alive when the first trust was started by Grandpa George in 1940.

Those limits are one of the great nightmares law students suffer through, known to generations of head-scratchers as the Rule Against Perpetuities. The concept dates back to 1682 and the *Duke of Norfolk's Case*. What the Duke taught us commoners is simple: a trust cannot be perpetuated for untold generations. In practical application, however, the concept can blow the mind of any high court chief-justice-wannabe. Learned professors, particularly Leach of Harvard, dissected the rule's applications over many years. The rule says, generally, that a trust cannot extend beyond a period measured by lives in being when the trust was created, plus twenty-one years.

Example

You create a trust now for the life of your daughter and, after she is gone, to continue for the lifetime benefit of her children. She has none at present, and could yet have a dozen if she puts her mind to it. The trust offends the rule, because it is designed to run for the lives of grandchildren who are not in being when you start the trust.

Similarly, caution was needed when Alice exercised her right to dispose of the assets of the trust created by Grandpa George, which started in 1940 when he died. The point of creation of the trust for the Rule Against Perpetuities was its very start in 1940, and not when Alice exercised her right of disposition. In order to extend the trust for the lives of her children, they had to be in being in 1940. Fortunately, Cindy and David were on the scene then, so the trust could be extended by Alice throughout their lives (and even twenty-one years beyond). If Alice's kids had come along after Grandpa George died, Alice could not have extended the trust for her children's lives.

There is a significant reward for what Grandpa George and Alice did: there would not be any further gift or estate tax on this fortune after the first trust was started in 1940, except for a smidgin of estate tax at the deaths of Alice, Cindy, and David, because of the absolute right to pull 5 percent out of trust in the year of death.

Pretty terrific tax shelter! That kind of program has been used by wealthy American families for generations, from Texas oil wildcatters to New England textile manufacturers to Wall Street bankers to Southern tobacco growers to Western ranchers.

After years of observing such wealth preserved virtually unscathed from death taxes, Congress decided it was all too much to bear. A new tax was invented to apply whenever assets pass on to grandchildren. Old trusts are protected from this tax, or, as the cognoscenti say, they are grandfathered. Old trusts are ones that were created before September 25, 1985, *and* after that date cannot be changed or revoked by the creator. So Grandpa George's trust, as extended by Alice, is beyond the reach of this tax, even though Cindy and David will die long after the new tax was invented.

Any additional property or cash put into a protected trust would attract the tax, so additions should not be made to a trust that otherwise would be pristine. But Alice's power to dispose of the trust in favor of her children is not a change, nor is it considered to be an addition. Even if she died in 1992, the trust is grandfathered; its creation date is fixed at 1940, when Grandpa George died.

The generation-skipping tax is not a gentle newcomer. The tax bites under varying circumstances. Here are examples:

Example

A gift or bequest to a grandchild need not be cash. A gift or bequest of jewelry, U.S. savings bonds, a car, or any investment, will be enough to trigger the tax, even if there is an occasion like a birthday.

Example

The grandchild need not be the only beneficiary or even the first beneficiary. If a parent creates a trust for the lifetime benefit of his or her child, and at the child's death the trust assets will pass to the child's children, the generation-skipping tax comes due at the child's death, when the grandchild's entitlement blossoms. The rate of tax is applied against the value of the fund at the child's death. Hence any growth occurring between the death of the parent-creator and the child's death leads to more tax.

Example

If a parent creates a trust and provides that income or principal may be used by the trustee at any time for the parent's children or grandchildren, as the trustee decides, payments made for the grandchildren fall prey currently to the tax.

The Exemption

Do not swoon yet. In each of these cases there may be exclusions or exemptions to prevent the tax from operating. Just as there is an exemption from estate tax, there is an exemption from the generation-skipping tax. Recall that the estate tax exemption is $600,000, minus whatever part of it was used up by lifetime gifts. For the generation-skipping tax, the exemption that every person has is $1 million, usable against lifetime taxable gifts or legacies at death.

Q: Is that an overall total exemption of $1 million?

A: Yes. Your spouse has the same exemption.

Q: How do I use my spouse's?

A: By lifetime gifts, in the same way you could use your spouse's $600,000 exemption against gift tax. For example, you write a check on your own account for $50,000 to your granddaughter. By obtaining your spouse's consent to the gift, you make use of four exemptions.

(a) A piece of your $600,000 exemption against gift tax.

(b) A piece of your spouse's $600,000 exemption against gift tax.

(c) A piece of your $1 million exemption against generation-skipping tax.

(d) A piece of your spouse's $1 million exemption against generation-skipping tax.

Q: How big are those pieces that are being used?

A: Remember that you have an annual exclusion from gift tax of $10,000 for a gift to your granddaughter, if you haven't used it already this year. That exclusion is doubled to $20,000 with your spouse's consent. So $20,000 of the transfer to your granddaughter is not taxable as a gift for gift tax purposes, and only the balance of $30,000 is a taxable gift. That has a parallel for the separate generation-skipping tax: the same $20,000 that is nontaxable for gift tax purposes can be (but is not always) a nontaxable transfer for generation-skipping tax purposes. The balance of $30,000 is a generation-skipping transfer.

Here is a bird's-eye view of how the total transfer of $50,000 to your granddaughter works out.

	For Gift Tax Purposes	For Generation-Skipping Tax Purposes
Total transferred	$ 50,000	$ 50,000
Less: Nontaxable part under *your* gift tax annual exclusion	(10,000)	(10,000)
Nontaxable part under *spouse's* gift tax annual exclusion	(10,000)	(10,000)
Less: Part of *your* $600,000 exemption from gift tax	(15,000)	
Part of *spouse's* $600,000 exemption from gift tax	(15,000)	
Less: Part of *your* $1 million exemption from GST		(15,000)
Less: Part of *spouse's* $1 million exemption from GST		(15,000)
Balance on which tax is due	0	0

Gifts that fit within the annual gift tax exclusion of $10,000/20,000 are therefore a way to duck the generation-skipping tax without tapping the $1 million exemption. Outright gifts would fit, but they give the beneficiary total control, and that may not be encouraging to the giver. Gifts to custodian accounts under the Uniform Gifts to Minors Act (UGMA) or the Uniform Transfers to Minors Act (UTMA) also would fit. But remember that UGMA arrangements end when the beneficiary is eighteen or, in some states, twenty-one, and UTMA arrangements end at twenty-one. That may not be to the bestower's liking.

Trusts for Grandchildren

The bestower may consider a trust in order to foster management of the assets until the beneficiary is more likely to be mature. But the choices are limited when the desire is to sidestep the generation-skipping tax via the $10,000/20,000 annual exclusion. The trust that runs until age twenty-one can be used, but that early termination may not please the bestower. Hope could be put in an alternative: a trust that continues until a later age, such as twenty-five or thirty, but that the grandchild-beneficiary has the right to terminate at age twenty-one. Either of these trusts satisfies GST requirements if it provides that if the grandchild-beneficiary dies before the trust ends, the trust assets will be part of his or her estate for estate tax purposes.

When gifts for children were discussed, we indicated that a different possibility was available: a trust that keeps going past twenty-one, or a trust with more than one beneficiary, so long as the beneficiary we are focusing on can withdraw a gift made to the trust of $10,000/20,000 in the year the gift occurred. That is a trust that has a *Crummey* power, which is the name (taken from a famous case) given to the beneficiary's right to withdraw.

For gift tax purposes, the government permits the use of *Crummey* trusts even if the beneficiary is so young that he or she would be oblivious to the gift, as long as a parent or guardian theoretically could exercise the power of withdrawal for the youthful beneficiary. But for the generation-skipping tax, this approach will work only when special provisions are in the trust. Those are that there may be only one beneficiary (who would be the grandchild in our situation); that he or she would take over all the assets when the trust expires, whatever the age may be; and that, if the grandchild dies prematurely, the trust assets will be part of his or her estate for estate tax purposes. When regular gifts are made to a trust for a grandchild, these requirements are not likely to be troublesome for the bestower, so the annual gift tax exclusion of $10,000/20,000 could be had. But they will cause obstacles with life insurance trusts involving grandchildren, a matter we'll look at in the chapter on Life Insurance (starting on page 151).

Other transfers for grandchildren that will escape the generation-skipping tax without using the $1 million exemption relate to payments for tuition and medical expenses. These may be either direct gifts by the bestower or payments from a trust.

Q: How do the trust payments work?

A: An example would be a trust that you create for your son or daughter, and that permits the trustee to pay tuition and medical expenses for your child's offspring.

Q: Suppose the trustee is allowed to pay for other things for a grandchild?

A: Allowing the trustee to do it is no sin. But if the trustee goes ahead and pays for something other than tuition and medical expense, that other payment is beyond the safe boundary. The $1 million exemption from the generation-skipping tax would have to be in play to avoid the tax.

When the generation-skipping tax cannot be avoided, the cost is rugged. The tax is a flat tax, whether the transfer that it is levied on is $5 or $5 million. The tax rate is the same as the highest rate prevailing under the estate tax. Today that rate is 55 percent. And remember, this is heaped on top of the regular gift tax or estate tax.

The threat of such a toll makes it important that the $1 million exemption be used to the hilt. Remember that every person, and his or her spouse, has that exemption. So within a family group, the exemptions of grandma and grandpa can be assembled to snuff out or substantially lower the tax. But also realize that the exemption that a person may call on in making gifts and bequests is a grand total of $1 million (plus the spouse's $1 million) and not $1 million per grandchild.

Here are examples for using the exemption:

Example

You wish to give some jewelry to your granddaughter and $10,000 to each of your grandsons. Everything else will be divided outright between your sons. If you wish to make lifetime gifts, the cash can be transferred under the protection of the $10,000/20,000 annual gift tax exclusion and your $1 million exemption is never even used. The jewelry as well can be given under the $10,000/20,000 umbrella, unless a real rock is involved. If you prefer to leave the jewelry and cash to your grandchildren in your Will, the $10,000/20,000 exclusions cannot be used, for they pertain only to lifetime gifts. But your $1 million exemption will be far more than ample to protect the grandchildren's inheritances from the generation-skipping tax.

Example

Your daughter, who is your only child, is quite competent and could handle her inheritance very capably. But she and you would like to pass a chunk of her inheritance on to her children without unnecessary taxes. In your Will leave up to $1 million of her inheritance in trust for your daughter's lifetime benefit, just as astute people did in the old days. Allocate to the trust your $1 million exemption from the generation-skipping tax. That trust will be sheltered from that tax at all times, and your grandchildren will have the full measure of their inheritance. Once the exemption goes into play at your death and shelters the entire trust, full protection remains intact even if the trust later grows many times over. If you are fortunate to have more than $1 million for your daughter's inheritance, consider leaving the excess to her outright, for if it goes into the same trust a portion of that trust will be taxed when your daughter dies.

Example

Your son, the doctor, earns a fine income, but he'll need help to foot the bill for his kids' education and other expenses. Create a sprinkling trust in your lifetime or by Will, so that payments from income and principal can go via the trustees' discretion at any time to your son and any of his children. Whatever income isn't paid out during the grandchildren's formative years can be kept in the trust. Don't fund the trust beyond the protection of your $1 million exemption. Once the trust is fully sheltered from the generation-skipping tax, it will remain so, even though clever investing and occasional retention of income cause the principal to mushroom. Payments for tuition would be protected from the generation-skipping tax even without

trust either (a) for the lifetime benefit of one of the children or (b) as a sprinkling trust for a child and that child's offspring.

In all of these illustrations a trust is used to funnel down the generation line to the grandchildren the amount ($600,000) that is exempt at the first decedent's death from estate tax. Even if a child is very capable of handling his or her inheritance, it is packaged in a trust to gain optimum tax protection. By that arrangement there is no estate tax at the deaths of the surviving spouse or the children, due to the shelter that the trust provides against estate tax. At the same time, the generation-skipping tax is also confronted. From the $1 million generation-skipping tax exemption enough protection is drawn, in the amount of $600,000, to shelter the assets throughout the trust's existence from that tax. That protection is fully intact even though down through the years the trust assets appreciate in value many times over from their starting amount of $600,000.

Alternatives are possible.

Example

The surviving spouse and the children are bypassed. The $600,000 exempt amount is left directly for the grandchildren, either outright or in trust.

In any of these situations, if the Will maker is already blessed with grandchildren, he or she may design the trust to continue for the lives of the grandchildren, with the trust assets eventually going into the hands of great-grandchildren. While $600,000 is the starting amount, clever or fortunate investment may cause the assets to multiply like rabbits by the time the trust finally expires some fifty or sixty years in the future.

So far our focus has been on a portion of the bestower's estate that is shielded from estate tax and generation-skipping tax at inception, again when the children die, and, if the trust runs long enough, again when the grandchildren die. But we have used only $600,000 of the Will maker's exemption from generation-skipping tax. We want to use the balance of $400,000 that remains of the Will maker's entire $1 million exemption, and we also wish to make use of the surviving spouse's $1 million exemption, which, to this point, may never have been touched.

The key to utilizing the bestower's remaining $400,000 exemption from the generation-skipping tax is to create a marital deduction trust of the QTIP variety, in that amount. The surviving spouse will be the lifetime beneficiary, but will not have control of the trust principal. At the death of the survivor, the disposition of the principal will be controlled by the bestower's Will. (For a refresher about the QTIP, look at pages 55–58.) Although that trust will be part of the surviving spouse's estate for estate tax purposes at his or her later death, the remaining $400,000 exemption that the creator had can be assigned to this trust.

We therefore have exploited the Will maker's entire $1 million exemption from the generation-skipping tax via two segments, neither of which is subject to estate tax at the Will maker's death. The first segment is the portion of his or her estate that is exempt from estate tax due to the unified credit, and would be $600,000 if none of that exemption had been touched before. The second segment would be a QTIP trust, aggregating $400,000 if the first segment was $600,000. If the first segment was less than $600,000 because some of the unified credit from gift and estate tax previously was used, the second segment comprised by the QTIP trust could be larger to make up the overall total of $1 million that is protected from the tax on generation-skipping transfers. The table on the following pages summarizes salient points about segments 1 and 2. You may find it helpful.

Segment 1

Beneficiaries: open choice; can be spouse, then trust for child, then on to grandchild.

a. Starts with $600,000.

b. Protected at Will maker's death from estate tax by unified credit.

c. Protected at spouse's death from estate tax by trust, which is a shelter.

d. Protected at child's death from estate tax by trust-shelter; protected from generation-skipping tax (GST) by $600,000 out of Will maker's $1 million GST exemption.

Segment 2

Beneficiaries: start with spouse, for lifetime benefit via QTIP trust; next, open choice; can be trust for child then on to grandchild.

a. Starts with $400,000.

b. Protected at Will maker's death from estate tax by marital deduction.

c. Subject to estate tax at spouse's death.

d. Protected at child's death from estate tax by trust, which is a shelter; protected from GST by remaining $400,000 of Will maker's GST exemption.

If any of the Will maker's estate remains, it would make up a third segment. This piece could be of any size and could be left under the marital deduction for the surviving spouse. Whether it be bequeathed to him or her outright, or in a classic marital trust with an unlimited power of disposition when the spouse later dies, or in a QTIP trust, whatever remains at the surviving spouse's death will be part of his or her estate for estate tax purposes. Although the assets in the segment 3 have to absorb that blow, much still can be done. Particularly, we can aim to use the surviving spouse's own exemption of $1 million from the generation-skipping tax to insulate the assets from that tax as they pass down through the generations.

Here is a table that may be helpful.

Segment 3

Beneficiaries: start with spouse; choose among outright provision or QTIP trust or classic marital deduction trust. If outright provision or classic marital trust, spouse has open choice for his or her disposition. Either open choice can be trust for child then on to grandchild.

a.　Any amount at start.

b.　Protected at Will maker's death from estate tax by marital deduction.

c.　Subject to estate tax at spouse's death.

d.　Protected at child's death from estate tax by trust, which is a shelter; protected from GST by surviving spouse's exemption up to $1 million.

The original bestower's third segment need not be the only source that the surviving spouse would call on to exploit his or her $1 million exemption from the generation-skipping tax. Alternatively, if the surviving spouse has independent assets, those could be wheeled into place for the same purpose. Or, the surviving spouse could use that exemption by melding together some or all of his or her assets with some or all of the bestower's inheritance, whether that was left outright or in trust, up to an aggregate of $1 million. Whatever the source of the assets, the survivor's exemption is availed of in one of these ways:

1. Separate shares for children. Each share in a lifetime trust for a child and, at his or her death, on to grandchildren.

2. Separate shares for children. While a child is living, income and principal can be sprinkled among the child and his or her offspring. When the child dies, the assets move on to grandchildren.

3. Children are bypassed and the assets are devoted to grandchildren, either via trusts or outright.

In some situations, the infamous Rule Against Perpetuities, which limits the length of trusts, will permit the assets to be continued in trust throughout the lives of the grandchildren. That permission under the rule would arise because the grandchildren were alive when the original creator launched the first trust in our sequence. With that trust plan, when the grandchildren die in the far future, there will be no estate tax or generation-skipping tax when the trust assets pass to the next generation, to the great benefit of the great-grandchildren.

In other words, what the wealthy American families could do before the invention of the generation-skipping tax still can be done, up to the maximum of available exemptions against the tax. That maximum exemption of $1 million per creator applies at the inception, when the gift or bequest is made. From the standpoint of growth, there is no limit on the expansion of the exempt trust from its starting place of $1 million. Careful planning and astute investment, coupled with the wonder of compound interest, can produce enormous growth for the benefit of future generations. If trustees can take an exempt trust of $1 million and grow it to a thousand times larger, so be it. The exemption will keep the IRS at bay.

Before embracing the opportunities too enthusiastically, bear in mind the issues we have discussed that are not tax-related but are absolutely critical:

- What are appropriate ages and terms for the inheritance that will fall into the laps of grandchildren and great-grandchildren?

- What safeguards can be erected to prevent them from becoming lazy, spoiled, unmotivated fat cats?

- What selection can be made of clever, wise, and fair-minded trustees?

Obviously, there is a lot of planning to do.

Even when the treacherous Rule Against Perpetuities would preclude any extension of the trusts throughout the lives of the grandchildren, critical questions remain. Even if none of the grandchildren was living when the original trust bestower died, the trusts created in his or her Will can run until at least twenty-one years after the death of the bestower's last surviving child. Under those circumstances, what choice does the creator wish to make concerning the appropriate trust terms and safeguards against a grandchild's gluttony and utter lassitude? And how about selection of trustees? The need for planning is hard to ignore.

CHAPTER

5

Trusts and Trustees

W hile England proudly lays claim to much, including Shakespeare and Winston Churchill, advisers particularly doff their caps to England for its invention of trusts. Here indeed is a great accomplishment!

The Trustee's Role

Trusts are a vehicle for transmitting gifts and inheritances. The structure is quite simple. The trustee is the owner and manager. So, if the trust holds real estate or shares of stock, the trustee decides whether and at what price to sell them, and he or she is the party who transfers legal title by signing the transfer documents.

The authority and powers of the trustee come from two sources. The law arms the trustee with a great deal of authority and power. How much and to what extent will vary from state to state. Additionally, the document that creates the trust can add to that authority and power, or, conversely, the document can diminish what state law otherwise would say. In the realm of authority, a major matter is the trust's investment policy.

The person who creates the trust can authorize the trustees to invest trust funds under any conceivable regimen, primarily for income or capital appreciation, circumscribed by tight restrictions or with the broadest scope. In days gone by, some anxious souls confined their trustees to investment in what was seemingly safe and sound: railroad bonds. Came the Great Depression and that investment policy was hurtful.

In more recent times, such restrictions are rarely imposed. Instead, the philosophy has widely developed of the creator's concentrating on selecting the trustees with exceeding care and empowering the trustees to invest trust funds as they may think best. Because of rapid changes, unforeseeable events, economic environments that fly from booming giddy highs to depressing lows, the recent philosophy seems best. For a bestower to write a rigid policy that is to prevail for years into the future and confidently expect it to succeed is the mark of stubbornness or colossal ego or grandiosity.

While I would not want my trustees playing the devil with my hard-earned capital that is intended to sustain my family, neither would I want my trustees restricted to investing in only this or that. Remember buggy whips and men's fedoras and carbon paper? All became obsolete, or nearly so. Who would have known? Remember when IBM was a fantastic growth stock and General Motors was king of the hill? They're pretty ordinary investments now. Who was so perspicacious as to see a roller coaster ride for oil and gas properties, or trouble ahead for tobacco companies or producers of products with asbestos? Who could foresee that tenants of good repute would become bankrupt and soil real estate holdings? Who could imagine that solid tenants would move out, even before their lease expired, under inducement to switch to other buildings whose owners slashed their rents in order to generate a flow of income, no matter how thin. Wisdom, flexibility, experience, wisdom, good sense, foresight, wisdom, experience, artfulness, good fortune, and wisdom and experience are what trustees need.

It has become apparent over time that the investment of trust funds is a critical business. As not every trustee has investment experience or the desired skill, the concept has taken hold of allowing the trustee to work closely with a respected and financially responsible investment adviser. The law in many states even permits the trustee to delegate the investment function to that adviser, so that he or she makes the investment decisions. So long as the trustee picked the guru with care, the trustee is not legally responsible for unhappy investment results.

There is a great deal of authority that can be granted to the trustee beyond the power to invest. For example, the trustee can be authorized to hire investment counsel and real estate experts, to provide guidance; custodians, to take charge physically of the trust assets for safekeeping; and lawyers and accountants, for professional work in their disciplines.

The trustee can be given considerable authority over the trust's economic benefits, which are the flow of income earned and the principal itself. We'll review various possibilities in our discussion of those benefits.

The Beneficiary

The folks who enjoy the gift or inheritance that is placed in trust are the beneficiaries. They come in all ages, under varied economic positions, with their own problems and needs, and they have divergent intellectual ability. The point is, trusts are not just for very young or disabled individuals. But it is true that, traditionally, youths and senior folk and people with special problems are beneficiaries of trusts.

Example

I want to take care of the education of my grandson Ronald, who is fourteen and a computer whiz — but maybe he'll be a doctor.

Solution: Put your gifts for Ronald in a trust. Gift tax might even be avoided. (See chapter 1 on Tax Opportunities.) The trustee can pay for education expenses. Let the trust continue until your grandson finishes his education or reaches a particular age (like twenty-five), whichever occurs *last*. Be mindful of the generation-skipping tax.

Example

I'm concerned about my mother, whom I help financially. If "something happens to me" before she goes, my mother may not have enough to live on. I don't want her to be dependent on my spouse, 'cause you never know how that may turn out.

Solution: In your Will put the exempt amount of $600,000 that is created by the unified credit (or less, if less will do) in trust so that the trustee can provide for your mother after your death. Don't select your spouse as trustee; use someone for that role who will be free of conflicts and to whom your mother can relate.

Example

My sister was in a bad accident last year and will always need physical therapy. Her doctor bills and expenses for medication could be rugged. I can't just give her the money, because she can't handle it — and I don't trust her husband. It's possible that she'll recover a lot of money in a lawsuit that she is bringing.

Solution: Pay her medical expenses directly. They are not considered gifts. (See chapter 1 on Tax Opportunities.) In your Will let the exempt trust, which is created by the unified credit, be on standby to help her, if other resources are lacking.

Example

My son remarried last year, and Gina is his third wife. He goes for the same kind of woman all the time and it never works. He's bright and sweet, but a fool when it comes to women. I'm afraid of leaving his inheritance outright to him; his kids will never see a dime.

Solution: Put his inheritance in trust. He'll receive the income and if he needs extra money for medical care or support or sound purposes, the trustee can help him with payments of principal. When your son dies his kids will inherit the trust. (Look at the chapter on Grandchildren, starting on page 87, concerning the generation-skipping tax.)

Trusts for Tax Savings

Trusts are sometimes created to exploit tax opportunities. This is illustrated by the $1 million exemption from the generation-skipping tax. Suppose your son is not only bright and sweet, but also very sensible and capable. Ordinarily you would leave his inheritance outright to him. But the opportunity is irresistible to protect that inheritance from estate taxes and generation-skipping taxes when he dies, and hand that protected inheritance over to his children. Meanwhile, your son will be the sole beneficiary of the trust during his lifetime.

This last situation is illustrative of what trusts can be made to do. Through the decades, wealthy American families, like the

Rockefellers and the Kennedys, the Astors, and the Fords, used trusts to pass inheritances down through generations. Trusts of that pedigree were expertly managed by professionals, and the principal multiplied in value over the years. Those trusts used to be impervious to death taxes, from one generation to another. But that glorious aspect has been substantially taken away for new trusts by the government, as described in the chapter on Grandchildren (starting on page 87). But, as that chapter indicates, some of that resilience to death tax has been preserved.

Q: That's all very well, but I don't want to tie up my son's inheritance, even if those taxes could be avoided.

A: The tax that can be avoided is about one-half of the value of the trust. The tie-up that concerns you is pretty mild. Your son not only will be the only beneficiary during his lifetime, but he can be one of the trustees who manages the trust.

Q: Why can't he be the only trustee?

A: In many states he can. But there's some disadvantage if you design the trust that way. If he is the only trustee, there are two means of his taking principal out of the trust without causing the entire trust to be taxed at his death. One is to authorize him to withdraw from principal each year whichever is greater: $5,000, or an amount equal to 5 percent of the current value of the principal.

　　The second way of safely opening principal to your son is to empower him to withdraw principal for his own support, maintenance, education, and health.

Q: Suppose he wanted to buy a house or a sailboat, or take his wife and children around the world?

A: If you named a co-trustee, that person could be authorized to give your son principal for those purposes, and other reasons as well, and the trust would not be taxed when your son dies.

Q: But wouldn't a co-trustee have to agree to everything?

A: No. You could direct that the trust's investments are controlled exclusively by your son.

Q: But I'd like my son to be able to provide for his wife out of his inheritance, if he wished.

A: You could give your son the right to say in his own Will how the trust is to pass at his death in favor of his wife, his descendants, and any other person or charity, and the trust still would not be taxed at his death. You can even direct that any provision he wishes to make for his wife can only be via a trust from which she receives income during her life, and when she dies the trust assets will pass to your grandchildren. By doing that, you allow your son to provide for his wife, but you keep the trust principal in your family.

Q: I'm still not sure I want a trust for my son.

A: Here are extra features in favor of the trust. If your son hits bad times, the trust can be pretty secure from any of his creditors. And, if his marriage isn't great, the trust can be a protector. In many states his wife could not get to the trust if they should be divorced. And she would not have any inheritance rights to the trust if he decided not to give her any benefits from it at his death.

Income and Principal

Traditionally, trust beneficiaries are divided into those who are in position to receive benefits currently and those who wait for their turn to come, which will be when the current beneficiaries are out of the way. Current benefits from a trust are denominated as income, comprising rental income, dividends, and interest. That last can be taxable interest for state and federal purposes (for example, telephone company bonds) or taxable interest for federal purposes and tax-exempt interest for state and local purposes (U.S. Treasuries) or tax-exempt for federal purposes that may be tax-exempt for state and local purposes (state and local governmental issues, lumped under the umbrella of municipal bonds).

Example

Dahlia, who lives in a suburb of New York City, will receive income from a trust that her recently departed uncle Quincy created in his will with a legacy of $250,000, to be held in trust for Dahlia's lifetime. The trustee is preparing to invest that money. Possible components of the income, and how the United States and state of New York would tax them, may be summarized this way:

Component	*US Tax?*	*NYS Tax?*
Dividends from stock like GE, GM, AT&T	yes	yes
Interest from bonds like Georgia Power, Con Edison	yes	yes
Interest from U.S. Treasuries	yes	no

Component	US Tax?	NYS Tax?
Interest from bonds of U.S. agencies such as Ginnie Mae	yes	yes
Interest from N.Y.S. general revenue bonds	no	no
Interest from bonds of other states such as IL, KY, and CA	no	yes

Principal is the fund that is invested. It may have started with cash or stock or bonds or real estate or something less common, such as oil wells or copyrights to books or plays. Over time, the original principal may be transformed by investment decisions the trustee makes.

Example

Natasha, who created a fabulous business in fitness through nutrition and exercise, placed one-third of the stock of her company in a trust for her children. Eight years later, the trustee sold all of the trust's stock to a group of investors at the same time that Natasha sold hers to the same group. The trustee then invested the trust's proceeds of sale, net of the trust's capital gains taxes, in a diversified selection of stocks and U.S. Treasuries, which are held by the trust.

Current beneficiaries either are entitled under the trust provisions to receive income yielded by the trust assets, or they are eligible for income distributions that the trustees decide to make, in the discretion of the trustees. Here are examples:

Example

A trust provides that income is to be paid to your spouse in monthly installments. He or she is entitled to the trust's dividends and interest and rental income net of expenses that income must bear. (More about those expenses shortly.) The trustees have no right to interfere with that flow of income. The trustees are obliged to produce a reasonable flow of income, and they cannot keep funds idle beyond very brief intervals.

Q: What if the trustees do not keep the funds invested?

A: They can be held liable in court by the income beneficiary, who is your spouse in this example.

Q: What if the income is inadequate, even though the funds are invested?

A: That possibility should have been foreseen when the trust provisions were written. One standby cure is to authorize the trustee to draw on principal to supplement the income so that your spouse can maintain a reasonable standard of living. This cure is in the trustees' hands. An alternative is to provide that your spouse is to receive a total return from the trust that is not less than a particular target (say 7 percent). If income is shy of that target in any year, the difference comes from principal. Another possibility is to have a definite target in dollar terms to protect the income beneficiary. For example, provide that if the income falls below a specified figure (say $40,000) in any year, the deficit will come out of principal.

Q: I like the dollar target. But, what if I specify a figure like $40,000, and inflation makes that amount inadequate?

A: The trust can provide that the targeted amount is to be adjusted by upward changes in the consumer price index.

Q: What happens to capital gains?

A: They belong to principal and do not go to the current beneficiary (your spouse here) unless the trust specifies that they should. That would be unusual.

Example

A trust is created for your granddaughter, who is eleven years old. The trust will end when she is thirty, and the trust assets will then be turned over to her. The trust could provide that until she is twenty-one (or any other age) the trustees decide how much income to pay to her. The rest of the income is reinvested in the trust. From the time she reaches the specified age and until the trust ends at thirty, the income must be paid to her and the trustees are without authority to withhold any from her.

Q: Who pays the tax on the income that is reinvested?

A: The trust. Your granddaughter pays the tax on income that is paid to her before the specified age, and on all the income after that age. It is possible, however, to deliberately burden the creator of the trust, while he or she is alive, with responsibility for the income tax. Some sophisticated people like that. We'll mention it again later.

Q: Who pays the tax on capital gains that go to principal?

A: The trust, out of its principal, unless the creator of the trust deliberately accepts that burden during his or her life.

Example

Your objective is to take care of a group of beneficiaries, depending on individual needs. You might create a trust like this for any children your daughter has. She has one now, expects to give birth in four months, and hopes to have more children. The trustees can be authorized, in their discretion, to pay as much income as they decide on for one or more of the children. The trust could provide guidelines for expenditures, such as education. The trust would say that undistributed income is to be retained in the trust and reinvested. The trustees completely control the income flow. This is a sprinkling or spray trust.

Although this trust will benefit grandchildren who will be born after it was started, it is entirely possible to design it so that it will not violate the Rule Against Perpetuities. For example, the trust could run until twenty-one years after the daughter dies (her "life in being" plus twenty-one years). Unless she dies in childbirth, the trust will be a resource for the beneficiaries until the youngest one is over twenty-one years old and the other children are even older.

Q: Why not specify that the income is to be paid equally among the grandchildren?

A: Greater flexibility comes about if the trustees have power to sprinkle or spray, as well as authority to retain income in the trust. For example, suppose one of the children has learning disabilities or severe asthma and needs special care? Or suppose the newborn turns out to be extraordinarily talented musically and in the child's teenage years lessons with a great cellist are recommended together with the purchase of an expensive cello. Equal payments of income won't do nearly as good a job for the grandchildren, unless a sizable amount is put in trust that will amply cover each grand-child, including those born later on.

The beneficiaries who wait in the wings for the current ben-eficiary to exit are concerned about the trust principal. They want it conserved and enhanced. Those waiting beneficiaries may eventually be entitled to receive the principal outright, to stuff in their jeans. Or they may be the next set of beneficiaries of a trust that will continue on and from which they will be paid the income that the principal would generate. Whichever future role is theirs, they now want the principal fattened up for their coming enjoyment.

The principal of the trust consists of the founding assets, ad-ditions along the way, and appreciation, including capital gains. Of course, the founding assets don't necessarily stay around. In-vestments may change along the way, and the original assets may have been transformed into something else.

It is frequently wise to authorize the trustees to use the prin-cipal for the current beneficiaries, in order to have flexibility. That authority can be broad or narrow, depending on the wishes of the trust's creator.

Broad authority arms the trustees with the ability to respond to any event or condition, including those that may not have been foreseeable when the trust was drafted. Experience, the great instructor, demonstrates that life is uncertain and can be precarious. Unexpected situations arise, which may significantly affect a beneficiary. There possibly may be illness or joblessness or financial misfortune or mountainous expenses not necessarily due to profligacy. And then, there are positive events that call for cash: a new baby, buying and furnishing a home, embarking on a bright investment opportunity, pursuing graduate school education, and traveling with family to distant places. If the trustees have been selected with care, and they are in tune with the beneficiary's reasonable and realistic needs and aspirations, much can be accomplished by timely use of trust principal.

Some bestowers want the principal to be conserved, and insist that the beneficiary tailor his or her needs to two sources: the available trust income derived from reasonable investments, and that individual's own earning ability. Despite life's vicissitudes, the trust may be drafted so that only very narrow use of principal is permitted, such as for medical expenses that are not covered by insurance.

Broad authority in the trustees to make payments from principal is apt to be conferred when the current income beneficiary is the prime object of the bestower's concern. That beneficiary may be the spouse or a child. Narrow authority to use principal for the current beneficiary is likely to be measured out when the bestower is anxious about preserving the principal for someone to come into after the current beneficiary either has died or is out of the trust for some other reason.

Sometimes that "preservation anxiety" is so great that no authority is granted to the trustees to pay out principal to the current beneficiary. An illustration would be a trust for a second spouse, whom the creator of the trust wishes to provide for. The trust may be eligible for the marital deduction for gift or estate tax purposes. In fact, the tax deferral engendered by the marital deduction may be the prime motivation for the trust in favor of the surviving spouse. But, when he or she later dies, the principal is to go to the bestower's children by an earlier marriage. Assuring the children's inheritance of as much principal as possible may be critically important to the creator of the trust. Hence he or she may deliberately decline to authorize payments from principal for the surviving spouse for any conceivable reason.

Beneficiary Conflicts

Conflicts may arise between the current beneficiary, who is entitled to income, and the people who anticipate that the principal will come to them, who are known in the law as remainder persons. (In bygone times they were called remaindermen.) There are different areas of possible conflict. Obviously, one concerns the last discussion about possible payment of principal to the current beneficiary. The remainder persons are not likely to be enthusiastic about such payments, unless the current beneficiary is someone they are affectionate toward and committed to (for example, their widowed mother).

In many trusts, where the current beneficiary is a child or grandchild, the trust may provide that it will terminate when he or she attains a particular age, such as thirty, and then the trust assets will be turned over to that beneficiary. The chance that he or she will not live that long may appear mighty slim to the remainder persons who are named to inherit in case the current beneficiary dies prematurely. They will view their chance of ever inheriting as less likely than hitting the Lotto jackpot. In that situation, they may be totally indifferent to the use of principal for the current beneficiary.

Other possible conflicts may relate to the investment policy of the trustees. The current beneficiary may crave high-income yields or substantial tax-exempt income over a prolonged period. The remainder persons, hoping for an eventual large inheritance, will have a strong bias toward capital growth. Satisfying these opposing preferences could be tantamount to walking on water. The creator of the trust should anticipate this polarization. If he or she fails to, much trouble may lie ahead. You can imagine the clash that may occur between the current beneficiary, seeking a nourishing flow of cash, and the remainder persons who want the assets to fatten up. Particularly, imagine the unhappy conflict if the current beneficiary is your spouse, and the remainder persons are children from an earlier marriage who are cool or even downright hostile to your spouse. When the opposing viewpoints heat up enough, a riot could ensue.

The trust document ought to tilt in favor of the current beneficiary when that is the creator's wish. That is accomplished by directing that the interests of the remainder persons are subordinate to the interests of the current income beneficiary. Additional preferences for the current beneficiary can be indicated, such as authorizing heavy investing in tax-exempt securities.

When a tilt in someone's favor is not the bestower's objective, explicit emphasis in favor of a particular beneficiary should be omitted. That will require the trustees to manage the trust in an even-handed manner. For investment purposes, that should mean that a reasonable level of income will be produced and a reasonable degree of appreciation will be sought. In the selection of securities for the trust, an even-handed policy is likely to engender investments of up to 60 percent in equities, or even higher when equities are strongly in fashion. Equities are usually thought of as the means of achieving growth, but over time good companies increase their dividends so that income also improves from successful equity investing.

Other conflicts can arise due to subtleties. When a trust has income-producing real estate, the current beneficiary receives the rental income after allowance for some expenses, such as real estate taxes and mortgage interest. The tax deduction for depreciation generally is allocated to the current beneficiary, providing shelter against income tax for him or her. That deduction, taken year after year, reduces the trust's cost basis for the real estate. Should the property be sold at a gain, the income tax for the gain would normally be paid from principal. So, the current beneficiary will have enjoyed depreciation deductions that reduce the trust's cost basis at the expense of the remainder persons, who later will receive the principal. Should that be the result? Or should some adjustment be made against the current beneficiary and in favor of the trust principal? The trust document could deal with this point once the bestower has decided on the results he or she prefers.

Example

If a trust has oil or mineral interests, and all the revenue from production is distributed to the current beneficiary, he or she profits while the asset is being depleted. What is the bestower's goal: to favor the current beneficiary or to keep the trust principal intact for the enjoyment of later beneficiaries?

Consideration also must be given to the anticipated expenses, and how they will fall. Income beneficiaries normally bear some, as we indicated with real estate taxes and mortgage interest. Principal normally bears some, such as attorneys' fees, mortgage amortization, and capital gains taxes. Some expenses are usually divided between income and principal. These expenses might be compensation for trustees, fees of investment advisers and accountants, and the expense of hiring a bank to be the custodian of the securities that the trust owns. But the charge for all expenses, even the so-called normal ones, is malleable. The bestower can cut the burden of expenses where he or she chooses. But one word of caution: that cannot be done in marital deduction trusts. Nothing may interfere with the regular tide of the law that would affect the spouse's right to income.

Selecting the Trustee

The burden of choosing trustees falls on the creator of the trust. It is his or her benefaction that will be administered, and it should be his or her selection of the person or institution that will undertake the responsibility.

First, let's distinguish the trustee from the executor. Their jobs are different.

The executor acts first. Responsibility starts immediately with the death of the Will maker. In fact, if in his or her last days the individual is incapable of looking after matters, the person named in the Will as executor may come forward and seek an appropriate means of dealing with problems. But, normally, the executor's job starts at the funeral; indeed it may include making funeral arrangements.

The executor is responsible for lots of things.

1. Having the Will accepted as valid, which is the essence of probate, and includes defending the Will against attack.

2. Collecting the decedent's assets, and being sure all are located. A nightmare for W.C. Fields' executor was that the actor, out of fear of being stranded in strange places, had opened bank accounts in whistle stops across the country. In doing so, he had often used fictitious names to assure privacy or secrecy. IRS form 1099 wasn't used in those days of vaudeville, so identifying the accounts was an enormous challenge after Fields died.

3. Scrutinizing claims that are presented for satisfaction; these may be run-of-the-mill, like the monthly telephone bill, or they may be complicated and lead to entanglements and law suits.

4. Settling taxes with the government, which would include not only estate taxes but also cleaning up open gift taxes and income taxes.

5. Reviewing investments to determine if changes should be made and what they ought to be. Even if the entire estate goes outright, changes may be called for. As an example, the decedent may have held an investment that was very speculative, or was still in his or her portfolio only because of the desire to avoid hefty capital gains taxes. The executor may decide that prudence dictates an early sale.

6. Raising cash to pay off obligations, such as claims, estate taxes, and cash legacies. Most experienced executors turn to this at an early time and prepare a budget that sets forth amounts needed and a calendar of payment dates. Bear in mind that the federal government's time for payment of estate taxes is very short: nine months after death. Many states have a similar timetable for their death taxes.

7. Paying legacies to beneficiaries. Often, substantial payments are made rather soon, even within the first year of the decedent's death. Final distributions usually coincide with the accounting to beneficiaries.

8. Accounting to the beneficiaries for everything done, including what became of every penny.

When the estate has been left in trust, distribution of the inheritance by the executor is made to the trustee. So the trustee takes center stage when funds and property are received from the executor.

The executor's job usually takes three years or so, depending on everything. It takes that long because the federal estate tax proceeding goes on at least that length of time, and sometimes longer. Once the indicated tasks, and others that may crop up, are completed, the executor is gone. But the trustee may be on the scene for decades, depending on the length of the trust. For example, if the Will maker created a trust for the lifetime benefit of his or her daughter, now age thirty-five, the trust could run for something like fifty years.

The trustee's job is less varied than the executor's. Investment is a major and challenging task. Producing income, and at the appropriate level, is a big responsibility, and so is protecting and enhancing the principal. Responding to beneficiaries is extremely important. First, the trustee must get to know and establish rapport with them, understand their needs, and gain their confidence. Patience and a willingness to listen are important keys to success. Second, decisions have to be made concerning investment changes, after weighing requests for more income and incursions into principal.

Sometimes the beneficiaries make demands or have expectations that are beyond the ability of the trustee to satisfy. Or the demands are unreasonable and should be turned aside. In a memorable situation, an individual created a trust for the lifetime benefit of his niece, who was unemployed and had extravagant ways. At the trustees' request, she submitted a budget for herself indicating that she required annual income of $80,000. When informed that the trust principal, which was under $600,000, could not produce that level of income, she impatiently informed the trustees that she didn't want to hear about it and the problem was theirs.

For reasons akin to that experience, relations between trustee and beneficiary are not always warm and cordial. Serving as trustee is quite a job!

Who should be chosen to fill it? Let's first discuss how many should be chosen.

Q: Why more than one?

A: Different candidates offer disparate skills. This one knows about investing. That one would have great rapport with the beneficiaries.

Q: But the one with people skills may not know a debenture from a crate of oranges.

A: You can carve out different tasks for particular trustees. For example, the trust document can say that the final word about investments is given to the person whom rich Uncle Leo used as a trustee for his family.

Q: How many would be the right number of trustees?

A: Don't choose more than can make a contribution. Never load up the trusteeship.

Q: If there is more than one, how do they decide?

A: You can write your own program. If you don't and there are three or more trustees, generally they decide by majority rule. If there are two trustees, they have to agree.

Q: If I pick two and they don't see eye to eye, there will be a deadlock.

A: You could give one of them the decisive vote. But weigh that notion carefully. The other one may feel that whatever he or she may think will be pretty academic, and the job isn't worth the effort.

In actually choosing, many people start with what it will cost. That's the wrong end of the spectrum. Suitable trustees are not everywhere. Your cousin Darlene may serve without compensation, but would you want her as your trustee?

Consider relatives, friends, and professionals, and select with care. Merely because someone is reputed to be successful at what that person does will not make him or her a good trustee. A client of mine chose as trustee a gentleman who is chief executive of a large hospital with a big reputation. But when serving as trustee his character was revealed. He was arrogant, sought to rule by intimidation, was uninterested in investment matters, was scornful of guidance from lawyers and accountants, and had no time or patience for anyone, including the children who were beneficiaries of their parents' trusts. Some trustee!

When I speak of professionals for the trusteeship, I mean those who are very experienced at the role and understand what is expected. The category includes some banks, some lawyers, some accountants, some investment advisers.

Q: How about using a bank?

A: Some are authorized to be trustee and others are not. Ask your banker.

Q: Are the authorized ones any good?

A: Some are and do it well. Others are humdrum or worse. A bank that has high visibility and advertises about loans and credit cards is not necessarily adept at being a trustee.

Q: How can I pick a good one from the group?

A: Study their track records, look over their investment results, sit down with their representatives, talk to your advisers, ask people you respect for recommendations.

Q: If I choose a bank, do I need another trustee?

A: Yes, if that someone else has something to contribute, like investment acumen or family rapport. Some advisers suggest always using an individual along with a bank so that a person with equal rank (the individual trustee) can see to it that the bank is responsive and does a solid job.

Q: A bank won't have a heart attack and die.

A: Right. Permanence is helpful. But so is consistent work by bank representatives. Some banks are notorious for moving their personnel around, so that the beneficiaries are constantly dealing with someone new.

You may decide to use only individuals. That would lead to other concerns. A bank will provide all services: investment, physical custody of securities, preparation of the trust's tax returns, record keeping, and administrative management. If a bank is not used, those services must be provided in any event. Lawyers, accountants, and investment advisers are often called on singly or in combination for what is needed by individual trustees. When cost is determined, using a bank for one-stop service is to be compared with the necessity of arranging for all service with individual trustees.

Q: You mentioned cost. Let's face it.

A: Each state has rules about compensation for trustees. Banks are likely to have printed material with information.

Q: If I have more than one trustee, doesn't that multiply the expense.

A: Each state decides if all of them share the compensation that a single trustee would have earned or if two or more sets of compensation are allowable.

Q: The whole thing upsets me. I'd like to have capable trustees, but the cost is bothersome.

A: You may be able to contain cost by making an agreement with the trustees you have in mind. Agreements about their fees will stand up.

Q: But if I use only my spouse and kids as trustees, there will be no cost.

A: How will they get investment advice, record keeping, physical safe-keeping of trust assets, tax return preparation, and other services? Someone will have to be paid for something.

Let's assume that cost is under control. Many points remain open for your consideration. For example, what is involved if you simply have the same people who would be beneficiaries also serve as trustees?

Example

Your Will creates a marital deduction trust for your spouse, who will be the exclusive beneficiary during his or her lifetime. When your spouse dies, the principal will go to your children. Name your spouse sole trustee, which is permitted in some states. Authorize the trustee to hire investment advisers and others, as needed. If you have faith in your spouse's judgment and his or her relationship with the children is good, this could be a sound arrangement. This trust will be included in your spouse's estate for estate tax purposes because it is a marital deduction trust that will not have been taxed at your death. Hence your spouse as trustee can have broad powers without adding any estate tax risks. But remember that the trustee makes decisions, for the investment adviser and other aides only give advice. If you are so persuaded that your spouse is capable, and this is not a multiple-marriage situation with children from an earlier union, why not forgo a trust and leave the inheritance outright to your spouse?

Example

Have your spouse and the children serve as trustees. In states where the current beneficiary cannot be the only trustee, you may have to start with this possibility. But are you realistic about their ability to work smoothly in deciding crucial issues, like investments and raising principal for your spouse? An acid test in weighing the feasibility of the children's being trustees for their surviving parent: if that parent were you, would you be content?

Example

With trusts for your children, be cautious about their serving as trustees for each other. It may be a good policy not to have a sibling involved in the financial affairs of a brother or sister. Misunderstandings, jealousies, and rivalries may erupt. If your daughter really wants your son's advice about investing her trust money, she can ask him even though he is not a trustee.

In any event, tax problems would be invited if brother Eric and sister Claudia are the trustees for both their trusts and, as trustees, they can pay out principal. The ability of each child to participate in taking principal out of that child's trust would expose the trust to estate tax when the child dies, unless principal may be used by the trustees only for support, maintenance, health, and education. Limiting use of principal in that way may be short-sighted. So broad authority to pay principal is wise, and the child-beneficiary ought to be barred from having a say about it in order to avoid tax trouble when that child dies.

If broader use of principal is sanctioned, and the child-beneficiary is precluded by the trust document from participating as a trustee in making principal payments from his or her trust, trouble may still be lurking. The government may assert that when Eric can pay principal to Claudia from her trust, and vice versa, they are scratching each other's back: you give me $10,000 from my trust and I'll give you $10,000 from yours. If that argument is raised, there is a risk that the trusts will be taxed at the children's respective deaths.

Letting a child be one of the trustees of his or her trust is sound. Assuming the child has capability and is able to work reasonably well with others, including him or her in the trusteeship offers pluses. It shows your confidence in the child. The trusteeship is a learning experience. Serving as trustee gives the child a sense of participation in his or her financial destiny.

Naming a co-trustee for the child's trust who is not a beneficiary would also be sound. Tax problems can be avoided. The nonbeneficiary, if well chosen, can be a steadying influence and can foster professional management of the trust.

Q: I have some individuals in mind, but each one presents a problem. For example, my sister is very able and she gets along well with my daughter, who is fifteen. But the trust could run twenty-five years, until my daughter is forty, and my sister is already fifty-three.

A: Start out with your sister as trustee. She sounds like a good choice. We'll confront the issue of backup or substitute trustees very soon.

Q: My daughter is married to a wonderful young man, who is a lawyer. I'd like him to be a trustee with her for her trust.

A: Consider a provision that in the (unlikely) event of a divorce, his right to serve as trustee shall end.

The Creator as Trustee

If an individual creates a trust in his or her lifetime, can he or she be the trustee or a co-trustee? If the strategy is to create a trust for children or grandchildren and achieve tax advantages, the answer has to be that, in most cases, having the creator in that role will surely deprive the creator of tax benefits. The powers normally granted to a trustee cause the problem. Similarly, if someone creates a custodian account under the Uniform Gifts to Minors Act (UGMA) or Uniform Transfers to Minors Act (UTMA), the powers that the custodian has makes it best from a tax standpoint that the creator not be the custodian who manages the account.

As a general practice I always discourage an individual from serving as trustee of a trust that he or she is creating for a child or grandchild. I give the same advice about serving as a trustee of a trust created by someone else, such as a grandparent, to which the individual would be adding property. I take that stance even in those situations in which it appears that the powers and authority of the trustee are restricted and would not seem to offend the existing law and cancel the sought-after tax advantages. I find it best not to gratuitously hand the government a chip to play with in any tax game that could arise.

Persuading the creator of the wisdom of not serving as a trustee is not always easy. That person may feel that he or she has special skills or, very simply, that making the gift is one thing, but divorcing oneself from all influence is another. But choices must be made. When tax advantages and avoiding costly or risky fights with the IRS are at stake, keeping the creator away from the trusteeship will avoid jeopardizing those goals.

Often, the creator's spouse may safely serve as trustee. That may be balm to the bestower.

Beneficiary as a Trustee

A beneficiary generally may serve as a trustee in many situations without endangering tax goals. Essentially, a beneficiary should not hold authority as trustee or co-trustee to make discretionary payments from income or principal to himself or herself. If those powers were held by a trustee-beneficiary, they would cause tax indigestion.

But there is a safe harbor in the estate and gift tax area relating to powers in one's own favor that often is exploited for a beneficiary. As a trustee, the beneficiary may safely hold a power as trustee to pay himself or herself principal for support, maintenance, health, and education. If it is desired not to be so constrained, and instead to enlarge the scope of the trustees' power to use trust funds for the beneficiary and yet avoid tax disadvantages, that enlarged authority should be lodged in the hands of a trustee other than the beneficiary.

Q: Does that mean I cannot let my son be trustee of his trust?

A: Let him, but preserve the tax advantages by directing that he may not participate in the trustees' powers to pay income or principal.

Q: That means someone else must be a co-trustee who holds important power.

A: Yes, if you want those tax advantages and also to make the trust principal available beyond support, maintenance, health, and education in order to meet life's bumps and surprises. Anyway, in some states, the only income beneficiary cannot be the only trustee. Hence, another trustee would be needed in those states even aside from the tax issues.

Our discussion here is focused on tax opportunities. The trust creator may have compelling reasons not to allow the beneficiary to be the trustee or co-trustee. Even when other trustees would be in office and would comprise the majority, letting a beneficiary who is difficult or rebellious or unintelligent into the trusteeship can be a mistake. Even though he or she can be outvoted, that trustee must be informed and consulted about all decisions. An unqualified trustee can gum things up, or at least slow down decision making.

When the beneficiary, particularly a child, is reasonable and intelligent, it is wise to name him or her as one of the trustees of that person's trust. Responding to the issues that arise for trustees, particularly investment questions that must be addressed, is a valuable learning experience.

Q: Why do you specify that such a beneficiary be a trustee of his or her trust? Why not all the trusts?

A: Because experience teaches that making a child a trustee of a trust for the child's sibling can provoke big trouble. Daughter Muffy may resent that her brother Cameron is involved in her financial life. Better to leave him out of her trust. If Muffy wants his advice about a trust issue, she can ask him. Even if Cameron is a whiz, don't foist him on Muffy. Even if that would require choosing an outsider for the trusteeship and providing compensation for that individual, it may well be worth it.

Substitute Trustees

Individual trustees characteristically are mortal. Indeed, none ever has been found who was not. Whether they are serving alone or as co-trustees with a bank, plans should be made to replace them.

Finding backups for the initial set of trustees may not be easy. Some people have difficulty in selecting a starting trustee, so that the concept of replacement is somewhat intimidating. Further, the trust that is being created may run for many years. It may be a trust for a young child or grandchild that is designed to continue until the beneficiary reaches age forty or forty-five; or maybe the trust will continue throughout the beneficiary's lifetime.

Even trusts for spouses may have a prolonged existence. Dad (age sixty-five) may have a new wife who is thirty-seven. At his adviser's suggestion he may select a marital deduction QTIP trust as the inheritance vehicle for her, which will protect the principal for the children from his first marriage. Well and good. But that trust may run for fifty years, and the trusteeship is a consequential role because the conflicting interests of the wife, as the current beneficiary, and the children, who have expectancies, may put the trustee on a hot spot.

Searching for trustees who are young enough to endure throughout long-running trusts is an added burden. Finding a man or woman of any age with the right makeup and skill to be a trustee is a task, no less finding a youthful one. And the young possibilities may not really be seasoned or experienced enough to inspire confidence. Here is a major reason why corporate trustees are selected, or at least thought of. But many people reject the idea of using a bank trustee, sometimes for reasons they feel to be sound, or simply out of instinct.

When a bank is chosen, the bestower may want an individual to serve as co-trustee, to lend a hand, or to assure that the bank performs, or to impart some special skill, which may be as fundamental as having a close relationship with the beneficiaries. Sometimes that individual co-trustee is put in place from the start in order to fire the bank if it fails to measure up. As that watchdog may die while the trust continues, he or she would need a replacement.

The role of substitute trustee must therefore be dealt with. One alternative is to name someone in the document.

Example

"If my brother Norman fails or ceases to serve as trustee, I name my nephew Adam to serve as trustee in his place. If neither Norman nor Adam is serving as trustee, I name my grandniece Debra to be Trustee."

Let us hope Adam and Debra will turn out to have the skills that the bestower feels are requisite for the position.

Suppose there is no Adam or Debra? Or, suppose when Norman, the starting trustee, dies, neither Adam nor Debra wants the responsibility of serving as trustee? Before an individual who has been selected to be a trustee actually takes on the job, he or she is free to say "No thanks" without explanation.

In the illustration recently used of a QTIP marital deduction trust for a thirty-seven-year-old second spouse, the worst fears of the Will maker may have been realized, as follows: after his death, she and the children fell out completely; she demanded heavy tax-exempt trust income, they demanded that principal be invested in varied equities for growth; her lawyer raised the devil; the children's lawyer raised the roof. Strident voices are constantly heard, and complaints about the trustee's decisions are endless. The starting trustee, the bestower's brother Norman, manfully weathered the storm and did his level best. But here, twelve years after the Will maker died, Norman goes the same way.

Nephew Adam wants no part of the trusteeship. He's too busy. The job is a family favor and brings no compensation; and even if it did, the pay could never be soothing enough to make up for the time and effort and stormy weather involved. Adam declines the position, much to his wife's relief.

As to grandniece Debra, who is next in succession, her life has changed dramatically since her great uncle, the Will maker, died twelve years ago. She completed her residency in family medicine, moved to Seattle, married a man who is a university professor, bore a child, and has little contact with the Will maker's offspring and none with her great uncle's widow. What does she need with that never-ending headache of a responsibility?

Q: How about naming a bank as backup trustee?

A: Might be a fine choice. But banks can also say no, when the position is offered. And some people won't use a bank, ever.

Q: What can be done?

A: One possibility is to authorize the initial trustee to select his or her successor. The selection is made before the vacancy in the trusteeship occurs. It's a standby selection.

Q: Isn't that risky?

A: If you had sufficient confidence in someone to ask him or her to serve as trustee, that ought to justify empowering the same person to choose a backup.

Q: Suppose I select two individual trustees to start. How does the selection work?

A: You could authorize each to select that person's backup. But if you are concerned that one of them will fill the vacancy with a person with whom the other trustee wouldn't want to work, a different approach is necessary. In that case, the backup is selected in a burst of togetherness by all the individuals who are serving as trustees.

Q: Suppose they select a backup and later change their mind.

A: The selecting person or persons can be authorized to switch to someone else as standby backup trustee. The last one selected is the nominee when the vacancy occurs.

Q: What happens if the nominee refuses?

A: In selecting a standby, an alternate should also be chosen.

Q: And if the nominee takes the job and later dies?

A: The selection process is handed down from the first trustee to the later ones.

An alternative procedure is to have the selection made by someone other than the first trustee. Some individuals anoint their lawyers or accountants with the responsibility of choosing. When used, that responsibility has been given to large organizations, which have the appearance of permanency so common among big organizations. In recent years, however, permanency is not always proving itself.

Q: Suppose the vacancy occurs and no one who was selected is willing to take the job?

A: The court will select a trustee. It is axiomatic that a trust will not be allowed to be without a trustee.

Q: Whom will the court select?

A: It might be someone the judge thinks of. Or, if the beneficiaries are not at each others' throats, the court might accept a suggestion made by the beneficiaries.

Q: That scares me.

trustee, the government does not relent. Its view is that the creator can compel the trustee to attend to the creator's bidding by the latter's ability to toss the trustee into the garbage bin. With such a point of view confronting the creator, it would be foolish for him or her to have any power to fire the trustee.

That state of affairs leads to the next logical thought, which is to give the beneficiaries the right to remove the trustee from office. That power could be given to the beneficiaries to exercise whether or not the bestower is alive. A removal power held by beneficiaries may not prove to be a healthy idea, for the trustee could be in danger of becoming the plaything of the beneficiaries. The government views the situation just that way. If the trustee has the right under the terms of the trust to make discretionary principal payments to the beneficiaries, the government's theory is that the beneficiaries hold the power to get at the principal via their ability to remove the trustee.

That contention would likely be made even if the trustee could only be replaced by a third party, not by any beneficiary. The notion is that a revolving door exists. If the beneficiaries find that the trustee won't do it their way, they'll spin the revolving door round and round until they find a compliant trustee. If the government succeeds in the argument that the beneficiaries control the power to reach the trust principal, tax disadvantages would follow. An exception to that would be if the power of the trustee were limited to making principal payments for the beneficiaries' support, maintenance, health, and education. Those are protected categories, even if the beneficiaries from inception, without any intervening subterfuges, could take principal only for those reasons.

Is there a surefire way to be able to remove a trustee from office? Some possibilities exist.

Example

If the trust is for the creator's spouse under the marital deduction, letting the spouse have power to remove the trustee will not aggravate the estate tax results that loom ahead. When the spouse dies, the trust assets will be part of his or her estate for federal estate tax purposes anyway. The spousal right to fire the trustee will not worsen that estate tax outcome. Of course, the question remains: is it a good idea to empower the spouse to get rid of the trustee?

Example

The creator has named a bank as trustee without much enthusiasm and put someone in place as co-trustee. If that co-trustee is not a beneficiary of the trust, he or she could hold the removal power.

Example

Lodge the removal power with one or more individuals who are outside the trust. They are neither co-trustees nor beneficiaries. They might be lawyers or accountants or investment advisers or just plain bystanders. They are like a board of review. If dissatisfied with the trustee's performance, they can swing the ax.

A person must be cautious about cooking up these or other arrangements for beheading the trustee. The discovery may be made that the best candidates for the trusteeship are reluctant to get involved if they can be summarily dismissed. Further, the process can be expensive.

If a trustee is fired, he or she will surely insist on an accounting, which is a procedure in the local court in which all the trustee's transactions will be spelled out in detail. Every original holding of the trust, every change in investment, every collection of dividends and interest, every distribution to beneficiaries, every payment of expenses and fees, is detailed. The current beneficiaries of the trust, and those who stand in the wings waiting to be beneficiaries, are given notice of the court proceeding. They may complain about what the trustee did or did not do. Many issues can arise, ranging from whether investments were appropriate to the payment of fees and expenses. Lawyers would have their say on each side of every issue, and the court would decide each point in contention. When complaints are raised, an accounting can be a prolonged affair. Even without complaint, the detailed presentation required for an accounting takes time.

The trustee's purpose in insisting on an accounting will be twofold. First, to clear the trustee of all responsibility for what he or she actually did. Rest assured that exoneration will be a high priority of the trustee's. And bear in mind that the trustee may have been removed even though he or she did nothing that can be complained about legally. A personality clash may be at the root of the matter, or maybe a feeling that the trustee was insufficiently attentive, or that the investment performance has been lackluster. None of those points would lead to liability, even though the trustee is ousted.

Second, the trustee will want to collect any compensation that has not been paid. In some states, the trustee is entitled to payment when he or she turns over the trust assets. If the trustee is a professional, such as a bank, that trustee will not go away without full payment. Indeed, the trustee may have refused to take on the trusteeship without some confirmation that payment for services will be made in the event of removal. Of course, if the ousted trustee was a family relative or friend who undertook the job as an accommodation, there would be no compensation issue.

Accounting proceedings also could generate serious fees for lawyers and accountants. Those fees may make the removal of the trustee an expensive business. A trustee is entitled to have an accounting. A trustee who is removed from office is surely not going to be dissuaded from insisting on one except for the very unlikely possibility that a trustee's hand was roaming around the cookie jar. So, a shortcut is unlikely. The prospect of incurring significant fees in a proceeding for removal may discourage anyone who is disappointed in the trust's performance from hoisting the trustee out of his or her chair.

CHAPTER

6

Life Insurance and Retirement Benefits

Life insurance and retirement benefits are blessed with special tax advantages. They are also key parts of the total portfolio of many individuals. For these reasons they merit special discussion whenever estate planning is under review.

Role of Life Insurance

There is a whole industry that markets life insurance. While some of the marketers get carried away and huckster outrageously, that characteristic is not by any means pervasive. There are many skilled and highly sophisticated industry representatives, some of whom are knowledgeable about finance and taxes. When dealing with them it is nevertheless critical to understand some points.

A large majority of those representatives concentrate their energies on selling. Their goal is to find your particular need for life insurance and satisfy that need with their product. If you aren't aware of a need, they hope to help you find one, and maybe more than one. When analyzing whether insurance is called for, and how much is enough, they are not neutral parties. Insurance is their life and marketing it is in their bones. Some representatives style themselves "estate planners," and they present computations and illustrations that delve into a prospect's affairs. But usually objectivity is apt to be missing and their presentation is tilted in a well-known direction: persuading you that insurance is the way of your future.

I do not suggest that you or your adviser should fend off these tireless sales people with a semiautomatic weapon. It is better that you drive to the point of what they are offering, know that you are being offered a product that has a cost, and consider. Many people do have a need for life insurance, and you might even be among them. Here are some examples:

Example

Families where there is little capital and a breadwinner's death would seriously diminish support for dependents and the opportunity of education for children. This risk may even be present in families with healthy incomes that sustain upscale living.

The point is that the breadwinner's salary or professional income stops when death intervenes. Without income-producing capital available, how will payments be made for a great variety of familiar obligations, from monthly mortgage payments to the children's orthodontia, from the car payment to the utility bills to credit card statements? All those obligations have been funded by a compensation stream that may flow no more — and will be sorely missed. Those deprived dependents may be a spouse, young children, a widowed parent, or someone else who currently is financially reliant on the earnings of that breadwinner. Insurance would create needed capital.

Example

There is accumulated capital, but there are economic risks. One risk may be the possibility of collapse of a business when the entrepreneur dies. That collapse may not be avoidable if death occurs before a family successor can be anointed, or if the entrepreneur's services are so special and personal that without him or her the business would shrivel.

In rough economic times, other reasons to fear the fragility of a business enterprise may be all too apparent. Insurance could bolster the family's situation.

Example

Even when there is capital, and it seems as solid as the rock that one insurer uses as its symbol, there may be a place for insurance. The need may be created primarily by the deadline for paying federal estate tax, which is nine months after the date of death. There may be other needs too: debts to liquidate, cash legacies to pay, heavy transitional expenses, money to support family members before cash flow can accommodate their requirements. These needs can be met by life insurance.

When a need for insurance is recognized, several questions arise. First, how much? If insurance were available for the asking, all of us would carry a truckload full. But there is an expense to be reckoned with, so how much is a function of cost. In some cases, the risk to be guarded against will not run on forever. If the concern is funding children's education should a parent die, the amount and the years of concern can be determined. A term policy may do nicely. Its cost is lower than the cost of a permanent policy. In some states, such as Massachusetts and New York, insurance at very low cost can be obtained at savings banks. A term policy from that source may be very affordable.

It would be wise not to start with settled preconceptions. Insurance companies have developed many new products and premium costs have fallen considerably. So even if a term policy may do to cover a specific need like education, some other plan may serve more than one need. An insurance representative's presentation of alternatives could be quite worthwhile. For example, a universal life policy, with a premium hinged to a reasonable interest rate, may be more attractive than a whole life policy. But careful consideration is necessary for each alternative that is presented. There not only is no free lunch; snacks have a price also.

Payment of Death Proceeds

When the insured dies, how should the insurance be payable for the beneficiary? Payment outright, in a lump sum, could be very nice for the beneficiary. But knowing his or her spending proclivities and inexperience with financial affairs, what is the attitude of the insured about outright payment? If management of the insurance dollars for the beneficiary seems advisable, choices are available.

One is to have the insurance company make installment payments over time, under one of its payment plans. These plans, generally known in the trade as optional settlements, have the promise of certainty for the beneficiary, so long as the insurer is solvent. That regular installment will come like clockwork. But these plans can be victimized by inflation.

Some fifty years or so ago, optional settlements were strong rivals to trusts as popular vehicles for handling insurance payouts. But trusts are far in the lead today. The mechanics are that the trustee is named as beneficiary of the policy, collects the proceeds, and invests them for the benefit of the true objects of

154

the insured's bounty. The trustee, therefore, serves as policy beneficiary under a strict fiduciary responsibility, and not for the trustee's own ends.

The trust can be any one of the trusts that we have touched on — for spouse, children, grandchildren, or otherwise. The insurance may be the mainstay of the trust, or it may be coupled with other assets that the insured channels to the trust, all of them to be managed for those selected beneficiaries.

If we put the issue of estate taxes off for discussion in a few moments, we can compare alternatives to reach the goal of melding all the assets, including insurance, together in one fund.

1. Make the insurance payable to the insured's estate. The Will would create a trust that will take over the insurance money and the other assets that the Will maker may have, such as cash, stocks, bonds, and investments. All financial matters will be governed by one document, the Will, which sets forth the trust provisions.

   A disadvantage is that the insurance becomes subject to the claims of the estate's creditors. If the insurance had been payable directly to a trust created outside the Will, or to an individual beneficiary, state law might have exempted it from creditors' claims. In hard times, that disadvantage becomes singularly apparent.

   Other disadvantages of making the estate the beneficiary of the insurance are: (a) it may forfeit a particular state's inheritance tax exemption for insurance and (b) the executor may be able to claim a fee for collecting the insurance. Another disadvantage would arise if the insured is hoping to diminish the surviving spouse's inheritance. This beneficiary designation would frustrate that desire by enlarging the "estate" from which the surviving widow or widower gets a slice.

2. In some states, the various disadvantages could be avoided by making the insurance payable to "the trustee under my Will." If state law sanctions that beneficiary designation, then the Will is the single document needed. It will set forth the trust provisions. If state law doesn't sanction that alternative, the insured should not be a pioneer.

3. Neither of the preceding alternatives may work. For example, your state's probate system may be antiquated and the local practice may be never to use only a trust in the Will to dispose of the bestower's property. The solution would be to create the trust separately during the insured's lifetime, and make it the repository of the insurance. If desired, other assets can go into the trust.

    The bestower would also have a Will, which would, at his or her death, add to the trust those assets that had remained in the bestower's name. In the trade, that is known as a pourover Will. If no attempt is being made to shield the insurance from estate tax, the insured can retain the right to modify and cancel the trust as he or she pleases, just as can be done with his or her Will.

We have not touched on saving taxes yet, because that may not really be a problem in every case. When the projected estate, including life insurance, is less than $600,000, the exemption from federal estate tax that is engendered by the unified credit may rub out the estate tax concern. If the projected estate is larger, the marital deduction may solve that concern, particularly if there are no children and the surviving spouse is to be the person whom the Will maker cares to benefit with everything. Even if some benefit is intended for others, their inheritance may be rendered tax-free by the $600,000 exemption while the marital deduction takes care of the widow or widower.

What if the taxes are more formidable? There are estate tax solutions. Before taking them up, let's take hold of income tax results, because they are not so much to grapple with.

Income Taxes

When insurance is collected outright, whether by an individual beneficiary, by the insured's estate, or by a trust, the insurance proceeds are almost certainly received free of income tax. That is so no matter how huge the insurance may be. Isn't that splendid? The insurance companies revel in that favorable result, and defend it strenuously whenever a hunt is on in Washington for more sources of tax revenue. The only exception to that delicious outcome occurs if an arcane principle known in the tax law as the transfer-for-value rule is in play. That occurs rarely. That infrequency and the boring nature of the rule mean it's not worth covering here. If you're really curious, or having trouble sleeping, please turn to the Glossary (page 286).

When the insurance company is holding the proceeds after the insured's death and making installment payments under one of its optional settlements, there is an earnings component in the periodic payout. That component is subject to income tax.

When a trustee collects insurance proceeds and invests them, the insurance comes to the trust free of income tax, assuming that the transfer-for-value rule has not made one of its very infrequent appearances. But when those funds are reinvested in the trust and a cash flow is paid to a spouse or child or other beneficiary, the usual income tax rules relating to dividends and interest will apply.

When a corporation or partnership collects insurance proceeds, the insurance is received by that entity free of income tax, assuming that the transfer-for-value rule stays on the sidelines. But the tax-free status for insurance ends there. When the corporation or partnership writes checks to someone, whether it be an employee, an heir of an employee, a shareholder, or a partner, the rules that prevail in the realm of corporate and partnership income tax, along with individual taxpayer principles, will dictate the ultimate income tax results. Often, income tax will be due.

Avoiding Estate Tax

On to the estate tax. The operative rules are not complex. Ducking them can be. One rule is that insurance receivable by the insured's estate is part of the estate for estate tax purposes. An offshoot of that rule is that insurance not payable directly to the estate, but receivable for the benefit of the estate, is also part of the estate for estate tax purposes.

Q: When is insurance receivable for the benefit of the estate?

A: When the beneficiary, whether an individual or a trust, has the obligation to use the proceeds to pay estate debts or taxes.

Q: You mean that if my son is beneficiary of my life insurance and decides to use that money to pay estate taxes on his inheritance, that makes the life insurance subject to estate tax?

A: Only if your son legally obligated himself to do that.

Q: That seems to clear up the problem.

A: Not so fast. The real trap is laid with trusts. If a trust document *directs* the trust to pay estate taxes or other estate obligations from the insurance money, the trap will be sprung.

Q: But I heard that insurance trusts were used to keep insurance safe from estate tax and also pay the tax.

A: Right. That works when the trustee is authorized to enter into transactions that will safely accomplish all of that. For example, the trustee is *authorized* to buy estate assets. When that is done, the insurance proceeds are exchanged by the trustee for illiquid assets that the executor has in the estate, such as real estate and business interests. Now those assets are in the trust and the executor has cash to pay estate tax. Incidentally, the estate should not have any capital gain when it transfers those assets for the insurance dollars, because of the transformation of basis that occurs at the bestower's death.

Q: So if the insurance is not payable to the insured's estate, and also not receivable for the benefit of the estate, all is well?

A: Not yet. There remains one rule to satisfy, and it has the greatest complexities.

Ownership of the Policy

The insured who hopes to keep the insurance free of estate tax could do so very simply by making his or her spouse the beneficiary, so that the marital deduction would operate. That deduction could be gained even if a classic marital deduction trust or a QTIP trust receives the insurance for the surviving spouse's benefit. But that is a one-estate solution. That is, the insurance will be shielded from estate tax when the insured spouse dies. But, when the beneficiary spouse dies later, what is left of the insurance proceeds, or the assets they were invested in, will be part of the surviving spouse's estate for estate tax purposes. So the goal is to accomplish more. Hit a home run, and not just settle for a single. The home run happens when the insurance money is kept out of both spouses' estates for estate tax purposes.

The first step to achieve that winner is to make sure that the insured spouse has no rights of ownership in the policy, or as they are called in the tax law, incidents of ownership. Those rights include such familiar items as the right to name the beneficiary, to borrow against the policy, to surrender the policy for cash, and to exchange the policy for a different one. To hit the home run, the insured must be rid of all rights in the policy.

If there already is an existing policy that the insured wants to win with, he or she must get rid of all rights of ownership. How? By doing two things.

1. Transfer all ownership rights, either to an individual or to a trust. Make the new owner the beneficiary of the policy. Transferring to the insured's spouse won't be a complete victory, because he or she will collect the proceeds later on and they will eventually be in the surviving spouse's estate. So a transfer to an individual should be to a child or grandchild or other favored person.

2. Live at least three years after the transfer. If the insured offends this rule by dying too soon, the tax avoidance effort will come to nought. That pull-back of the insurance into the insured's estate is due to a rule known as the contemplation-of-death rule. It used to apply on a wholesale basis to all kinds of transfers, but its sting has been lessened a great deal. It still applies, however, to transfers of insurance policies. If the insured trips over the three-year rule, what is catapulted into his or her estate for estate tax purposes would be the full amount of the death proceeds under the policy.

Q: Aside from the three-year survival point, what else is involved in transferring the policy?

A: The policy holder must accept that control of the policy is passing from his or her hands. Borrowing against the policy or cashing it in will not be up to him or her.

Q: How about changing the beneficiary?

A: That control is gone, too, except if the policy is transferred to a trust and it has flexible provisions. For example, a husband could transfer a policy to a trust that provides benefits for the wife who survives him. If the wife is not named by her given name, and if the husband divorces and remarries, the policy should benefit his new wife. This is a delicate matter. If our husband hero shows the trust to his wife during the planning stage, and she notices that her name is missing, there may be some trauma involved. A likely happening is that the husband will blame the lawyer who drafted the document. C'est la vie.

Q: Are there tax issues involved in transferring the policy?

A: That would be a gift for gift tax purposes. The policy facts determine the amount of the gift. As the policy does not yet pay off, the death benefit has not matured, and the policy should be worth less than its face amount. Very likely it will be worth far less. The size of the gift is likely to be near the policy's cash value.

Q: In whose favor is the gift?

A: If the policy is transferred to an individual, such as a child, the gift is to that person. If the policy is transferred to a trust, the gift is to the group of beneficiaries according to their interests in the trust income and principal.

Q: Can the gift be offset by the $10,000/20,000 annual gift tax exclusion?

A: Yes, if the policy is transferred to an individual and the $10,000/20,000 exclusion has not been spoken for in that year by other gifts to that individual.

Q: Suppose the policy holder transfers the policy to a trust?

A: Ordinarily the $10,000/20,000 exclusion could not be claimed because at present no benefits will flow from the policy to the trust beneficiaries. That shortcoming can be overcome if the trust confers a power of withdrawal on a leading beneficiary.

Q: That sounds simple.

A: Not quite. Those powers are known as *Crummey* powers, as their genesis is the court decision in *Crummey v. Commissioner*, a gift tax case of several years ago. We'll discuss them when we review paying premiums (pages 172-74).

New Policies

The goal of safeguarding insurance from estate tax is easier to reach when new insurance is being considered. If someone other than the insured applies for the coverage and becomes the policy owner from the outset, the transfer hurdle need not be cleared. As the insured's hands never touch the policy, no rights of ownership have to be transferred away from those hands. That means that the contemplation-of-death trap cannot be sprung, even if the insured dies shortly after the insurer issues the policy.

Q: Who applies for the policy?

A: That could be an individual, such as a child, or a trust.

Q: Can it be a trust that the insured has created?

A: Yes, even a brand-new trust.

Q: Can the insured be trustee of the trust?

A: If the insured created the trust, absolutely not, if you hope to achieve tax success.

Whoever becomes owner of the policy should also be the beneficiary, to avoid a tax mistake. For example, if the insured's daughter applies for a policy on her father's life, she should be the beneficiary. If she allows her children to be the beneficiary, a gift by the daughter will occur at her father's death. It is at that moment that the daughter, as owner of the policy, loses her opportunity to change the beneficiary to herself. The amount of the gift that she is deemed to make under this scenario would be the full face amount of the policy.

Avoiding a transfer of the policy by the insured also avoids any gift on his or her part with respect to the policy itself.

Insurance that will benefit grandchildren is a means of leveraging the $1 million exemption from the GST (generation-skipping tax). Only a moderate amount of the exemption may have to be called on to fully insulate the insurance from the tax. Remember, the insured is not transferring the proceeds of the policy. What he or she is transferring would be cash to pay the premiums and, if the policy is already in existence, an amount roughly equivalent to the current cash value of the policy.

Example

Devlon, who is sixty and doesn't smoke, creates a trust that applies for a $1 million whole-life policy on his life. The beneficiaries of the trust will be his grandchildren, Janeen and Rick. The annual premium for the policy will be about $40,000, which Devlon will pay (more about this premium payment in a few minutes). To protect the insurance from generation-skipping tax, Devlon need apply only $40,000 of his $1 million exemption annually to cover the premium payment. If he dies at age seventy-four, after fourteen premiums were paid, the aggregate use of his GST exemption would be $560,000 to transfer proceeds of $1 million to his grandchildren. If he dies at sixty-nine, after nine premiums were paid, the aggregate use of his GST exemption would be even less ($360,000).

Generation Skipping

When the policy is successfully cleared out of the estate of the insured, and also out of the estate of the insured's spouse, estate tax has been avoided. But that does not insulate the insurance from operation of the generation-skipping tax. That tax has a life of its own, separate and apart from the estate tax.

Assume that a trust has become owner of a policy on the insured's life.

Example

Kyle creates a trust that owns insurance policies on his life. The policies are payable to the Standard Trust Co. as trustee. The trust is for the lifetime benefit of Kyle's daughter Star, who is thirty-eight. When Star dies, the trust will end and the principal will pass to her children, Kyle's grandchildren.

It makes no difference if Kyle's trust initially had applied for the policy, or if Kyle once owned the policy and transferred it to the trust more than three years ago. Either way, there is a generation-skipping tax issue when Kyle's grandchildren take over the trust's benefits. Only by tapping the insured's $1 million exemption can that tax be skirted successfully.

Second-to-Die Policies

Insurance companies are forever seeking to develop new products for their energetic representatives to sell. Recently the companies put a sparkling finish on a product that has gained wide appeal. It is often referred to as a second-to-die policy, or survivorship insurance.

This insurance is on the lives of husband and wife, but it pays off only when the surviving spouse dies. As two deaths must occur before the insurance company has to release the proceeds of the policy, the mortality risk is much different from what it is with a policy that insures one person and will mature when he or she dies. The lower survivorship risk allows for lower premium charges than single-life policies call for. Further, second-to-die coverage conforms to the need for estate tax dollars in many situations. It is common with a married couple to plan so that the combined result of (1) the $600,000 exemption spawned by the unified credit and (2) the marital deduction leads to no estate tax at the first spousal death. Because the marital deduction serves to defer estate tax until the surviving spouse dies, the day of tax reckoning arrives then. Enter the second-to-die policy, to assist the heirs when the last surviving spouse has died.

These policies are typically marketed with emphasis on the premium, which is attractive when compared with traditional single-life policies. In the marketing, a special burnish is applied by the pitch that the premium will "vanish." That is marketing talk meaning that the pain of paying premiums won't last. A computer presentation will show that after a particular number of years, no further premiums need be paid. The projection is that after premiums for ten years or so are paid, the policy carries itself. No further infusion of cash on the insured person's part will be necessary. Presto! Coming from a knowledgeable insurance representative, who may be styled an estate planner, that can be heady stuff. Right there a thoughtful pause is wise.

Q: Seems to me that you are hinting that there's something amiss.

A: The presentation that you receive is likely to be from the individual salesperson's computer, not from the home office of the insurance company.

Q: Is that misleading?

A: The computer presentation is a blizzard of numbers. They can make anyone's eyes glaze over. But the same blizzard occurs even when the insurance company cranked out the numbers. Tucked away somewhere in the presentation is the crucial statement that the numbers are only illustrations, not guaranteed results.

Q: What does that mean?

A: The policy that the home office of the insurance company issues calls for regular premium payments, year in and year out, without vanishing. If, and only if, all of the assumptions that are the foundation of the projections come true, will the policy, via dividends that are projected, be able to carry itself at the predicted time.

Q: What could upset the plan?

A: The insurance company's expenses could significantly increase, for example, expenses connected with bad real estate mortgage loans. Recently, a change in the way insurance companies are taxed boosted their expenses. Another possibility is a change in mortality experience, which turns out to be much worse than the company's actuaries had predicted. That might occur because of a wave of unexpected deaths due to some dreadful health problem like AIDS. If untimely deaths cause policies to mature faster than originally expected, that's a burden on the finances for remaining policy holders.

Q: How about an economic bust?

A: A downturn in the insurance company's earnings will hurt the ability of a policy to carry itself, because there will be a shortfall in the accumulated fund within a policy. This could occur when the economy dives or if a particular insurer's portfolio goes sour. It is wise to ask the presenter to produce a new set of projections that is based on a lower dividend assumption for the insurance company.

Within the presentation of all those numbers, some points should be probed. What exactly happens to the premium and the cash value when the first spouse dies? Does it matter if that happens next year or in twelve years? Are paid-up additions boosting the total death proceeds? What kind of insurance is involved: term or whole life?

Different projections and actual results will be produced if term insurance is part of the mix of insurance coverage. A dose of term along with whole life will reduce the annual premium. But the more term insurance, the more uncertain will be the chance of vanishing premiums. Thoughtful insurance representatives may caution their prospects not to let more than 25 percent of term insurance intrude into the package of coverage.

Other features are possible. Some companies offer an option for dividing the policies between the spouses in case of divorce, so that each ends up with a policy on his or her own life. Some policies pay at the death of the first spouse and afford the survivor the opportunity to buy coverage on favorable terms on his or her life. A trust can be used to make the purchase in order to achieve estate tax savings.

A skeptical approach to all products is fruitful. For example, if the insurance company in a straight second-to-die policy rates the chance of both spouses dying young as slight, why not adopt that concept and do a home-grown program to pay the estate tax when the surviving spouse dies. If the amount needed for premiums is set aside on a persistent basis, say in a trust for children, shrewd investing might produce what will be needed to restore the amount taken in taxes. In other words, insurance for this purpose is an investment alternative. Of course, insurance has an advantage. If the unexpected occurs and both spouses die before their time, the insurance dollars will be delivered, while an investment fund could not suddenly mushroom because someone died.

After reflection, a couple may decide to invest in this insurance coverage. If a very large amount of insurance is involved, they may wish to diversify by obtaining parts of the overall coverage from different companies. All insurance companies are not the same; some are financially stronger than others. We have learned that insurance companies can have bad times, too.

How Much Life Insurance?

It won't raise your eyebrows to note that insurance coverage of any kind costs money. The greater the coverage, or the older the prospect, or the more health problems that are present, the larger will be the cost. The cost may be sufficiently considerable to cause gift tax problems, which elevate the costs further. From a planning point of view, some pointed questions must be addressed because of the costs.

How much money should be spent this way? Some will conclude that all that should be sought is protection against risk of an untimely death, so that support and education of dependents can be handled. Others will want to go farther and provide an inheritance for heirs through insurance dollars. Those dollars may be sought after to provide cash to pay estate taxes, thereby avoiding the need to liquidate holdings, such as investments in business. But even when raising cash to pay estate taxes is not a problem, because cash and other liquid assets abound in the estate, insurance may seem very attractive as a means of replacing capital that is expended on estate taxes.

Those who consider insurance coverage as a financial solution for paying estate taxes or replacing capital, whether via single-life policies or second-to-die coverage, will reach varying conclusions. To some, getting lots of insurance dollars on board is desirable, even obligatory. Others will invest a limited amount in such coverage. Anyone who has thoughtfully reached either conclusion may be very wise and may have done what is exactly fitting for himself or herself and his or her family. Others will not be tempted at all to put their money into insurance programs to defray anticipated taxes or to fill in the gash that paying taxes causes. They might seek to reduce their estates substantially by gifts or lay aside a fund to cope with the day of reckoning or adopt the attitude that nothing should be done. That last conclusion may stem from the idea that the children have been raised and educated and are properly on their own, and whatever spendable dollars husband and wife may have will be used for living and not on preparation for dying. In their view, the children will just inherit less, after the government collects its inheritance.

The public is bombarded by proposals to finance their estate taxes or replace capital that is taken to pay off the government. These proposals all have life insurance at their core as the funding medium. Insurance professionals with knowledge and creativity promote the theme, as do firms that once were known primarily as stock brokers and lately have taken to marketing life insurance under the label of financial planning. Sure, they provide a service to some folks. But their message is played like a siren song, as if insurance costs nothing and only a stubborn fool would resist, probably because of either failure to understand or patently wrongheaded advice from independent advisers.

Q: I have seen newspaper ads comparing this kind of insurance to doing my own savings. The insurance looks good.

A: But remember why. The insurance company says that the insurance is there if both you and your spouse die tomorrow or next month or next year. But the chance of two such deaths so soon is pretty slight. If it weren't, the insurance company would be charging much heftier premiums. The realities are that everyone expects at least one of the spouses to be around for a long time. The insurance won't pay off until the second death.

Aside from the realities of comparing the cost of life insurance with other plans for accumulating wealth, other thoughts are pertinent.

It is not foolish or stupid or even unconstitutional to decline to buy life insurance for the purpose of paying estimated estate taxes. Some very astute people I know have declined. They have concluded that they do not owe that undertaking to anyone, including their children. And I say this not forgetting for one moment that some of my best friends are in the life insurance business. Insurance is an idea, not an article of faith.

Paying Premiums

When an individual owns a policy on his or her life (for example, the individual can change the beneficiary), then paying the premium is strictly a matter of having cash available. If the policy has a value that can be borrowed against, then a loan can be obtained to provide cash for the premium that is due. Two things will occur. Interest will run, and the policy holder will owe that. Also, if death occurs, the policy proceeds will be reduced by the loan and any unpaid interest that has run. The falloff in the death proceeds could be cured by using dividends from the policy to purchase term insurance, which will bring the death proceeds back to snuff. If the loan runs for a sustained period, the interest cost will spiral and a greater amount of the dividend will be needed to buy term insurance because of the advanced age of the insured. Incidentally, the interest cost is not deductible for income tax purposes.

Other issues are presented if the insured does not own the policy. It makes no difference if the insured once owned the policy and transferred ownership to someone, or if the policy initially was taken out by another individual or a trust. If the insured pays the premiums, a gift results. When the ownership of the policy is held by an individual, for instance, the insured's child, the gift is eligible for the $10,000/20,000 annual exclusion for gift tax purposes. (You will recall that to be the privilege, which we discussed at pages 15–18 in the discussion of Tax Opportunities, to give $10,000 each year free of gift tax to each of an unlimited number of recipients, increased to $20,000 when the giver's spouse consents.) That seems painless. But remember our observation in the discussion of Tax Opportunities in chapter 1 (for example, page 16) that once the exclusion in a particular year is fully used, the exclusion is exhausted until the next year. And if next year the premium for the insurance again will be due and the insured expects to pay it, next year's exclusion is also spoken for. Hence, no further gift can be made directly to that child during that time span that could be offset by the annual gift tax exclusion. Of course, if the premium is smaller than $10,000/20,000, then a gift arising from payment of the premium only chips away some of the annual gift tax exclusion and the rest remains available to offset a further gift that year.

If the insurance premium is very large, bulging beyond the coverage of the $10,000/20,000 annual exclusion, the $600,000 exemption from gift and estate tax will be called on to avoid payment of gift tax.

The difficulties will be heightened if ownership of the policy is held by a trust. While the insured is alive, no economic benefits flow from a life insurance trust to its beneficiaries. Under the tax law, that would ordinarily deprive the insured of claiming the annual exclusion of $10,000/20,000 from gift tax when he or she provides funds to pay the policy premium. But a present economic benefit can be artificially created by a trust provision that authorizes a beneficiary to withdraw funds from the trust. This is the *Crummey* power. But bear in mind that the *Crummey* power is not anointed with a special gift tax exclusion right of its own. Instead, giving the *Crummey* right of withdrawal to a beneficiary is a means of making use of the giver's privilege to transfer up to $10,000/20,000 to that particular beneficiary. Thus, the giver cannot double up the annual gift tax exclusion by writing a check to an individual, say a child, for $10,000/20,000 and for the same year authorizing that child to exercise a *Crummey* power to withdraw from a trust another $10,000/20,000.

The game plan is to give a *Crummey* power to each primary beneficiary, say the two children of the insured. That sets the stage for two annual exclusions. The power is exercisable when a policy is put in the trust and each time a premium is to be paid. So an exclusion will be available in each year when one of those events occurs, up to the overall annual limit of $10,000/20,000 per child. In a particular year, the insured writes a check to the trust for the premium. The children observe the unspoken ground rules of the game, and refrain from exercising their withdrawal rights. That allows the trustee to have funds available for the premium, which the trustee pays.

The government does not find the *Crummey* power to be a barrel of laughs. For example, it has taken the position that a *Crummey* power will be recognized as creating a $10,000/20,000 exclusion only when it is held by a primary beneficiary. For example, assume that the insurance trust provides that when an insured parent dies, the trust income will go to the daughter for her life and at her death the trust assets will belong to the daughter's three children. A power of withdrawal has been given to each trust beneficiary, including those three children. The government has been insisting that only the daughter's power has tax validity. So, instead of four $10,000/20,000 annual exclusions for gift tax purposes, the government sees but one. Although the government lost this argument in a recent court case, it persists in its view.

The *Crummey* power is very much part of the scene, however, and despite IRS growling, action by Congress would be needed to put the power on the sidelines. In the meantime, several complex issues arise for the power holder relating to income tax, estate and gift tax, and even generation-skipping tax. The usual attitude of advisers is to let those issues play themselves out, because the higher priority is to create an annual gift tax exclusion of $10,000/20,000 for the insured when he or she pays premiums.

A word of caution about the *Crummey* power, even if it endures: its role is to ameliorate gift tax. The power does not help with the generation-skipping tax. For GST purposes, a different approach is needed.

Example

Yolanda creates a trust that takes out insurance on her life. Yolanda will pay the premium of $15,000 annually. The trust beneficiaries are her grandchildren, Brandon, Carlette, and Perri. The *Crummey* power of withdrawal held

ter from the credit, the marital deduction may be the savior from estate tax.

The marital deduction, which can shelter a spouse's inheritance from estate tax, coincides neatly with a major point that is imposed by the tax laws. The Internal Revenue Code prescribes that a surviving spouse cannot be deprived without his or her written consent from enjoying a joint-and-survivor annuity arising from the dead spouse's participation in a qualified pension plan. Putting it succinctly, a joint-and-survivor annuity would start in favor of the employee, at his or her retirement, and at the employee's later death, the payment would continue in favor of the surviving spouse for his or her lifetime. The survivor's payments must be in an amount that is not less than 50 percent of what the deceased employee had been paid.

If the employee-spouse died *before* retiring, the widow or widower would be entitled to annuity payments, but not necessarily right away. The payments would begin to flow at the date the pension plan prescribes as the earliest time when the late employee could have retired.

Example

> Craig, employed by Widgets, Inc., dies suddenly at fifty, leaving wife Robin, who is thirty-nine. Widgets has a pension plan in which Craig participated. Robin will get annuity payments because she never consented to anything. But Robin will have to wait for her annuity until the earliest time when Craig could have retired under the Widgets pension plan. That may be about fifteen years in the future.

In a profit-sharing or stock-bonus plan, should death occur before benefits have been completely distributed to the employee, his or her spouse cannot be cut off from the death payment without the spouse's written consent.

Written consent is critical in these cases if the employee wishes to have someone else as the beneficiary of the benefits. That is the case also if the employee wants to have the benefits collected by a trust for the surviving spouse, instead of by that spouse directly. It matters not if the surviving spouse has a plentitude of assets from other sources, or had been a shrew of a wife or a monster as a husband. The tax law has an inflexible rule of protection for the surviving widow or widower.

The surviving spouse's right to an annuity is eligible for the marital deduction for estate tax purposes. That would stay the government's hand in collecting estate tax, but not so for other taxes.

One of those other taxes is sure to intrude — the income tax — and we'll shortly look it over. Another tax possibility would apply if there were an excess retirement accumulation. Were an employee to retire and have an excess accumulation, there would be a 15 percent tax on the excess distribution in any year. Should the employee who has an excess accumulation die before retirement, the 15 percent tax threatens at the time of death. It would be imposed as an add-on to any estate tax. This surcharge cannot be wiped out by either the $600,000 exemption from estate tax or the marital deduction. Even if the estate would otherwise escape estate tax, the 15 percent add-on would occur. Some solace might be gained by deducting this added cost as an expense of the estate.

The major hope for avoiding this surcharge would come to pass if the surviving spouse is the beneficiary of all retirement and IRA benefits, and that spouse elected to deem the decedent's excess distribution as the spouse's when he or she later retires. That election would create a deferral. Without the election, the special surcharge would be due when the first spouse died.

When does this add-on tax become an issue? A complex calculation sets the acceptable amount of retirement accumulation. Briefly, you first value all of the late employee's interests in IRAs and qualified retirement plans as of the time of death. Then, using actuarial principles, you subtract the discounted present value of an annuity that would have been paid to the late employee over his or her lifetime, up to the maximum amount that the tax law tolerates (that maximum tolerable amount in most instances would be $150,000). If after the subtraction is made a difference remains, that is the excess accumulation to which the 15 percent surcharge applies.

Income Tax

Employee benefit rules are complex and intricate. We have had a tiny taste in looking over the estate tax and surcharge rules. Things get indigestible when the income tax issues come onto the plate.

We shan't undertake an exhaustive review, for that would surely make you drowsy. And we definitely will avoid discussing rules that apply when the employee retires, because that would put me under as well. Suffice it to say that the rules are abundant, and inescapable. No matter what plan the employee may entertain, the government's income tax bombardment cannot be dodged. The only exception is if the employee makes charity the beneficiary of the death benefits under his or her retirement plan. Charity would receive those benefits free of all taxes. But that can't be duplicated for individual beneficiaries.

Because these retirement benefits are income tax laden, an important truth must be grasped. These benefits are not wholly spendable by the heir.

Example

Cameron, a divorcee, decides to make his retirement pension payable to his daughter, if he dies before retirement. The benefit is worth $300,000 today. Cameron seeks to balance that by leaving $300,000 of cash and securities to his son. Everything else, which is not much, will go to Cameron's girlfriend.

Result, the plan is not in balance and the daughter will be the loser. Her inheritance is subject to income tax, while the son's is not.

Why is there income tax? Because (1) contributions to the retirement plan were deductible when they were made on the employee's behalf and (2) while in the retirement plan, those contributions were invested and spawned dividends, interest, and gains that were not taxed. The government gets even when the retirement plan benefit is paid to the employee at retirement, or to the heir when the employee dies.

Making one's way through all of the optional methods of collecting the retirement benefits and the maze of income tax rules is an onerous and bewildering task. It is akin to being in Wonderland with Alice. There are two occasions when the challenge might have to be faced. One is when the employee retires, and must select the right twisting path. The other is when the employee dies and his or her beneficiary must choose the path to take.

The starting point is what payment plans are available under the particular retirement plan. All corporate plans are by no means alike, nor are all Keogh plans. Illustrative is the defined-benefit pension plan, whose objective is to fund a retirement payout of a specified amount for the retiree. Defined-benefit pension plans that are sponsored by large corporations infrequently offer lump-sum payments to the retiree, or to his or her

(1) was a participant in the retirement plan before 1974 and (2) reached age fifty before 1986. That would permit using capital gain rates for a portion of the lump-sum benefit.

When the retirement or death benefit would come in a lump sum, another option is available. The would-be recipient may have the option to decide not to collect it yet. For example, a retired employee may have other income coming in and would like to defer payment of tax on the retirement benefit. The same thought may occur as to a lump-sum death benefit that would go to a spouse. He or she may prefer to postpone collecting the benefit and having to pay income tax. A deferral is available to the retiree and the surviving spouse-beneficiary. They can roll the benefit over to an IRA, keeping it on ice until the ages when the would-be recipient is ready to take payments or is compelled by the tax law to start doing so. We'll touch on those ages in a moment. The rollover continues the income-tax-free earning status of the retirement money. While the money is on ice in the IRA, dividends, interest, and gain continue to accumulate without income tax. A rollover can be made with all of a lump-sum distribution or part of it, so the decision about deferral does not have to be all or nothing.

The rollover fund must be tapped at some point. There are tax disadvantages to leaving it on ice too long. The distribution rules are intricate. Basically, a takedown must not be postponed beyond age seventy and one-half. The earliest time for payments from a rollover IRA to start without a tax penalty would be fifty-nine and one-half. So, when a retiree or a surviving spouse considers a deferral of the lump sum, the age brackets for the takedown have to be thought about soberly. The decision to defer is not a lark for avoiding taxes. For a rollover, lump-sum income tax treatment is not attainable any longer. A rollover involves surrendering income averaging, and also capital gain rates if they ever would have been available. Instead, when rollover money is taken, it is taxed like a payment made over time and not like a lump-sum distribution.

An important point concerning rollovers by a beneficiary of the benefit at death relates to who the beneficiary is. Only a surviving spouse may achieve income tax deferral by a rollover. No other beneficiary may do so: not child, not parent, not live-in special companion. Again, marital status is unique.

Benefits that are paid over time from any of these retirement arrangements are basically taxed as ordinary income when collected. So, if an annuity is paid to a retiree for life, and thereafter a payment stream continues for the life of the surviving spouse, all of these payments are ordinary income to the recipient.

Note that two taxes can apply to a death benefit. If the benefit is not payable to the surviving spouse under protection of the marital deduction, there can be estate tax. And there certainly will be income tax. There is some relief for this double bombardment. The recipient of the death benefit is entitled to a deduction (not a credit) on his or her income tax return for the estate tax that is attributable to the benefit. While this is welcome balm, it will not make the tax hurt go away.

We have reviewed only the income tax highlights. There are so many persnickety rules. They deal with several issues, including contributions that the employee made to the retirement plan, distributions from the plan to the employee before age fifty-nine and one-half, delaying distributions of a retirement payment or death benefit too long, and piling up excessive amounts in a retirement account. Scrutinizing these issues may induce a stupor, so we'll avoid such scrutiny with but one exception. We touched on the point of excessive accumulations in connection with the estate tax, and highlighted the 15 percent death tax that would have to be faced if an employee with an excessive accumulation died before retirement. Were that employee not to die but instead to retire and not do a rollover, the government would impose its 15 percent tax at retirement, concurrently with the income tax. If a rollover occurs, the potential surcharge will overhang the rollover fund and have to be faced when the deferral ends and payments flow.

Another caution is in order. We have talked about retirement plans that are qualified under the tax law for advantages. If an employee makes a special deal with his or her employer that is not qualified for those tax advantages, different rules will apply. Each contract must be reviewed to determine the impact of the estate tax and income tax when there is a specially prepared retirement program and a benefit to be paid at the death of the employee. Basically, the estate tax cannot be countermanded, and the income tax, at most, can only be deferred. There are no free meals.

CHAPTER

7

The Family Business

Of all the challenges that an individual's assets may present, none can top the problem of dealing with an interest in a family business. The issues are myriad. There are tax difficulties, considerations of who the business heirs rightfully should be, taking care of those who are not the chosen business heirs, and personal conflicts aplenty.

The family business could be one of several varieties. There is the long-lived business, started decades ago by some forebear. Maybe that ancestor was a parent of today's business person or maybe that ancestor lived a century ago and never laid eyes on the heir who is today's business person. As to the heir, sometimes that person is actively in charge, and sometimes that heir is the spouse or in-law of the active manager of the enterprise. Then there are businesses that were started and nurtured by today's business person. Sometimes the business was bought from a third party who was the founder.

Sometimes the executive runs the show alone, and sometimes he or she has a partner or two. That partner could be of any dimension: smart, honest, gracious, cooperative, unassuming, a vital force in the enterprise, a guiding light, crafty, scheming, manipulating, domineering, untrustworthy, stupid, a drag on the enterprise, a nonentity, an embarrassment, or many other things.

Sometimes today's executive is not behind a desk or in a Brooks Brothers or Ann Taylor suit. He or she may usually be on the run, sometimes hunched over a computer terminal, even have grimy hands and be tailored in jeans or khakis. The business itself could be farming, manufacturing, selling, servicing, processing, consulting, developing, assembling, managing, designing, constructing, or lots of other things. It never ceases to amaze how entrepreneurs make money and what it takes to make a go of the enterprise.

The business may be incorporated or it could be a partnership or an enterprise that is neither. Its assets may include real estate, tools, equipment of all sorts, vehicles, finished and unfinished goods, raw materials, minerals in the ground, cash, securities, accounts receivable, patents, copyrights, and much more. It may have no debt to speak of, or it may be laden with debt. It may have few employees or thousands, who are or are not union members.

Whatever it is, whatever it may have, however it came to be, estate planning issues have to be addressed.

Will the Business Last?

Some businesses are personal service enterprises. When the leader dies, that may end the business. It is important to face this issue squarely. Maybe the leader totally personifies the business and cannot be replaced. Maybe he or she has special skills or a way with customers that is unique. If the business cannot be handed down, there may be little else to wrestle with respecting the enterprise. After the funeral, it will be liquidated and gone.

If the business could endure, should the family continue with it? In some cases, that would entail high risk. It could well be an acceptable risk now, because the entrepreneur is capable of turning to other pursuits and earning a living if the business gets excessively rocky. But there may be no family member who could emulate today's leader. It may be just too chancy to risk the net worth of the business after the leader is gone. That may dictate that plans be developed to sell the business advantageously, even while the leader remains alive.

The business may survive and it may not present undue risks, but who will be there to lead it? A replacement for the entrepreneur may have to be hired, and the salary and perquisites he or she may command could cut too deeply into profits to make it worth the family's while to continue. Sometimes a candidate to assume the leadership may yet emerge. Possibly the entrepreneur has hopes for a child or nephew or niece, who is still too young or inexperienced to take up the reins today but might do so in a few years. Here the question may be the continued good health of the entrepreneur until that heir apparent can emerge.

Let's proceed, assuming that a successor is already on the scene or is likely to emerge.

Educating the Successor

Succession is a very delicate affair. There are plenty of examples of an entrepreneur who ought to share the leadership role with a family successor, even relinquishing the reins while staying in place. But the reins are not handed over, or even shared. It may be justifiable, because the entrepreneur is still contributing mightily to the enterprise, or feels that the lady or gentleman in waiting is far too green. It may occur out of habit or misgivings or cursedness or egomania. Overstaying one's time is unwise, but how many are clever enough to recognize when time is running out.

Bringing in family successors, training them, preparing them for the future, and doing it all in a timely fashion, is a high art. Fortunate is the family in which the art is practiced, especially if it is practiced well. Where the entrepreneur has hesitated or resisted, an effort should be made to bring the issue of succession into the open. Of course, this is a delicate affair. Offending the older person is easy to do. But he or she must be brought to realize that time goes by. Stifling a candidate for succession is also easy to do. That can retard the enterprise. New techniques, new ideas, fresh approaches, and up-to-date attitudes inject vitality into a business and create growth. Younger people must be encouraged to come forward, try their wings, take responsibility, and learn to face up to hard decisions and assume the burdens of leadership.

The different generations have to resolve the matter. Resolution is far more likely to go well if it precedes death or incapacity. If not, the successor walks into the spotlight in a time of crisis. The older person has to plan an exit, and get out of tomorrow's way. The younger one must show patience — and humility wouldn't be amiss — as experience is garnered and time swings around to his or her advantage. It is far better if the succession dance proceeds at a pace that suits both. It should not be done overnight. But neither should it proceed like a marathon.

All too often, the entrepreneur grouses about other planning problems, such as taxes, without doing anything constructive about the succession issue. That's an error, and it can be fatal. Overstaying one's time can lead to a decline of the business, and frustrate the heir apparent. If that individual is deeply discouraged, he or she may go elsewhere to try out his or her dream. That may be an irresistible idea because the entrepreneur could be tough to handle, anyway. On the other hand, the younger person may be too much in a hurry, not sufficiently seasoned, or short on endearing personal qualities. Pressing too hard for an early coronation could lead to a setback or disappointment. I know of a grandfather-grandson case where it led to a dismissal. This dance is quite something. Busby Berkeley never produced one like it in all his Hollywood years.

Let's go on, assuming that the succession issue is being addressed.

Fairness to Heirs

In many families, one or two children are interested in the business while others are not. The parent may want the business to be preserved. But above all, the parent must understand that there ought to be fair dealing for all the heirs. If that primary element is missing, great woe can occur. Sibling can turn against sibling, and severe hurt can be felt for years and years. If the family is lucky, there will be sufficient nonbusiness assets to leave for those who are not in the business. That would provide everyone with an appropriate inheritance. That program also goes well with the concept that it's best not to tie all those young people together for the future. Being economically independent of each other may be the supreme tonic for siblings.

But frequently that is not the way it is. Very often the business is the dominant parental asset. It must be the source for an inheritance for the surviving spouse, for those children who want to succeed to the enterprise, and for those children who want to be out of it.

Example

Corinna, a divorcée, has built a successful executive search and personnel business. Five years ago, her daughter Carly came into the business at entry level. She has progressed rapidly since then. Corinna feels that Carly is a natural and should someday take over the business, known as Executive Placement Corp. (EPC). Corinna's other child, Torrance, is a high school teacher in Maryland. Corinna's major assets are:

Item	Estimated Value
Stock of EPC	$1,800,000
Condominium apartment	350,000
Cash, U.S. Treasuries, and tax-exempt bonds	500,000

If Corinna hopes to treat her children equally, some interest in the business must be left for her son Torrance. Remember that the available assets will be depleted by estate taxes.

In these situations, the parent-entrepreneur may have particular goals. A familiar one is that those involved in the business are to operate it without interference. So Carly is not to have to suffer from Torrance's sideline sniping. Another goal ought to be that so long as the other heirs, such as Torrance, are tied to the business, they must not be victimized by high salaries, perquisites, and expense account hijinx by the operator of the enterprise, who is Carly. This balancing of goals takes some doing.

A serious risk of squabbling can interfere with goals and overshadow any set of circumstances. Indeed, the risk may be of lasting warfare. If the would-be heirs, such as Carly and Torrance, are already estranged, or well along in that direction, no plan and no goal will assure peace in their time. But tolerable irritations could be aggravated by the testamentary outcome.

Suppose in a particular family that brother comes into the business and succeeds, and sister inherited a chunk of cash as her portion. No matter how large the chunk, she may feel that brother was unfairly given the advantage of a going business that will outperform any investment that she would make. Conversely, if, in that family, sister is provided for by some secondary interest in the business because sufficient other assets were not available to give her a full inheritance, she may resent being involved in her brother's inherited business. And he will be deeply offended by her carping about her subordinate inheritance, not to mention gratuitous remarks from her husband. Most likely, the trouble between the siblings is ancient history, but the areas of disagreement and communication breakdown can be easily intensified after the parent's death.

These family snapshots only touch lightly on the deep issues that are involved. The family business is in the center of the picture, and it commands attention because of its economic importance. But at the edges of the snapshot are glimpses of the sibling relationships and the divergent views of those in the business and those who are doing something else. Each one is sure that his or her view is accurate and reasonable. Adding to the maelstrom will be the comments and incitements from the other players: sister's husband or husbands and brother's wife or live-in companion of either sex. Truly, these scenarios outdo any daily drama on the TV tube.

Income Needs

Another serious issue is getting income to those who are not compensated by the business for services and work actually performed.

Example

If the late entrepreneur's spouse does not work, or works for insufficient compensation, how is he or she to be sustained? This issue is heightened by the most likely choice of the vehicle for the spouse's inheritance: a marital deduction trust. The tax law requires that the trust be productive of income for the surviving spouse. Hence, if an interest in the business is the spouse's inheritance, then that interest has to carry some cash flow.

Example

If those children who are not in the business nevertheless are to receive something from the business as their portion because there are no other assets to provide for them sufficiently, what exactly flows to them?

Solutions are possible. If the business is operated as a partnership, the spouse and uninvolved children could get cash flow from limited partnership interests. Those interests do not involve them in management, because that is the exclusive purview of the general partners, who are the children involved in the business.

If the business is operated as a corporation, nonvoting stock that has a cash flow could be the inheritance of the surviving spouse (outright or in a trust) and the uninvolved children. Preferred stock, which pays dividends before the common stock gets any, and also has a priority for being paid off if the corporation is wound up, is one possibility, with the common stock held by the managerial children. But preferred stock dividends are expensive, as they are not deductible by the corporation on its income tax return.

A possible corporate variation is offered by the so-called S corporation, which resembles a partnership for income tax purposes in that the income tax burden does not fall on the company. Although an S corporation cannot have preferred stock, it can have nonvoting stock. The nonvoting stock would be left for the uninvolved children. That plan permits corporate earnings to be shared by all of the shareholders, with voting control lodged in the managerial children.

Solving income problems may not dispose of all concerns. Those not in the business may be eager for capital, which they would be free to use as they please. Free capital can mean some degree of independence.

Example

> Orlando inherited all the voting stock of Waggles, Inc., a distributor of widgets and squiggles. His sister Dyan inherited the nonvoting stock. It is an S corporation, so corporate profits are taxed directly to Orlando and Dyan as the stockholders. Each received a cash dividend last year of $40,000. In addition, Orlando as president receives a salary of $125,000 and enjoys such fringe benefits as health insurance and contributions for him into a retirement plan. He also is reimbursed for his substantial travel and entertainment expenses. Dyan feels that her brother is doing a solid job and is not overpaid. *But* she would like to get out of the business, where she has no voice and no active involvement. She now has a golden opportunity to invest in the investment advisory firm where she has worked for ten years and at which she is highly thought of.

Hence the uninvolved children, such as Dyan, would like to sell their interests, and the likely buyers are the managerial siblings, such as Orlando. The latter, in turn, may be eager to buy the others out, in order to increase the distance between the siblings and reduce the cash flow that would be outgoing from the business on a persistent basis. Working out such an accommodation between the likes of Dyan and Orlando may be quite a challenge. The major problem is funding the buyout. Borrowing money to purchase the Dyan interest may be costly. An additional issue for the siblings could be arriving at an agreement about the price. That could require negotiations that experienced statesmen would shy away from.

The Business Partner

If the entrepreneur has a substantial partner, matters may take a very different course. ("Partner" here means a business colleague who is an owner, whether the form of conducting business is a partnership or a corporation or a joint venture.) It may or may not be a 50-50 partnership. The point is that the other person has a major position, and may refuse to accept a plan whereby he or she could end up being in business with the entrepreneur's family. That may be a reciprocal idea: the entrepreneur may not wish to have any involvement with his colleague's family.

The solution in many of these situations is a buyout of the interest of the partner who dies first. If that turns out to be the person for whom we have been considering these planning issues, they all fall to the wayside. The business interest will be sold. Succession within the family would cease to be an issue. The proceeds of sale will be divided among the heirs, and who among them might have been a manager and who an outsider would become academic.

But the existence of a buyout arrangement does not always cut through those issues. The other partner may die first, with the person for whom we are planning ending up with an increase in his or her stake in the enterprise. All of those other issues remain open and need to be resolved.

Another situation in which a buyout does not resolve everything is when the partner is a family member and the insider-outsider plot continues.

Example

Clint, age seventy-one, and his son Torrance, age forty-six, own their business 50-50. They have an agreement that provides for Torrance to buy his father's interest when Clint dies. Clint plans to leave the proceeds from the sale for his third wife, Rochelle, age forty-five, and his daughter Lacy, age forty-three. It is therefore important to the women that the agreement between Clint and Torrance not be a sweetheart deal.

Whenever an agreement between partners is made for the purchase of the interest of the first to die, two issues predominate above all others.

1. *How is the price to be arrived at?* This is challenging because the interest is not being sold now. Unless someone is clairvoyant, no one can be sure when the sale will occur. The business may take off, nosedive, or muddle along before the time for sale arrives. So it cannot be said with certainty that this partner's interest will be worth $5 hundred or $5 million when the critical buyout time arrives someday. The price has to be arrived at by some method that is flexible and can be applied at buyout time without serious contention.

    Often the approach is to have the partners set the price initially and adjust it periodically. This has the merit of allowing the most knowledgeable people to express their opinion on a very important matter. A common failing is that once they set the price, they neglect this task as years go by and don't keep the price current. A fallback method is often invoked under those circumstances. That fallback method should be sound, so that a fair deal results. One such method I have seen used is to take the last agreed-upon price and increase it (by, say 5

195

percent) for every year that has passed since that last agreement was made.

2. *How is the price to be paid?* That must be fair to the heirs, who should not be required to wait for their inheritance. Further, they may need cash to pay the government or deal with other obligations. The price and terms of payment must also be reasonable to the survivor, otherwise; the business may collapse under the payment load.

    Often some sizable amount is payable at once, and the balance is to be handled over time. The down payment is often funded by life insurance. Insurance representatives adore these situations, because they can market policies for all of the partners. The other payments should bear a reasonable interest rate and be fairly secured. To prevent a breakdown in installment payments in the future, restrictions are often imposed on what the survivor can pull from the business in terms of salary and dividends, so that the security of the collateral remains intact.

Valuation for Tax Purposes

A significant matter is valuing the business for estate tax purposes when the entrepreneur dies. Or, if the entrepreneur decides to give some or all of the business to others during his or her lifetime, a gift tax valuation has to be made. Valuation is an issue that must be addressed carefully.

The government is in the enviable position of requiring the taxpayer to make the first move. That is an entry on the gift or estate tax return of a value. When the government has received the return, it can challenge the taxpayer by asking the searching question: "How was this value arrived at?" There is more about this tender subject in the chapter on Paying Taxes and Dealing with the Government (starting on page 199). But suspense need not be created; the discussion in that chapter will underline the need for a valuation strategy for the taxpayer.

The entrepreneur and family must adjust themselves to realities. In valuation matters, the government can be a tough opponent. Sustaining a low value for tax purposes is a major challenge to the adviser. If the business has been a success, a magic wand may be required to persuade the government to believe otherwise.

Paying Taxes and Dealing with the Government

There are unpleasant aspects of estate planning. One can be the business of confronting your feelings about your spouse, kids, friends (particularly the special ones), and various relatives. For some people the confrontation may not prove to be unpleasant after all. But for most, coming to grips with expectations, disappointments, frustrations, if-onlys, and might-have-beens is not a happy experience. It may be a particularly heavy adventure for a person who is very elderly or seriously ill, and is taking stock of what life has been. Only the very young, with naive ideas of immortality and interminable new chapters yet to begin, would dismiss such a survey as a foolish duty.

A universally felt unpleasantness of planning is paying taxes. No matter how much one may plan, no matter how clever the design or ruthless the conniving, the government is an implacable adversary. It is glorious to triumph now and then in tax escapades, but inordinately difficult to disinherit Uncle Sam permanently. So, at some point, a return will be due to report gifts or an estate's holdings. Because of exemptions and exclusions, tax may not always be due, yet. But at some point, maybe with the next return, a check will have to be enclosed.

Gift Tax Returns

We should say more about returns that are due even though a check may not be required. This commonly arises with gifts. If a gift is made, say of $20,000, to one person, gift tax may not be payable because of the $10,000/20,000 annual exclusions of the donor and the donor's spouse who consents to the gift. But that consent must be signified to the government on a return. Hence, husband and wife each must file a gift tax return that the filer signs and that is also signed by the consenting spouse.

Q:　Are you saying that if I make a gift of $20,000 to my daughter and no return is filed, my spouse's consent doesn't count?

A:　Exactly. You and your spouse must each file, and sign the other's return, in order to claim two annual exclusions of $10,000.

When larger gifts are made, but they are sheltered from gift tax by the $600,000 exemption, a return is due even though no tax is payable. The government wants a running record of those uses of the $600,000 exemption, so it knows if you have exhausted the exemption and your next event requires you to pay tax.

The gift tax return is due on April 15 following the year in which the gift is made.

Example

Carter makes a $50,000 gift to his son, Lowell, on November 15, 1992. The gift tax return will be due on April 15, 1993.

Example

Delia makes a $50,000 gift to her daughter, Moira, on January 5, 1993. The gift tax return will be due on April 15, 1994.

If tax is due, it is to be paid then. An extension of time to file can be requested and is not hard to obtain. That alone does not extend the time to pay: April 15 will still be the payment date. If an extension of time to pay is granted along with the extension to file, then both can be done after April 15, on the adjourned date.

If the tax is not paid on time, the government will charge interest. Even if an extension of additional time to pay is granted, interest will begin running on April 15. Starting on that date, the government is entitled to the use of the money. If payment of tax is tardy, the government may charge a penalty for late payment unless it accepts the taxpayer's excuse for tardiness. Not every excuse will fly.

The taxpayer may never hear a word about the gift tax return that was filed. The alternative is not so welcome: word from the government that it wants to conduct an examination.

Q: How long does the government have to examine?

A: Normally three years from the April 15 filing date. If the taxpayer received an extension of time to file, the three-year period runs from the extension date.

Q: What does the government look at?

A: The examination could focus on the value of the item that was given or the taxpayer's right to claim the annual $10,000/20,000 exclusion or anything else the government feels is pertinent.

Q: Can the government ask for more time?

A: Absolutely.

Q: Tell me more about valuing the item that was given.

A: That's a big subject. Let's survey it when we come to valuation in the discussion of the estate tax (starting on page 211).

Estate Tax Returns

Estate tax returns are special in a few ways. First, the return is filed by the executor, for the decedent is normally unable to sign the return. The time for filing and paying the tax is nine months after the date of death. Very often that date comes on like gang-busters, and there is feverish scurrying to meet the deadline. The filing date can be extended by the government, and it is usually not difficult to obtain an extension of six months. But that doesn't change the date for paying the tax. If an extension of the time to pay is granted together with an extension of time to file the return, then both will be done on the adjourned date.

If the tax is not paid on the nine-month anniversary date, interest will be due the government. That is so even if the time to pay was extended. The use of the money starting from that nine-month date cannot be denied the government. If payment is late, a penalty may be exacted in addition to interest.

A major exception to paying the tax at that nine-month date relates to business interests, a matter we'll discuss later. Aside from that exception, the tax is due, ready or not, and the government likes cash.

A return may be due even if no estate tax is required to be paid. Whenever the gross estate exceeds $600,000, the estate tax return must be filed. The fact that a combination of the $600,000 exemption and the marital deduction wipes out the tax does not relieve the executor of the responsibility to file.

The government always responds to an estate tax return. How promptly after the return has been filed varies from locale to locale. But generally a response is had by one year after the filing date. That response tells the executor whether his responsibility is satisfied or if more remains. One frequent response is a letter from the IRS advising that the tax has been paid in full. That is welcome for two important reasons. First, the government has decided to expend its energy elsewhere, leaving this estate alone. That is a relief to everyone involved and can lead to a moderation in professional fees for whoever was handling the estate tax aspects. Second, getting rid of the government early means the estate can be wound up more rapidly.

A very different response can come: notice that the government wants to conduct an examination. It usually wants its representative to look over many records of the estate and the deceased, including his or her bank statements, checkbooks, brokerage statements, partnership agreements, and lots more. In addition to records, other matters are commonly scrutinized, and will be pursued. Those issues can be

- what is the proper value of an asset;

- whether a claimed deduction for an expense or a debt is to be allowed;

- whether a trust is eligible for the marital deduction;

- whether assets have been erroneously omitted from the return, such as life insurance, income from a trust to which the deceased was entitled but from which he or

she did not collect, and property that the deceased transferred but kept some kind of control over; and

• whether the decedent's gifts had been properly counted,
for that would influence the computation of the estate
tax, as the estate tax rate picks up where the gift tax rate
had left off.

In an estate tax examination, other taxes can be involved: for
example, gift tax. One aspect is whether the decedent's lifetime
transactions included gifts he or she failed to report. That could
lead to a government claim for gift tax, interest, and penalties
for failure to have paid the tax way back when.

Another subject can be the decedent's income taxes. Did he
or she file all required returns? Was something mishandled in returns about which the government still has time to raise questions? Are all assets reflected on the income tax returns properly
accounted for in the estate tax proceedings?

Example

If the income tax return for the year before death shows
interest income from a Citibank account, is the account
listed on the estate tax return? If not, what became of the
funds in that account?

Example

If the income tax return for two years before death shows
General Motors dividends, are shares of General Motors
listed on the estate tax return? If not, why weren't the
shares shown as sold on an income tax return?

The government has three years from the filing date to complete its administrative work in examining the estate tax return.
That date is nine months after death, or a later date granted under an extension of time to file. The time limit cannot be ex-

tended. If all issues cannot be resolved within that period, the return is headed for litigation.

Valuation Fights

For both gift tax and estate tax returns, frequent spats with the government occur concerning the value of an item listed on the return. Any kind of property could be involved: a home, an office building, a family business, a promissory note, an investment represented by stocks or bonds, rights under a contract, a painting, a Chinese vase, a boat, a diamond necklace, an oil well, baseball cards, a collection of seventeenth century armor — or anything else you can imagine. The starting point for these contests is the value that is reported on the return. That is the opening gambit. The taxpayer must be prepared to explain his or her initial move, for the usual salutation of the IRS representative is, "How did you arrive at this figure?"

To be prepared in advance is extremely wise. Preparation should start with a valuation strategy.

Q: Why is that necessary? Why not give the government guys your number and let them shoot at it?

A: If the number is not supported by some acceptable valuation approach, the taxpayer has no credibility with the government. Once again, credibility is key, as it is in relationships. Although you may not equate the IRS with some special person in your life, you will find that saying believable words counts heavily in both experiences. Without credibility, the taxpayer's arguments will get no respect and the IRS will go on to do as it pleases. The value the IRS goes for will skyrocket.

Q: What's an acceptable valuation approach?

A: It depends on the asset.

Example

For a home, it could be comparable sales.

Example

For commercial real estate, it could be a multiple of cash flow or comparable sales.

Example

For a painting, it could be auction prices.

Example

For a business interest, it could be asset value or a multiple of earnings or, in some cases, a reflection of market value for a comparable business that is a public company.

A persuasive presentation of an acceptable valuation approach requires homework. Details and numbers have to be assembled. That is often done by someone who has credentials, such as an appraiser for art or real estate, an investment banker for business interests, a dealer in fine arts or a curator for Chinese porcelain, a petroleum engineer for oil interests, and so on. Whoever is chosen will expect a fee for his or her work.

Q: Why not get the lowest number from the cheapest guy?

A: Because that may not do. You want a solid presentation to maintain credibility. Someone with a good reputation will have respect from the IRS. And when the government starts poking at your number, you want the expert you hired to sit alongside you at the negotiations with the IRS and dazzle the examiners with backup and articulate arguments. You get what you pay for. The cheapest guy probably would blow it, or charge much more to show up and negotiate.

Q: This could be expensive.

A: The fees are deductible.

Q: I still don't see why you can't just give the IRS a number on the return. Maybe it'll get by. If it doesn't, so what. Just pay the extra tax.

A: Not so fast. Getting by isn't so easy. The government is looking for these situations. If the low value doesn't get by and the tax goes up, interest is charged as well as more tax. The IRS interest rate is higher than the taxpayer is likely to earn on money before it is paid over to the government.

Q: So it costs some interest. Can't that be deducted?

A: Not for income tax purposes. No deduction is available if it was a gift tax battle before the taxpayer dies. Yes, if it was an estate tax contest, interest would be deductible in computing the estate tax, or in settling any gift tax that was an open issue when the person died. But the costs don't end there. In addition, there are tough penalties if the value was really low and is raised substantially.

Example

A gift or bequest of a business interest is reported by the taxpayer on the return at $100,000. After battle with the IRS the value comes out at $200,000. The government can exact a penalty equal to 20 percent of the tax on the $100,000 increase in value. If the contest with the IRS concludes with the value for the business interest zooming up to $400,000, the IRS penalty would be 40 percent of the tax on the $300,000 increase in value.

Example

Government regulations call for the taxpayer to submit financial and other data that are the basis for the value used on the return for a business interest. If that material isn't provided, a separate penalty of 20 percent of the tax on the increased value can be imposed for negligence or disregard of regulations.

Valuation Strategy

Developing a valuation strategy is prudent and self-protective. Preparation just can't be matched by anything else, even prayer or good-luck charms. Doing the job right can save lots of grief. A theory of value should be hatched, and it must be backed up by financial data. The taxpayer is free to develop a theory that favors a low figure. But the wise strategist anticipates what the government reaction is likely to be and is ready to counter government arguments that favor a higher value.

In the battle with the government, don't underestimate the adversary. The government has had years of experience in all sorts of valuation issues. Its representatives have heard every spiel, every sad story, every explanation. In my professional experience I have been involved in myriad valuation struggles, including disputes involving skyscraper office buildings, Impressionist paintings, mansions, yachts, diamonds, timber and oil interests, sports franchises, business of many kinds, and so on. I always found the government to be ready for battle: knowledgeable and prepared with data. The government also can hire experts from the private sector. It is a formidable opponent. Can it be beaten? Absolutely. Sometimes compromise is necessary because of the expense that would be generated by prolonging the fight.

Valuation strategy is more sophisticated than simply coming up with a number that can be defended. Sometimes the taxpayer doesn't want the lowest number.

Example

Cameron Harris dies and his estate is divided into two segments: (1) a $600,000 bequest to his children, which is
shielded from tax by the $600,000 exemption, and (2) the
rest, which is left to his widow Blaine. There will be no
federal estate tax because of the unified credit and the marital deduction. The assets that Blaine inherits include a vacation condo near Vail and a business venture. Blaine's adviser feels that these assets may be worth $1.5 million.

There is no one figure that is the correct value for the condo
or the business. Reasonable people can disagree about the values for those assets. There is a range of values that would be in
the ballpark. It could be a major mistake for Blaine to use the
values at the bottom of the range on the estate tax return. Why?
Because of the point we looked at in discussing Tax Opportunities in chapter 1, that the cost basis is transformed at death. That
takes place even though no federal estate tax is payable at Cameron's death. How can that change in basis help Blaine?

Example

Blaine may want to sell the condo. If she sells it for more
than the amount shown for the condo on the estate tax return, she will have to pay capital gains tax. As the condo is
not Blaine's principal residence, she cannot dodge the capital gain by reinvesting the proceeds in another place, or by
using the $125,000 exclusion from income tax.

Example

If the business venture is sold for an amount that is more
than the value shown for it on the estate tax return, a capital gain will result. (Just like the condo.) But more could
be involved. If the venture is a depreciable asset, like an in-

terest in a building, then income tax benefits are based on
the new basis for the venture.

Blaine would do better with a higher value for those assets on
the estate tax return. That would improve her basis position and
wipe out, or at least reduce, any potential capital gain. Here,
higher values could save real tax money.

Q: How much higher?

A: As close as possible to the eventual sales price.

Q: But Blaine may not sell the condo right away, and certainly not the business venture. And while she's figuring
those things out, the time will come to file the estate tax
return. What does she do?

A: The normal due date for the estate tax return would be
nine months after Cameron's death. But an extension of
six months can usually be obtained from the government without much difficulty. That means the filing
date for the estate tax return is moved to fifteen months
after Cameron's death. That extra period may give
Blaine the time she needs to work out the higher value
that suits her situation.

Don't embrace the higher value approach as a "can't miss"
idea. Higher values may not be more favorable to Blaine. If she
wants to make gifts of the condo or business venture to her children, higher estate tax values in Cameron's estate would be a bad
precedent in projecting Blaine's gift tax responsibility. If Blaine
is elderly or seriously ill, her own estate tax return may not be
so far distant, unfortunately. A low value would be desirable in
Cameron's estate tax return in order to be in tune with a low
value in Blaine's estate tax return. Remember, when Blaine
dies, no marital deduction will be available. At that time, large

estate tax is certain to be more important to the children than raising the cost basis for income tax benefits.

What Is the Value?

Valuing an item is not an offhand affair. The bromide is that fair market value is the amount a willing buyer would pay to a willing seller, both having reasonable knowledge of the relevant facts, the seller not being under compulsion to sell and the buyer not being under compulsion to buy. It's a standard that is easy to conceptualize, but it can be very hard to apply.

Some of the familiar tests that are used to find fair market value are not foolproof. Take a house that is an asset of an estate. Even though there is one on the next block with the same square footage and lot size and architectural design that was sold seven months ago, that is not absolute proof that someone will pay the same price now for the estate's house. The next block is a different street; seven months ago is not today; the built-ins and equipment may be different there; the deterioration here may be worse; the lawn and bushes may be nicer there; the feel of the place may be more comfortable here. Valuation is not an exact science. But, short of divine intervention, comparable sales may be the best approach that the appraiser and the IRS can apply to get to the fair market value. Clearly, if the estate's house were sold within a reasonable time after the valuation date, the market price would be the best indication. What is a reasonable time? That depends on the market. If it is jumpy, a sale more than ninety days after the valuation date could be in an entirely different marketplace because either buyers or sellers are scrambling for cover. But when the market is steady, a sale within a year, or perhaps even eighteen months, may occur in a market just like the one that prevailed at the valuation date.

The government has rules. Some of them will surprise you.

Example

A car is valued at the price it would sell for in a showroom or on a used car lot. That is the retail price, which is higher than the price a dealer would pay.

Example

Jewelry is valued at retail.

Example

The value for a work of art worth more than $20,000 will be reviewed by the Art Panel in Washington. That is a rotating board drawn from art galleries, auction houses, and unaffiliated experts, which is convened under the aegis of the IRS. Neither the taxpayer nor the taxpayer's appraiser will be present when the Art Panel does its thing.

Example

Goodwill may be an element in valuing a business interest.

Example

If a minority interest is involved, say 10 percent of the stock of a business, a discount may be allowed in the valuation process. The size of the discount will itself be a debatable matter. The taxpayer will shoot for 50 percent and the government will stand still for 10 percent. Usually a compromise figure is the result. When a controlling interest is involved, the government may try to add a premium in getting to the fair market value.

Example

For estate tax purposes, in valuing certain farm real property and business real property, the law allows a lower figure than the highest possible value. This is designed to determine the worth of the land as a going farm, or in a going business, rather than what a developer might bid the price up to. The reduction in estate tax value is aimed at avoiding forced sale of family farms at death. Lots of minute rules must be complied with to be eligible. The maximum decrease in value is $750,000.

One on One

Valuation is a prominent estate and gift tax issue. Others can loom large, too. They may run the gamut, from intricate questions, such as whether the trust which the decedent created eight years ago belongs in the gross estate because of some connection the deceased maintained to the trust, to seemingly simple issues, such as whether an accountant's fee is deductible. These issues are first thrashed out by the IRS representative and whoever speaks for the taxpayer. Most gift and estate tax returns are handled in this one-on-one context. The government's person is not a palooka. He or she is doing a job and deserves respect.

Over many years, I have found the great majority of the government's representatives to be scrupulous, honorable, thoughtful, and reasonable. We didn't always agree, but that was never the point. I also found the people I was dealing with to be well trained. For the most part, IRS representatives who handle audits of gift tax returns and estate tax returns are lawyers.

Here and there, a bad apple turns up — not a dishonest person, but a government representative who is unreasonable, or on a crusade, or trying to prove how smart he or she is. Those representatives are terrible to deal with. Fortunately, they are very few, but they give the IRS a black eye.

Sometimes a position taken by a government representative is prompted by a policy emanating from the national IRS office in Washington. Those occasions can be anxious, as the government tries out a new approach or a novel theory. Most of the time, however, the examination centers on plain issues: (1) for an estate, did the taxpayer report all of the assets that are part of the estate for tax purposes; were the values correctly set forth; are the deductions in order; is any generation-skipping tax due now; and (2) for a gift tax return, was every gift for the year reported at the right value; was the taxpayer entitled to the $10,000/20,000 exclusions that were claimed?

The examination proceeds until all the issues are out in the open. Then the horse-trading begins. The taxpayer gives way on this issue, and the government compromises on that one. When valuation issues are present, they are frequently resolved by mutual give and take. Because of that long-standing method, it is unfortunate to be involved in an examination where issues have inadvertently or unnecessarily been handed to the government. For example, if the decedent insisted on being trustee of a trust that he or she created in his or her lifetime for a child, that enables the government to assert that the trust is subject to estate tax. In order to win a clean bill of health for that trust, something may have to be offered in sacrifice, such as a higher value on a piece of property outside the trust.

When all issues cannot be resolved, the experience will be prolonged. There are higher levels of the IRS that may be tried, including its appellate division. It is common for the government to take a tough stand when agreement cannot be reached with its first representative. Not only will the contentious issues remain open, but items that were resolvable by compromise will also be declared to be fair game. The government will keep all the chips in play, refusing to allow the taxpayer to push some of them out of reach.

The trading process will persist at the upper administrative levels also. If resolution cannot be achieved, the remaining step is to proceed to court. Sometimes the taxpayer would like to resolve all matters, but the government's posture is to refuse to bend or compromise on a particular issue as a matter of policy. So the taxpayer is hauled to court while the government seeks judicial sanction for one of its theories. That can be a bad adventure, akin to being on a runaway bus. It also can be an expensive experience.

Estate Tax and Business Interests

There is a recognition that estate tax that is attributable to a family business can be a wrench. As we emphasized, valuation is a central issue. Sometimes the family is stunned by the government's view of the worth of a business interest. Sometimes the family is incredibly unrealistic about how valuable is a business venture that sustained not only the decedent, but his or her spouse and children, siblings by the score, and cousins by the dozens. Sooner or later, with or without pain, a tax figure will be arrived at. If a number of criteria are met, the estate tax will not have to be paid at the usual nine-month deadline. Instead, the estate tax relating to the business can be paid over an extended period.

A business interest has to be a substantial part of the estate to come within this rule. That test is met if the value of the business assets is more than 35 percent of the full gross estate less the expenses that are deductible. The business assets are only the ones actively needed for business operation, and would not include a portfolio of such marketable stocks as Pfizer or Boeing. Nor would the business assets include excess cash or its equivalent, such as certificates of deposit or Treasuries. Of course, what is "excess" can be heatedly debated.

Another requirement is that the enterprise be "closely held." That phrase is commonly used by lawyers and business people to mean an enterprise that is owned by a few people. Those owners may be members of a family, such as father and daughter, siblings, and their offspring. Or the owners may be few, but not related, such as Sylvester Ford, Garth Moore, and Raoul Carson, who met fifteen years ago when they worked for a large corporation and decided to try their luck together in a business they launched. The Internal Revenue Code, however, has a more precise test for a closely held business. Its standard is met if there are no more than fifteen shareholders or partners.

An alternative way of meeting the requirement of being closely held ignores the number of shareholders or partners and concentrates instead on how much of the entity is in the gross estate: in the case of a corporation, it would be closely held if 20 percent or more of the voting stock is in the gross estate; with a partnership, it would be closely held if 20 percent or more of the partnership's total capital is in the gross estate. If the enterprise is a trade or business that is conducted as a proprietorship, that automatically satisfies the test of being closely held. Here are some examples of the way the alternatives work.

Example

Kirk and his cousins Moira and Camilla each owns 25 percent of the stock of Widgets Corp., and Camilla's son Merton owns 10 percent of the stock. The remaining 15 percent is owned by T.J. Dudley, who is an old family friend, but is unrelated. The net worth of Widgets Corp. is about $2 million. As there are no more than fifteen shareholders, Widgets is a closely held business as to each shareholder.

Example

T.J. Dudley also owns 250,000 shares of the voting stock of General Blast Inc., whose stock is listed on the American Stock Exchange. T.J.'s holding is more than 25 percent of the voting stock. His stock is worth over $200 million. For T.J.'s purposes, General Blast is a closely held business (more than 20 percent of the voting stock will be in his gross estate for estate tax purposes). But if you bought 100 shares of General Blast Inc., your interest would not be closely held.

Example

T.J. Dudley and seven golfing buddies each owns 12.5 percent of a partnership, known as Putting Partners, that owns some land on the fringe of Junction City. That would be a closely held partnership for each of the partners because there are no more than fifteen of them. The value of the land is about $200,000.

Remember that having a closely held business is only one test for eligibility for payment of estate tax over an extended period. Don't forget the first requirement: the value of the closely held business must be more than 35 percent of the gross estate minus deductible expenses and debts. Knowing how wealthy T.J. Dudley seems to be, only his stock of General Blast is going to pass the 35 percent test.

Another crucial point to underline is that the law allows the estate tax to be paid over an extended time only for the active business assets. That breathing space is not available for the rest of the estate. The regular nine-month deadline applies for the tax on the so-called passive business assets, such as "excess" cash and the business's holding of stock in public companies, and on the decedent's nonbusiness assets, such as house, car, bank accounts, life insurance, and pension benefits.

Q: What's the break they give you in paying tax on active business assets?

A: For the first five years, only interest on the deferred tax is due. On the fifth anniversary, the tax installments begin and they can be stretched out to ten payments of tax.

Example

Noel died on May 1, 1992. The normal due date for filing
the estate tax return and paying the federal estate tax is
February 1, 1993. All tax is due then except for the part attributable to Noel's closely held business interest, which
satisfies the tests we have surveyed. For that segment of tax,
interest starts running on that date and has to be paid on
every subsequent February 1 until all tax has been paid.
The first installment of tax on the active business assets will
be due on the fifth anniversary of the due date for the estate tax return, which would be February 1, 1998. Up to
ten installments can be elected by the taxpayer, so that the
installments can be strung out to February 1, 2007. That
would be a period of fourteen years and nine months after
Noel died.

The taxpayer has to pay interest on the deferred payments. A
segment of the interest is a bargain: 4 percent on the first
$153,000 of tax. So when a medium-size business interest is in-
volved, a real break in financing the tax payment is presented to
the taxpayer. The balance of tax above $153,000 draws interest
at the going rate. That rate is keyed to the market and is adjusted by the government quarterly. In recent times this charge
has soared as high as 12 percent, which is rough going. But
quite lately the interest charge has moderated considerably, in
line with general interest-rate cuts. Fortunately, the interest is
deductible for estate tax purposes as the payment period unfolds,
and that softens the impact of the financing cost.

We should not step away from this taxpaying business without
noting that figuring out who really takes the impact of the tax
payment is a crucial matter. That goes for the regular estate tax
and the tax on the business interests. If you have reached this
point in the book, you know that I cannot be counted on to pay

your estate tax. Similarly, I don't expect you to pay mine. So, who is left? I venture to say that the responsibility will fall on those who benefit from our respective estates. But are all the beneficiaries to be hit for the tax money, or only some of them? We'll look at that issue in chapter 10 (pages 268–71).

Marital Deduction Decisions

A crucial decision in planning is whether the Will maker will use the marital deduction, and, of great significance, how it will be taken.

Example

> Barton Marsh is planning a new Will. He projects his estate to be $2 million. He will use the $600,000 exemption for his children. He will devote the balance of the estate to his wife Aliana, who has a profession and has substantial assets in her name. He is undecided whether to leave her inheritance outright, or in a QTIP trust that will provide income to her for her life and at her death pass the principal to their children.

Outright or in trust; that is the question. The marital deduction for Barton's estate will be available either way. The decision has obvious economic implications for Aliana and the children. If her inheritance is outright, she is answerable to no one about what she does with it. If a QTIP trust is used, her entitlement is to income only, and she has no control over how the principal will go at her death unless Barton also gives Aliana a power exercisable by her Will to direct the disposition of the principal at her death.

Aside from those consequential matters, there are tax points involved. Recall that by his Will plan, no federal estate tax will be payable when Barton dies, but everything Aliana inherits and neither consumes nor gives away in her lifetime will be taxed at her death, unless her $600,000 exemption covers it. So the lower estate tax brackets Barton could have allowed to apply at his death will not. Instead higher brackets will hit Aliana's estate. That would be an unfortunate result if Aliana outlived Barton by a short time. What might be done?

Example

Barton dies. After leaving the $600,000 exemption for his children, his Will leaves the marital deduction bequest outright to Aliana. Barton's Will could provide that if Aliana disclaims any part of the inheritance, the segment of Barton's estate that she gives up will be held in a trust for her life. Payments can be made to her from income and principal of the trust. By disclaiming, estate tax will be due currently on the segment of Barton's estate that Aliana declines to accept as an outright bequest. That segment will be taxed in lower estate tax brackets in Barton's estate instead of higher brackets that are forecast to apply when Aliana dies later. Should Aliana disclaim? This decision is likely to be more sensible to Aliana if she is elderly, say eighty-one, than if she is forty-one. Gaining a differential in tax brackets at an older age is not so speculative then. Further, trading some of her outright inheritance for a trust is not so meaningful a surrender of Aliana's sense of independence when she is a more senior woman.

Time limit: Aliana must make her disclaimer within nine months after Barton dies.

Example

Barton's Will leaves the marital deduction bequest outright to Aliana. His Will provides that if she disclaims, the property is to be held in trust for her lifetime benefit and at her

death it passes to their children. Aliana dies very soon after
Barton. Aliana's Will leaves whatever she has at her death
for the children. Aliana's executor disclaims part of the
outright bequest intended for Aliana, causing it to go via
the truncated trust to the children. The disclaimed part
therefore cannot be eligible for the marital deduction for
Barton's estate. The lower estate tax brackets will apply in
Barton's estate to the disclaimed part, before it goes to the
children. But the portion that the executor does not disclaim will be good for the marital deduction in Barton's
estate, and therefore not taxed in his estate. But that portion will be taxed in Aliana's estate, before it goes to the
children. Because nothing is involved in the disclaimer but
tax results, Aliana's executor can punch numbers for hours
in order to come to the decision about precisely how
much to disclaim.

Time limit: Aliana's executor must act within nine
months after Barton died.

Example

Barton's Will leaves the marital bequest in a QTIP trust for
Aliana. In strategy sessions, Aliana and her advisers discuss
the tax wisdom of how much of the QTIP trust should be
made eligible for the marital deduction. (Recall that the
final step in making a QTIP trust eligible for the marital
deduction is the executor's electing on Barton's estate tax
return whether all or part or none of the trust is to be
counted for the marital deduction.)

Time limit: The estate tax return for Barton's estate is
normally due nine months after Barton's death. But without any strain, an extension of six months can be obtained
from the IRS to file the return. That moves the deadline
for making the executor's QTIP decision on the estate tax
return to fifteen months after Barton died.

Assume that, in the course of planning, Barton basically decides to leave the marital deduction bequest outright to Aliana. But he wants a hedge in case she is very ill, or if she dies soon after him. If a disclaimer is to be made of an outright inheritance, the time limit for Aliana or her executor to disclaim part of the marital bequest is nine months after Barton dies. That would be the only way to swing assets away from the upper estate tax brackets for Aliana's estate to the lower brackets for Barton's estate. Can the time limit be pushed back to fifteen months, as in the last example? The hedge Barton wants can be exploited over fifteen months in a subtle manner. In Barton's Will, leave the marital deduction bequest in a lifetime trust for Aliana, *but* direct that if she is living one and one-half years after Barton's death, the portion of the trust that is made eligible for the QTIP marital deduction by the executor's election is to terminate and all of the marital deduction assets will go outright to Aliana. If any portion of the trust is not made eligible for the QTIP marital deduction by an executorial election, that segment will stay in trust throughout Aliana's life and eventually pass to their children. The trust income would continue to be payable to Aliana. Now, the time for quantifying the marital deduction decision can be extended to fifteen months after Barton dies, so long as the IRS grants the extra six months for filing Barton's estate tax return. Economically, Aliana need only wait a short time to receive her marital deduction inheritance outright. In the interim before that occurs, she will be entitled to all of the trust income, including that from the truncated QTIP trust.

CHAPTER

9

Avoiding Probate

Wouldn't it be neat to do it all without lawyers? I include in that dreamy wish the planning, and when death comes, the handling of the estate. That's the major theme in everyone's mind when avoiding probate is mentioned. It's the damnable lawyer's fee that they hope to escape.

Well, I understand. I'd like to avoid lots of fees, myself. The doctor's when surgery is indicated. Who needs that! Surely the dentist's, for his work is a bore, anyway. I'd like to duck the interior designer's fee too, for I know what colors I like, and fabrics are a cinch to select, aren't they? Certainly I don't need to pay someone to counsel me on investing my money. I know a callable convertible debenture from a crate of oranges — don't I? And when I sell my home, I don't like one bit having to pay some broker a fee for bringing around a prospect whom I could have fetched via an ad in the newspaper. That fee particularly galls me; my having to pay a broker for giving advice about my home to the buyer!

Oh yes, there's another charge I resent. It's all the commissions that a life insurance representative makes when he or she sells me one of those fancy policies that will cover my estate taxes some day. I'm very aware that out of the first year's premium, half — and maybe even more — is going to the insurance person. And that's not the end. In some of the succeeding years, a piece of the premium is going to him or her as a further commission. I don't mind some payment, for some of my best and dearest friends are insurance representatives. But should I support my friendly insurance representative?

So, I understand, absolutely. But let me share some professional insights with you. As a lawyer, there's lots of money to be made in the estate business when people start out seeking to avoid my services. When they try to do it themselves, often with those drippy forms that are printed, they invariably mess it all up. Then there are problems everywhere. To my mind that's just ducky, for cleaning up the mess is very rewarding work for me.

Let's level with each other. You don't want to pay one red cent more than is absolutely necessary to put your planning in order and, when the inevitable occurs, to handle your estate. For the adviser's part, he or she wants to be paid for time, and for dealing with complex problems, and for ideas that produce results. You say that there are no complex problems. I'll wager that you're overly optimistic. But if you don't need those services, fine — someone else will. Let's examine what you want and what a skilled adviser could contribute.

The Planning Stage

All the things we looked at in the previous chapters are part of the planning stage. I say part, because there can be much more, such as charitable foundations and charitable lead and remainder trusts, personal residence GRITs, private annuities, stock redemptions, GRATs, personal loans, guarantees, family partnerships, net gifts, sales and leases within the family, attempts at freezing values, deferred compensation agreements, survivor annuities, and other assorted stuff that creative planners get into. If either the tried and true approaches or the fancy maneuvers are for you, I assume you will pay for the services rendered. Those services would include the cost of producing documents that carry out the plan.

For this work, lawyers charge primarily for the time spent. For extraordinary effort, including creative ideas that are fruitful and solve hard puzzles, a premium may be requested. But the basic ingredients — and usually the most important criterion — would be the time of the lawyer and his or her colleagues.

The anticipated time can be lengthy. Be prepared! A lawyer spends a fraction of the billable time in discussion with you. Most of the hours are spent after you have left the lawyer's office. There are myriad details to work out in order to put all of the pieces together. There are ideas to ponder and alternative solutions to work out. Numbers are crunched, presentations are made to you, and your responses are weighed. There are lengthy documents to produce and then send to you for review, and they will be revised as you change your mind. You doubt that you will change your mind? Why should you be different from everyone else?

There are clients who want to revise the language in the documents. Contrary to what you may believe, the language has not been used deliberately to baffle you. First, the most artful drafter is writing a document for the eyes of judges and tax representatives, not for the amusement of casual readers. As an example, the word "support" rings bells in the office of the Commissioner of Internal Revenue. It is to be used sparingly, if at all. Second, the document is not meant to entertain or beguile. Granted that many lawyers write in a dry, even a stuffy, way. Who among us enjoys reading "notwithstanding" or "provided that" or "contingent on" or "in trust nevertheless"? And "of sound mind and disposing memory" is an unnecessary and self-serving declaration. Setting boredom or triteness aside, you are entitled to understand every sentence in the document. But many skillful lawyers will use certain language because it has stood up over time, though it will never earn a Pulitzer prize. When you expect short punchy sentences and flowing structure, you want far too much. Your Will or trust cannot read like a Hemingway novel or a Cheever short story. Those documents are going to have phrases like "discretionary common trust funds" or "the last survivor of" or "apportionment of estate taxes," and requests to have your lawyer make the language more literary are not productive and, worse, will cause the lawyer to spend more time needlessly. And you must expect some reference to "issue per stirpes" (or maybe "issue by representation"), for that short phrase is the way drafters handle this scenario among countless others:

Example

Holly left two daughters, Dara and Florine. Holly created a trust for each, for that daughter's lifetime. When a daughter dies, the assets of her trust are to pass to her issue, per stirpes. Our crystal ball reveals that the following will play out among the family descendants:

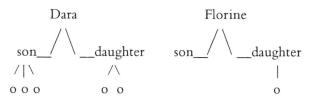

In each case, the son dies before his mother (Dara or Florine) and all the other descendants will be alive when the trust ends. The result under "Dara's issue, per stirpes" will be that half of Dara's trust will be shared equally by her deceased son's three children. The other half of Dara's trust will pass to Dara's daughter. The daughter's children do not inherit because their parent in the line of descent (Dara's daughter) is alive.

The result under "Florine's issue, per stirpes" will be that her daughter takes all. As the son is dead and left no descendants, the share of Florine's trust that the son would have inherited swings over to Florine's other child (the daughter) who also inherits the other half of Florine's trust in her own right. Florine's only grandchild may have charmed her grandmother, but she doesn't inherit.

Notice that no spouse of a descendant inherits. Even though Florine's son and Dara's son have widows, they are not in the blood line of descendants and do not inherit as "issue." It makes no difference that Florine really adored her widowed daughter-in-law.

There are traits some clients have that cause additional effort, even though the client may deny that he or she is really responsible for eating up the adviser's time. Changes of mind, whether or not accompanied by entangled explanations, are a particular bane. Each time that you reverse course and decide that your jewelry should go to your children and not your spouse, or that small legacies ought to go to long-standing employees or dear friends, or that you will, after all, put only part and not all of your spouse's inheritance in a QTIP trust, or whatever other initial decisions you change, the document has to be redone. Even state-of-the-art word processing equipment does not substitute for the lawyer's careful input of changes and review of the revised document to see if the changed plan fits together now as it did before you made alterations.

A lawyer's time is spent in other ways in dealing with your concerns. Let's just touch on garden-variety subjects that come along. If you want your lawyer's advice about life insurance, time will be consumed in reviewing the life insurance representative's presentation and discussing it with you as you seek an in-

dependent view. Going over the premarital agreement that you
have with your spouse and discussing it takes time. Considering
with you to what extent you wish to make current gifts to your
children and grandchildren, and whether trusts, Uniform Gifts
to Minors Act (UGMA) accounts, or the more recently developed Uniform Transfers to Minors Act (UTMA) accounts
should be used, takes time. Discussion of health care documents
and powers of attorney for you and your spouse takes time, as
does producing the papers involved. Review of your employer's
retirement benefits and discussing them with you takes time.
You want your accountant or investment adviser to be consulted
by the lawyer on some aspect of the plan? Fine, but that takes
time. Sophisticated subjects consume more time, and sophisticated subjects bob up more and more these days.

Finally, some tax position of the government may be pivotal
to your planning. That position should be checked to make sure
that your program is on solid ground. A lawyer can be very
knowledgeable and experienced and up-to-date and still have to
see if Washington has subtly changed its position on whatever
may be the issue, such as personal residence GRITs or split-
dollar life insurance or discounts for minority interests. The material cascading monthly out of the government's various orifices
would dam up a river. The lawyer owes it to you to check the
latest and consider how it all impacts on your plan.

Going into the planning stage is when you should ask the
lawyer about his or her fee. Most likely the response will be an
estimate or a range, particularly if you are a new client. The
lawyer cannot know in advance what your style is, for some of
your own doings could require more of the lawyer's time. Do
you change your mind a lot? New instructions from you will
require more of the lawyer's time. Ditto if you like to have lots
of meetings. The lawyer may willingly and patiently go over the

documents with you two or three times, but time is piling up with each session.

Do you procrastinate? I have experienced situations with very sophisticated clients who sat on their decisions for a year and more, before edging forward. That requires me and any other lawyer to get back into the situation by reviewing all the parts again and being reassured that the program and documents are fine.

Do you like to check things out with cousin Harry? I have wrestled on several occasions with questions or suggestions from the wings, posed by relatives or friends to whom the client went for commentary. The outcome is almost invariably the same: the questions or suggestions are irrelevant or worse, and at best are repetitive of the very comments I gave the client. Nevertheless, cousin Harry's offerings require a response, and that means more time.

Another point you must face up to concerns your notion that you and your family will benefit by avoiding probate. That quest takes more lawyer's work and additional documents at the planning stage, for which the lawyer has to charge. Might that extra cost be worthwhile?

Avoiding Probate, Actually

Probate is not what most people are truly concerned with. Probate is acceptance of the Will by the court as a valid document. In most states, in an overwhelming number of estates, that is a simple affair, and the time and effort involved is moderate or small. The real issue therefore is something quite different.

What citizens fear is being bogged down in court procedures after the Will is accepted as *the* valid expression of the decedent's plan. Or, as is more likely the case, there is a fear that the lawyer will cook up a fat fee that is uncalled for, undeserved, and absolutely unconscionable. Let's examine the issue.

Messy court procedures do prevail in some states, Michigan and California among them. The executor in those untidy states cannot manage the estate without constant trips to the courthouse for official confirmation that he may do this or that. All of that is an expensive nuisance. A state with untidy and drawn-out procedures ought to get up-to-date. If your lawyer advises that your state is such a place, then you should explore what can be done to sidestep the quicksand. Avoiding the probate court's grip in those locales is a solid idea.

The notion about lawyer's fees is embedded in many minds. Wearing my professional hat, I can tell you that the notion carries a lot of misunderstanding. Certain things have to be done after the funeral, no matter how skillfully the estate may be guided away from the probate court. First, there is the matter of analyzing the estate's obligations for taxes, debts, reasonable expenses, legacies to beneficiaries, and the like. What are they about and how is the money to be raised to handle that burden? The lawyer plays a heavy role in solving those puzzles. Second, insurance and retirement benefits have to be verified. Third, there are tax returns to file, tax payments to be made, and tax authorities to deal with. All of that takes lots of lawyering.

Q: I thought avoiding probate could reduce taxes.

A: Not one cent ever. There is no hope for it. Indeed, in some ways, avoiding probate might raise taxes. More about this when we look at how you can go about avoiding probate.

Next, there are plans to be made to distribute the estate to the major beneficiaries. That includes when, how much at a time, and with what assets. And speaking of beneficiaries, they often cause extra time and effort. They seek explanations, pose questions, and ask for their inheritance — sometimes early on and frequently.

Next, the estate managers are entitled to have their responsibilities resolved. That may require an accounting for their transactions, which is presented for approval.

All of those steps are normal and occur repeatedly. They must be taken whether or not you avoid probate. If nothing further need be done, the lawyer still will have spent yards of time in attending to those steps.

Then there are the abnormal events. Actually, abnormal is a misnomer, because unsettling issues arise so often that the so-called abnormal is common. There are claims that are disputed, such as a doctor's final bill. There are business problems that make waves; back claims for income tax; contests with the government in the estate tax proceeding; and maybe lawsuits that were pending when the Will maker died. Even worse: a disappointed heir may challenge the Will; a former spouse may have grievances; the surviving spouse may seek to upset the premarital agreement; the decedent's partner, who survived, may be rocking the business boat; the nice couple who contracted to buy the decedent's home may try to back out; and a beneficiary may assert that a bank account in joint names of the deceased and someone else should go into the estate, and not to that someone else. Any of these, or other assorted uproars, could create turmoil, a fight in court, and a whopping bill for legal services.

When it comes time for the bill, the lawyer should be straightforward about how the bill was arrived at. The executor who receives the bill should not be unrealistic. The bill will mirror what was done with the situation presented. Contrary to popular belief, even without abnormal events, the estate almost certainly was not simple. In over three decades of day in, day out experience, I have never worked on a simple estate. Either the assets (often a business) created problems or the government presented tax issues or the decedent's beneficiaries were difficult.

Q: You must be exaggerating. The assets and the government I can understand. But the beneficiaries?

A: Come along and stand in my shoes and use your eyes and ears. Folks who are a delight as dinner companions or tennis partners can be unbelievable cranks when an inheritance is at stake. There are disappointed expectations, or rivalries with others, like siblings, or just plain greed. There are old family wounds that are reopened. These and other misfortunes turn countless rational people into complaining, unreasonable, feisty grouches. Much of a lawyer's time in many estates is spent dealing with these folks.

If you have misgivings about my remarks, look around your own family and judge for yourself. If a parent of yours should die, would you expect smooth sailing with all your siblings, their husbands and wives, and their assorted children? If you are in a second or third marriage and your current spouse were to die, would you have an easy time with your spouse's children by an earlier marriage? If you were to become the decedent, would your children work together harmoniously? How would their spouses interact in the situation? And let's include your husband or wife in the scene: is it a peaceful picture before your eyes or a battleground?

Previously in this book I recounted the brother and sister who served as co-executors and would argue over whose signature went first. That was an ordinary fight. When it comes to multiple-marriage situations, the carnage can be limitless. But within the context of single-marriage families, I have watched real bloodbaths: twin brothers litigating against each other; children in court against their mother; an aunt cursing her niece;

arguments galore among the whole family over dividing jewelry and works of art; sisters who cut each other dead; nephews accusing their uncles of stealing from them; brothers and sisters vying for the upper hand; and a grandson who pocketed some of grandma's nice things when backs were turned. Of all the horror shows that I have witnessed, none has surpassed the response I received in a dispute concerning a man's estate between an adult daughter and her own mother, who was the widow. I asked the daughter, who had hired me as her lawyer, what she wanted. Her reply was succinct: "I want to see my mother cry."

Although the major element in a lawyer's bill is time spent, problems wrestled with and results produced are important and deserve a place in the bill. Why? Suppose the estate presents a knotty tax problem and a good bit of your money is at stake. Let's say that I come up with an idea that works. Assume I spent two hours developing the idea and testing it at my desk and another hour persuading the enemy that my approach is correct. By doing that, assume that the family is saved $50,000 or so. Let's say my hourly billing rate is $250. Am I to be rewarded with $750 for my creativity and persuasive powers? That seems awfully mean. I would have earned a fair payment for my contribution in warding off the government, and $750 is well short of fair.

A tax problem, or any of the other assorted issues I alluded to, will arise whether or not you seek to stay away from the probate court. So the whole idea of avoiding probate is very unlikely to reduce attorneys' fees. I have been involved in several estates in which avoiding probate was the late client's goal, and we accomplished the sought-after avoidance. The postmortem work proved to be the same as if we had proceeded in conventional fashion. Because of that work, the fees were not at all diminished.

When to Avoid Probate

Still, there are times to stay away from the probate court. That is accomplished by having the prospective Will maker create a trust during lifetime for his or her own benefit that converts to a substitute for a Will when that individual dies. We'll shortly review how all of that is done. For the present, let's review the reasons for going the trust route.

I mentioned one earlier: the messy procedures in certain states for handling a decedent's affairs. I pointed out that California is one of those states. Because of that, California lawyers habitually advise their clients to take steps to keep away from the probate court. Ironically, California lawyers have their own reason for that advice. The California probate court regulates attorneys' fees in estate matters rather strictly. But lawyers are free of that strict regulation when their clients steer clear of the probate court. So the lawyers in that state see very good reason for their clientele to avoid probate.

There are other familiar reasons that are advanced for avoiding probate. One is privacy. The client is advised that when he or she dies and leaves a Will, anyone can hike over to the probate court and read it. In contrast, if another vehicle is used for transferring the client's estate, such invasion of privacy is not possible. I have these reactions. First, not every probate court in the lower forty-eight states plus Alaska and Hawaii is so free with Will details. Yes, I know that some hometown papers print some information from the probate court. But most of that is innocuous, and it doesn't happen universally. Second, seeking another way will not work everywhere. For example, in some probate courts in New York State, the trust that is used to substitute for the Will must sooner or later be placed in the probate court's file. So inquisitive eyes can alight upon the sensitive material anyway.

Above all, let's be real. Are you so renowned or notorious that you need protection for your Will against busybodies? Maybe, if you are Bob Hope or Richard M. Nixon or Dolly Parton. If you aren't any of them, why are you anxious? Are you really concerned that someone will be insatiably curious about your plans for family and friends? Bear in mind that your Will would not list your assets or specify the amount of your net worth. In all the years that I have practiced law in New York City, where many celebrated people have died, I have never once wandered over to the courthouse to read some individual's Will out of curiosity. And I know the way to the courthouse! The privacy business is far, far overblown.

If you plan to provide for some special friend who has warmed your heart lately, or did so in years past, then special steps could be necessary. You want things handled discreetly and effectively. Avoiding probate is not the real key to your objective. Special steps would not only offer greater privacy than an explicit provision in a Will, they would provide more protection from attack by aghast family members against a Will or even a trust that was designed to avoid probate. A special step might be an insurance policy for that person, or an account jointly held by you and that special someone. Either would take effect outside of the Will or trust. But no matter how cleverly you proceed, the facts may be exposed after death occurs because of the need to report the policy or account for estate tax purposes. If a family member will be the executor, he or she will know about the tax report, as the executor must sign the estate tax return. A professional executor, like a lawyer or a bank, may be a better choice in these circumstances.

Another reason often advanced for avoiding probate is that using a trust in place of a Will assures that a challenge to your testamentary plan by a disappointed heir can be avoided. Don't believe it! The trust that would be used in place of a Will can be challenged, too, although the challenger has more trouble to go through. Additionally, one New York probate judge has ruled that it takes greater mental capacity to do a trust than a Will. That would mean that a determined challenger may have a better opportunity to upset your plan when you use a trust as the vehicle, if the attack is based on mental capacity.

Other reasons given for avoiding probate I can subscribe to. One is that when a trust is used, the trustee can work with the trust assets immediately. If there are appreciated assets that the decedent hung onto out of distaste for paying capital gains tax, the trustee can sell them promptly after the date of death. The trust assets would be part of the gross estate for federal estate tax purposes. That means a change in basis for those assets at death and, therefore, the avoidance of capital gain. The executor named under a Will needs to be officially placed in office by the probate court before he or she can deal with the assets. That may take a week or two, at a minimum, and maybe longer, causing delay. Action therefore can be much more immediate with a trust. But such immediacy isn't needed in every estate.

The other reason I find valid for avoiding probate relates to transferring assets. With a trust, the individual's bank accounts and stocks and bonds should have been transferred to the trust when the trust was started, or shortly afterward. So, with a trust properly in place, transferring assets due to the death of the individual should not be a heavy item. But for a Will maker, transfers cannot begin until after the funeral. Some asset transfers take time — even weeks or months. Until transfer occurs, the executor cannot use an asset or sell it, no matter how urgent the circumstances may be. So, if the stock market comes apart and the stocks are awaiting transfer, significant losses can be inflicted on the estate during the transfer period.

How about saving taxes, any kind of taxes? It is repetitious of me to say it, but the point is so important that it deserves emphatic underlining: *not one penny will be saved in estate taxes or gen-eration-skipping taxes when you avoid probate.* Honest! Not one, even a little one. Avoiding probate is not a tax-saving adventure.

How to Avoid Probate

Let's assume that you have thought it through and you opt to avoid probate. How do you do it?

At the outset, accept that you will need to make a Will any-way. The odds are many thousands to one that something you have owned will still be yours at your death and will not have been placed in the trust that is the vehicle for avoiding probate. Maybe it's your car, or your jewelry, or your collection of Amish quilts, or your Paul Revere sterling silver tea service that has been in the family for over two hundred years. Whatever the objects may be will be passed out of your hands at your death by your Will. I never met a client who didn't need a Will to trans-mit something at death. Your Will may very well direct that the assets you owned at your death are to be added to the trust you created during your lifetime. In lawyer's jargon, that is called a pourover Will, but in anyone's language, the needed document is still a Will. How much in the way of assets your Will handles at your death will depend on what assets you will have kept in your personal ownership until your death.

In order to avoid probate, you need to create a trust. That is a separate document your lawyer will prepare. And that will un-doubtedly increase the fee charged at the planning stage.

These trusts can be designed in different ways. The most likely design has these features. The benefits of the trust will be devoted exclusively to you while you are alive. Because you are the lifetime beneficiary, the trust is probably going to be called a living trust. That label has become common, but all it means is that it is the sort of trust a person creates for himself or herself.

As you reserve all of the trust's benefits, you have not made a gift for federal gift tax purposes. You will reserve the right throughout your lifetime to change the trust or cancel it entirely. Your ability to pull all the assets out of the trust, or to change the trust terms as you please, are other reasons why embarking on such a trust plan does not produce a gift for federal gift tax purposes. If you cancel the living trust, all of the assets will go back into your personal ownership. That will return your affairs to the old status. You would then need a classic Will to dispose of them at your death.

If you do not cancel the trust, it will convert at your death to the equivalent of a Will, spelling out what happens when you depart this earthly realm. For example, it may direct that upon your death, those of your assets that are governed by the living trust that are exempt from federal estate tax (which could be $600,000) will go to your children, and all the rest will be held in trust for the lifetime benefit of your surviving spouse.

Those provisions of your living trust that go into play at your death will apply to two groups of assets:

1. the assets that you had placed in the living trust during your lifetime and

2. the assets that still were in your personal ownership at your death, and are placed by your pourover Will in the living trust when you die.

It is remarkable how many people who are intent on avoiding probate never follow through and do it. Oh, they consult a lawyer, all right, and have him or her prepare the necessary documents, which are the living trust and the pourover Will. So far, so good. But more needs to be done. The effort to avoid probate will abort unless the individual takes the trouble to actually put assets in the trust during his or her lifetime. Remember, whatever remains in the individual's ownership will pass under his or her Will. Those assets don't avoid probate. So, after the trust is signed, the creator should transfer to it his or her bank accounts, home, stocks, bonds, real estate investments, and other assorted assets. A transfer just doesn't happen by itself; it requires time and effort and papers. For example, if the creator owns a home that he or she wishes to put in the living trust, a deed and other transfer papers have to be prepared and signed to make the trust the owner. More work from the lawyer is required in the planning stage.

Some individuals find it to be a nuisance to make those transfers and live with their assets in a trust. Those people have to decide what their priorities are. If avoiding probate is that urgent, whatever inconvenience may be created by enveloping their assets in a living trust will have to be endured.

These trusts can serve another very worthwhile purpose. They can protect the assets of a person who is incapable of looking after them because of illness or incapacity. When an older person seems to be having some problems, it could be worthwhile to guide him or her toward creating a trust for his or her own lifetime benefit. That living trust can serve as a safe harbor for the individual's assets. It is far preferable to use a living trust with a keen trustee for the creator's security than to fail to take protective steps, have the property remain in the disabled person's name, and rely on either a durable power of attorney or a court-appointed guardian to manage the person's property. Guardians are expensive and cumbersome. By all means, avoid that alternative! A power of attorney is never so flexible or dependable as a trust. If the power of attorney was signed years ago, a banker or stockbroker who is asked to honor it today may question its continued viability. Staleness is never an issue with a living trust. Using a trust for a senior family member seems wise, but remember: it will cover only the assets that are actually placed in the trust.

Finally, a living trust *may* aid you in attaining a cherished goal. If you are intent on disinheriting your husband or wife, a living trust *might* be helpful. In some states, the protection for a surviving spouse's inheritance rights may be limited. *Possibly,* they could be circumvented if you moved assets out of your name into a living trust. Even though that trust is for your benefit, your spouse might not get a crack at it at your death if the law of your state has blinders and only permits the spouse to share in that "estate" that is disposed of by Will. Your lawyer would have answers for you about this. But note, this maneuver is not likely to help you in the event of divorce.

The Trustee for the Living Trust

Who can be trustee of the living trust? As the trust is the creator's alter ego, he or she would probably want to have the position, all alone. In some states that aspiration fits in with the law. In other states it may not be clear if the creator can be his or her own trustee.

Q: Suppose it offended the law for the trust's creator to be the only trustee. So what?

A: Then the law may not officially recognize the trust, and the effort to avoid probate would fail. And even if the trust's existence is recognized, if you hoped to use the trust to disinherit your spouse, the effort may fail if you were your own trustee. That coziness may not be allowed to keep a disinherited spouse from successfully challenging the trust.

If the creator starts out as sole trustee, a newcomer has to take over when the creator dies. Here all the considerations concerning the role of trustee that we looked at in the chapter on Trusts and Trustees (pages 129–30) merit review.

When a living trust is created by someone who is losing a grip on things because of illness or decline, that individual couldn't handle the trusteeship. So some living trusts have third parties as trustees from the start. In some situations in which a person who is still able to handle his or her affairs creates a living trust, that individual starts out as the trustee. The trust goes on to specify that if a doctor states that the individual has lost capability, the trusteeship goes into the hands of others who were standing by. Those others may be children or professionals or any suitable choices.

Should You Avoid Probate?

Here we are at the bottom line. Should you aspire to avoid probate? My answer is unflinching: it depends.

If you live in a state with messy probate court procedures, I think you should.

If you are Madonna or Warren Beatty and dislike publicity about your affairs, I think you should. If you are not so well known, but your hometown paper reports in detail about probate court doings and that rankles you, then avoid the probate court.

If you are really afraid that there will be a hiatus after your death — when none of your assets could be sold for a couple of weeks until an executor is officially appointed — and volatile markets could inflict losses, I think you should.

Otherwise, I think not.

Q: But everyone says I'll save money with a living trust.

A: Everyone also said that Dewey would beat Truman. Stop listening to sidewalk superintendents who have little information and no experience and are really unable to judge.

Q: But you're a lawyer. You're biased.

A: My dear, I really don't care whether or not you want to avoid probate. If you're burning to, I'll assist you. In the end, I'll have lots of work to do and I expect that my services will be paid for.

What really motivates you? If you think that you will save taxes, you are dead wrong. Everything in the living trust at your death will be part of your estate for federal estate tax purposes. Income taxes could be even worse for two reasons. A trust cannot use a fiscal year, while an estate is able to start with one. In particular cases, fiscal years can pare down income taxes or defer the time for paying them. Second, trusts are subject to the nasty throwback rule that relates to income that is retained in a trust and not currently paid to beneficiaries. That rule makes trustees, accountants, and lawyers grind their teeth in their sleep. Estates do not have to contend with the throwback rule. Aside from what it does to teeth, it may cost your beneficiaries income tax money some day when income that was retained in the trust years ago finally is distributed.

Let's return to the real point. Overwhelmingly, folks want to avoid probate in order to save attorneys' fees. I believe that they will not. My response is primarily based on experiences that I have had. But whenever clients wanted to avoid probate, I didn't fight back; I joined them. I prepared their living trusts and pourover Wills. Some of those people have died. I saw their affairs through to completion. I found the postmortem work to be the same as in cases in which only Wills were used to convey the clients' wishes. After all, tax proceedings were necessary, probate of the pourover Will was necessary, money had to be raised to defray obligations, claims had to be scrutinized, budgets had to be prepared, beneficiaries had their lists of questions, distribution of assets had to be worked out, and on and on. The purported savings in the lawyer's time and effort were an absolute fantasy. If I practiced in a state where the probate court proceedings were a hindrance, time and effort might be less when probate is avoided. I can believe that. But in all other states, the work hardly differs whether only Wills are used or pains are taken to avoid probate.

The nub of the matter is the lawyer's role and what he or she contributes. Over the years I have witnessed important contributions that lawyers make to the personal lives of many clients and their families. The role of the trusted family adviser, as depicted in nineteenth century English novels, persists today. Indeed, the complexities of modern life; the intrusion of taxes; and the difficulties that illness, stress, and misfortune visit upon families place the adviser in a central role as never before. Those who would aspire to avoid probate for the purpose of shaving legal fees might gain more if they found a lawyer with whom they could work closely, and obtain from that lawyer the skill and counsel he or she has to offer.

CHAPTER

10

Odds and Ends

We have come a long distance together. Before we part, a few more points should be discussed.

Powers of Attorney

There may be times when your affairs need attention but you cannot tend to them. You may be housebound or in a hospital or, more happily, wandering through Westminster Abbey or the Roman Forum. While you are unavailable, your instructions or your signature may be needed.

Someone you trust could be given the right to act for you. The legal document that does the job is a power of attorney. You name an agent to speak in your name. In olden days, a power of attorney lapsed if you lost your mental capacity. A few years ago, that became outmoded with the development of the durable power of attorney, which continues to have vitality no matter what your mental condition may be. But a power of attorney is immediately cancelled upon your death.

What can the agent do? That depends on what authority you give him or her. In many states, a durable power of attorney automatically empowers the agent to carry on a list of activities for you, such as banking transactions and stock and bond transactions. You can add to those by specifying additional things your agent can do in your name. Among powers you might want your agent to have is the authority to sign your tax return and deal with the IRS. Some people even give their agents the authority to make gifts from their property. This is to assure that the annual privilege to give $10,000/20,000 will not be lost because the person is ill. The potential recipients, such as the person's children, can be identified in the power of attorney so that the agent cannot get too generous with the principal's money.

Q: I'm not comfortable giving someone the broad power to act for me when I don't know what the issue is.

A: Then you can grant narrow authority, even cancelling some powers that the law would ordinarily grant to your agent. For example, you might want your agent to sign checks only on a particular account you have.

Obviously, a crucial decision is to whom you give authority. If you want to be sure that there will be some safeguards, you can give the power to two or more people and specify that they must act unanimously. But whether you choose one person or two, there are fundamental tests that the prospective agent must easily satisfy. Loyalty to you, absolute integrity, and common sense are certainly required. Standout candidates may be your spouse, a child or two, a sibling, your trusted lawyer or accountant, or some exceedingly close friend.

Q: I'm still uneasy. I can look after myself. What I need is someone to act for me if I'm too ill to handle a situation.

A: In some states a power of attorney can be granted on a deferred basis. It won't become usable unless a doctor certifies that the person who granted it is no longer mentally capable. If you give your power of attorney that way, no one can act for you if you're laid up but still mentally competent, or if you're out of town.

Q: I'm not worried about temporary situations that last for a week or two. I'm only concerned about long-run situations.

A: Fine. The power of attorney that is dormant unless you lose mental capacity is better suited for you. But remember what we said in the chapter on Avoiding Probate (starting on page 223): a trust for your lifetime benefit is superior to a durable power of attorney if you fall out of it.

Q: Why?

A: Because trusts have had acceptance for generations. Banks and brokers are accustomed to them. Trusts never get outdated, while old powers of attorney have been questioned.

Example

Desmond, a client's son, has been trying to move his grandmother's bank accounts around under a durable power of attorney. Grandma is ninety. A bank where most of the money is wants proof that she had mental capability when she signed the power of attorney. I'm certain that the issue would not come up if grandson Desmond were acting as trustee under a living trust grandma created.

Take note that the power of attorney we have just discussed is usable when issues arise concerning your money or business affairs or taxes. In contrast, that is not the way to handle issues of your personal well-being. Should you have surgery? Should you have radiation therapy? Should you go on life-support systems? Should you enter a nursing home? Those are not handled under a power of attorney that pertains to money and property. They fall under a different title: your health.

Health Care

The nation is tuned in to health care issues. One substantive issue is whether life support systems would be kept in place if an individual were far gone and terminal. Another is whether major surgery should be undertaken for an elderly or out-of-it person.

These are very difficult issues, fraught with medical aspects and economic and emotional sides. And the context is that the victim is in the hands of doctors and hospitals that are striving to save lives. Some individuals want everything done for them that medical science could concoct. They would undergo surgery and radical treatment, no matter what, in pursuit of any chance to remain alive. Others would say that avoiding pain and helplessness is their major objective. If they are brain-dead and hopelessly terminal, their life is over anyway, and the machines should be shut down. If their life would be severely altered by procedures or medication or surgery, they would not have it. In between, and on both ends, there are lots of variations in viewpoints.

The essential point is that the individual must understand his or her own feelings on the crucial subject. Those who want to be relieved of pain in the event of a terminal illness, but not kept alive artificially if the prognosis is hopeless, should understand that their wishes as to treatment and course of action have to be made known. There are many points at issue, including whether hydration and nourishment should be maintained, whether resuscitation should be tried, and what the rules are concerning blood transfusions and breathing tubes. And there are many, many more. The usual course is to designate someone to be a spokesperson, i.e., to give instructions to medical personnel, whose orientation is to save lives.

Q: Will a regular power of attorney do?

A: No, something special is needed. A regular power of attorney is for material things. Health care is in a different realm.

Q: Why can't I just say what I want without naming someone to speak for me?

A: Because new techniques and treatment are always being developed, and your general instructions may not cover them. Even for well-established procedures, the medical staff wants clear instructions. A doctor under pressure to act would not welcome a piece of paper that he or she has to read and interpret. Also, medical facts and physical condition can never be precisely predicted. Three years from now, a procedure might be recommended for you that is only in an experimental stage now. If you are not alert enough to decide, a spokesperson is important to handle the unexpected and unforeseeable.

What are your wishes? The various states have adopted positions about expressing an individual's wishes. A living will is the popular description of the document that is used. Although that may be the commonly accepted and shorthand title of the document, official names vary. In some states, it is officially called a power of attorney for health care; in some states, the document is named a health care proxy. Whatever the nomenclature, the point is that the person expresses his or her feelings about prolonging life under severe circumstances and names a spokesperson.

How these documents work and how effective a spokesperson may be is impossible to say. The law has been developing slowly. What is clear is that without those precautions in place, a patient who is said to have expressed a wish in general terms not to be on life-support systems or to have ruled out radical treatment may not have those wishes respected. That has been the result in a few court cases so far, even when someone who holds the patient near and dear has pressed for those quoted wishes to be honored. Many courts want certainty about your wishes, not generalities. There is a presumption that self-preservation is a primary instinct. To have that put aside by this or that friend or relative's simple statement that, in a past discussion, the patient said he or she would not follow a life-preserving course of conduct is a lot for the medical and legal worlds to absorb. At a minimum, better evidence of those wishes is needed.

The choice of a spokesperson must be made with sensitivity. Imagine your having the burden of making such decisions for your husband or wife, or for a parent or child. The last of life can be a heart-rending business.

Premarital Agreements

More and more, lawyers are called upon to counsel men and women about financial arrangements to be made in anticipation of their marrying (usually called premarital agreements, but sometimes called antenuptial agreements). While not all engaged couples go down that path, many do, especially people who were previously married, particularly if there are children from the earlier union to whom the expectant bride or groom wishes to devote her or his accumulated assets. There also are first-timers who consider a premarital agreement in order to protect against a marital mistake that could be costly economically. This delicate subject arises in marriages in which one party is well-to-do and the other is not. It is prompted by the concern that the less economically well-endowed may be motivated toward marriage by something besides palpitations of the heart.

There are two major issues at stake under these agreements. First, what should be done in the event the wedded bliss fizzles? Without a premarital agreement, the result would turn on the divorce law of the particular state. In states that observe community property, that kind of property is divisible by the court between the splitting spouses. Community property is made up of assets that were acquired during the marriage, but not property that came to a spouse via gift or inheritance. Also left out of community property is what each spouse can prove was already his or hers when the marriage began.

Most states do not have a full community property system. But what they do have is a look-alike when it comes to divorce. That is, marital property is up for division by the divorce court, while separate property is not.

Please keep in mind that each of the fifty states has its own law about divorce, marital property rights, alimony, support, and the like. But there are some common themes.

Q: What is separate property?

A: In most places it comes in two types: (1) what the person had in the way of assets when the wedding ceremony was performed and (2) gifts and inheritances received from anyone either before or after the wedding ceremony.

Q: And what's marital property?

A: In general it's property acquired during the marriage, but not by gift or inheritance. That is not a total answer, however. In some states, any appreciation to separate

251

property occurring during the period of the marriage can be marital property. And income from separate property may be marital property. So separate and marital property can be intertwined in a particular state.

Q: What can the divorce court do?

A: Generally, the divorce court can divide marital property between husband and wife.

Q: Is the division right down the middle?

A: Rarely. Many factors are taken into account. Among them are the length of the marriage, what each spouse contributed to the marriage in or out of the home, age and health of the parties, the inheritance rights that would be lost because the marriage is over, tax consequences, future prospects (including the ability to be gainfully employed), whether support will be paid for any period, the standard of living the parties are accustomed to, what separate property each party had when the marriage began and can now turn to, and so on. The court strives to divide the marital property in an equitable manner, as the circumstances point the way. Equal division is not necessarily equitable, so equal sharing may well not result. Generally, who was "at fault" is irrelevant, although that point can influence judges.

Q: What happens to separate property?

A: Separate property owned by one spouse cannot be awarded to the other, but separate property can be reached in some ways. First, it can be reached for child support. Second, a dependent spouse can be given a money award, which the wealthier spouse has to pay from any source available to him or her.

Q: It sounds awfully tricky.

A: It is even trickier than you may imagine. The spouse who claims that particular property is not marital or community property could find himself or herself with the burden of proving that. If proof is lacking, the property will be tagged as marital or community property, which the court has the right to divide between the spouses. So being able to trace a particular cash balance or investment back to its origin may be key.

These prickly aspects of marriage and property persuade many people to make premarital agreements. That persuasion is heightened when it comes to inheritance rights. Among the forty-two states that do not have community property, the surviving spouse generally has a right of inheritance. That right attaches to both separate and marital property.

Example

Todd has a large bundle of assets that are clearly traceable back to an inheritance from his grandmother. Todd and his wife Edwina do not have a happy life together. From time to time, one or the other thinks about divorce. Under the law of the state where Todd and Edwina live, Todd's inherited property and its accumulated appreciation are safe from Edwina's claims for a portion of the couple's assets if their marriage comes apart. If divorce occurred and Edwina sought a share of Todd's total assets, she would only have a claim to their marital property, and that property is pretty modest. But, if Todd dies first, the law of their state gives Edwina the right to take outright a minimum share of one-third of Todd's estate. That estate would include Todd's valuable separate property as well as the modest marital property.

The inheritance right, which generally cuts across marital and separate property, is another reason some individuals feel driven to make premarital agreements.

What these agreements will say depends on the parties and their attitudes, strengths, negotiating tactics, and tenacity. The agreement might give husband or wife nothing in case of divorce or death. At the other end of the spectrum, the agreement might provide for significant division of property in the event of divorce, and a more substantial share at death if the husband and wife are still a couple. Often, a moneyed person may have more generous feelings about provisions to make for the spouse if death interrupts the marriage. That is particularly so when there are no children of an earlier marriage. Presumably, that termination of their life together was not the other one's fault. So a softer attitude is often the context for deciding what inheritance to provide under the agreement. That softer attitude is fortified by the knowledge that rejection is not an issue at death, as it frequently is on divorce.

It is important to understand that premarital agreements only take away or limit entitlements that husband or wife would otherwise have by law in the event of divorce or death. If a spouse voluntarily wishes to be more generous than the agreement requires, the sky can become the adopted limit.

Example

Gardiner and Roselle have been married for eight years. Each was married before and has adult children. When Gardiner and Roselle married, they made a premarital agreement under which each surrendered all rights to inherit from the other. Gardiner is so blissful about his marriage that his new Will leaves half of his estate in trust for Roselle's lifetime benefit.

Notice that in the last example, the inheritance was set aside in trust, not left outright. That is a common practice for a spouse who wants his or her children from an earlier marriage eventually to inherit what that person had. The trust will preserve the assets for the children. Preserving the assets via a trust may be an objective even when there are no children from a prior marriage. In that situation, the spouse who has assembled the assets may not want to lose control of their eventual disposition, even without children to endow. So, generosity toward a spouse does not equate with relinquishing the reins over the dead spouse's estate completely to him or her.

Lawyers who are consulted about premarital agreements know of results all over the place. I once counseled a young woman with modest earthly goods who was engaged to marry an older guy who just had emerged from a bruising divorce. For his new marriage, he insisted on a premarital agreement. The young woman told me over and over that she would not sign a premarital agreement unless it assured her of XYZ. The draft agreement from the expectant bridegroom's lawyer said nothing about XYZ. The day before the wedding was to be celebrated, the couple had a showdown about the agreement and XYZ. She was tearful, and he was stubborn. She said, "No XYZ, no wedding." He said, "No XYZ." He won and the ceremony went off right on time. In contrast, a fine, but impecunious, young man whom I represented in a premarital negotiation was able to obtain an assurance that if his marriage to an heiress fizzled, he would be favorably treated if they had children. The winning argument in his favor was that he should not appear shabby to any kids they might have when he took them for visitation.

If you have concerns that a premarital agreement might lessen, go to it. But these agreements are not easy as pie. Imagine! Discussing what will occur financially if there's a divorce, and the marriage hasn't happened yet. The dialog will go far beyond practical subjects that couples are accustomed to, such as whether there will be kids, what religious practices will be followed, how household expenses will be met, where the couple will live, how the couple will invest its savings. Premarital agreements call for pointed discussion of unpleasant possibilities, of which divorce is the most jarring. Among young romantics, these agreements can be particularly disillusioning. They will shortly vow to cherish and honor, but first divorce and death have to be dealt with, each person consulting with a lawyer.

If the necessity for a premarital agreement doesn't grab you, do without. The risk of derailing a romance by discussions of what ought to happen in case of divorce can be worrisome.

Government Help

Lawyers find themselves these days being asked to help qualify a client for government assistance. Often the request comes from children or grandchildren, who are eager to preserve parental or ancestral assets for themselves, and want to safeguard those assets from being spent on nursing or health care.

The health care problem in our country already affects millions, and millions more are anxious that they will also become affected. So it frequently happens that family members, particularly offspring, want the government to pick up the tab. This would be done by trying to make the older person eligible for Medicaid. That program was designed to aid financially disadvantaged people. To be eligible, an individual must come underneath income and asset limits. The attitude that is spreading is that members of a family, knowing that mom or dad or a grandparent is not eligible, want to strip away their parent's or grandparent's income and assets so that the elderly person can fit within the eligibility requirements. The objectives are not only to put the senior citizen on the government's list of beneficiaries, but also to conserve the income and assets for the younger family members.

It is ironic that the mindset that leads to those objectives is often found among individuals who speak out forcefully about welfare cheats and parasites who soak up lots of government revenue. Those voluble speakers may seek to justify taxpayers' money being used for mom or dad or grandma because in younger years he or she was a taxpayer contributing to the national treasury. But how about personal responsibility, which is supposed to be a guiding beacon? If the elderly or ill parent or grandparent has resources to afford needed care, why shouldn't they be used? Sure, they may be exhausted by expense eventually. Well, then is the time to apply for Medicaid. Why is that application to be made now? And what does the taxpaying record of mom or dad or grandma have to do with his or her offspring's claim to an inheritance? After all, it is the determined claim to an inheritance, as a matter of right, that motivates the offspring to assert that governmental assistance is merited so that resources can be preserved.

It is a nearly universal perception that the nation's medical system and custodial care setup are unworthy of the world's greatest power and strongest democracy. But more than that is at play here. There is a me-tooism among many people, an idea that they deserve a slice of the pie at anyone's expense. The pie in this case is what their ancestors accumulated, and the expense to provide that accumulation to them is supposed to be borne by the rest of us.

Lawyers will be embroiled in this. It may be their clients who have aged and need care. Typically, a child or grandchild will expect the lawyer to assist in stripping that lawyer's client of his or her savings and investments so that the eligibility rules for assistance can be met. Sometimes the child or grandchild hopes to use a power of attorney to effect transfers of assets out of the client's name. Curiously, the parent or grandparent who is to be shorn may well have been an independent soul and fiercely protective of his or her funds. The lawyer who has such a client should not rush in to aid in the shearing. Further, the lawyer should ask the crucial question: who is my client? If the answer comes back, the older person who would be shorn, the lawyer may well hesitate to do the bidding of the offspring who have emerged from the wings.

As to the stripping operation itself, there is much to be wary of. The federal law requires that the assets that are no longer in the individual's hands have been gone for at least thirty months before eligibility for assistance can be gained. Additionally, each state may have its own rules. Some states count husband and wife as a unit, so the resources of either are looked at in weighing eligibility. Additionally, any stripping of assets may be scrutinized thoroughly. Fraud is a very possible accusation if there was sly maneuvering that leaves an unpleasant aroma. The family may discover that it has a lawsuit on its hands when the state government demands reimbursement for money it spent on the elderly or ill person for his or her care, or the care of his or her spouse.

If you saw your neighbor's kids walk away with your neighbor's assets while the state paid for the neighbor's daily care, what would your reaction be? If you wouldn't mind, then nothing I have been alarmed about would disturb you. But if you would mind, be aware that there is a cottage industry at work in the stripping business.

Joint Ownership

Many husbands and wives own assets in joint names. The family house is very likely to be owned that way. So might the primary bank account. In some families, every significant asset is owned that way: stocks, bonds, and all bank accounts, as well as each residence.

Some of this togetherness surely emanated from the couple. But often the notion to make the ownership joint was inspired by real estate brokers, bank personnel, stockbrokers, and others. They, and the couple who end up with joint ownership, may believe that they will thereby reap tax savings. That is not the case. In fact, tax troubles can be generated by joint ownership.

Let's first look at the tax that would come into play when the joint form of ownership starts. That is the gift tax.

Joint Ownership: Gift Tax

If you put an asset in the joint names of yourself and someone else, the law generally permits that other person to break up the joint arrangement and walk away with her or his half. So, when you create the joint arrangement, you are endowing the other person with control of half. That causes a gift of one-half for federal gift tax purposes, unless a special rule intervenes. A slight variation on the theme occurs if husband and wife acquire a home in both names in a state that recognizes their ownership under the quaint old English label of tenants by the entirety. Neither spouse alone can break up that joint arrangement, but, for simplicity's sake, the tax law also treats that as a gift of half.

Q: Do you mean that when my spouse and I close on our new place I'll have to pay gift tax if we own it together?

A: Maybe. When the other joint owner is your spouse and your spouse is a U.S. citizen, the gift is eligible for the marital deduction. The gift is rendered nontaxable by the deduction. If your spouse is not a U.S. citizen, you cannot use the marital deduction, but you have an opportunity each year to give your spouse $100,000 free of gift tax. After that is used, the $600,000 exemption would be available. So, if the equity in the property is greater than $200,000 when you and your noncitizen spouse become joint owners, the gift being one-half of that equity, a bite would be taken out of your $600,000 exemption.

Q: Suppose I put General Motors stock in joint names of my daughter and myself?

A: That's a gift. You may call on your $10,000/20,000 annual gift tax exclusion to lighten or cancel the gift tax. If you already used up your annual exclusion, or if your daughter's half-interest in the stock is worth more than $10,000/20,000, your $600,000 exemption would be pressed into service to save you from actually paying gift tax.

There are some gift tax special rules here. In many states, when you put funds in a joint bank account with someone else, such as parent, child, spouse, or special dancing partner, the gift does not occur quite yet. That is because the local law allows you, willy-nilly, to reverse course and take everything out of the account. A gift would occur when the other person makes a withdrawal. At that point, the marital deduction (for a citizen spouse) or the $10,000/20,000 annual opportunity may be helpful.

Example

Brady and Marina, who live in one of the states with such a rule, have been going together for some time. Once they started to make plans to marry, Brady put aside money every month in a joint bank account with Marina. No withdrawals were made. That went on for fifteen months. Last week Brady and Marina were married. If now she were to make any withdrawals, gifts would then occur, but they would be eligible for the marital deduction as Marina is a U.S. citizen.

With United States savings bonds, a special rule applies. No gift is made when the bond is purchased in two names. If the individual who provided the money for the purchase wanted to redeem the bond, the government would pay him or her. So that individual has not lost control by the purchase. But if the other person redeems the bond, a gift would occur then.

A gift can occur more than once with the same property.

Example

Mervin buys a home in the suburbs in joint names with his daughter Kim, who lives there with her children. Mervin makes monthly mortgage payments and also pays for improvements to the place. A gift from Mervin to Kim occurred at the original purchase, equal to 50 percent of the cash in the deal. Each later payment is a gift of one-half of the amount involved, whether it be on the mortgage or for an improvement. If the gift in any year exceeds Mervin's $10,000/20,000 opportunity, his $600,000 exemption must be invoked to avoid paying gift tax.

But don't conclude that Mervin can slyly outwit the government by using joint ownership to limit his gift to only half of the value of Kim's home. If Mervin ever gives up his 50 percent ownership right, that step is a further gift consisting of the other one-half of the home that Mervin had owned, at its value at that time. If Mervin keeps his 50 percent ownership throughout his lifetime, the estate tax will whack his estate.

Joint Ownership: Estate Tax

The federal estate tax has two separate rules concerning joint ownership. The simpler rule applies when a married couple owned the property and the surviving spouse is a U.S. citizen. When one spouse dies, half the value of the property is in his or her gross estate for estate tax purposes. Valuation is taken at the time of death. The marital deduction will prevent that half from being taxed. The other half-interest is not part of the deceased spouse's estate at all.

This 50-50 treatment isn't necessarily favorable. It has an impact on the cost basis that the surviving spouse takes over. Only the basis for half of the property is adjusted at death.

Example

Jared and Robin hold securities in a brokerage account in joint names. Jared dies. Robin is a U.S. citizen. Among the securities are 300 shares of stock of a drug company. Robin inherits them automatically at Jared's death. Robin recently read that its products include a drug that can cause dangerous side effects. Robin wants to sell those shares. The 300 shares were bought eight years ago for $9,000. On the date of Jared's death they were worth $21,000. Only half of those shares will be in Jared's gross estate for estate tax purposes. The marital deduction protects them from estate tax. Robin's cost basis for those 150 shares will be transformed to date-of-death value, or $10,500. Her basis for the other 150 shares, which are not part of Jared's gross estate, will be measured by their original purchase price, and therefore will be $4,500. Robin's combined basis for all 300 shares consequently will be $15,000. At a sale for $21,000 she will have a $6,000 capital gain.

In contrast, if all the shares had been in Jared's name, the cost basis at his death would have changed to $21,000. If all the shares had been in Robin's name, the original cost basis of $9,000 would continue, as none of the shares would be in Jared's gross estate. So, as between spouses, when the survivor is a U.S. citizen, the rule that half of the jointly owned property is in the gross estate primarily has an impact on the survivor's basis for the property. That impact may be hurtful, as Robin discovered.

The other estate tax rule for jointly owned property applies in two situations: (1) if the joint owners are spouses, but the surviving spouse is not a U.S. citizen, and (2) if the joint owners are not spouses. In those cases, when one joint owner dies, all of the jointly held property comes into the gross estate unless the property originally was owned by the survivor, or if the survivor can prove that he or she provided the funds to purchase the property.

Example

Elvin and his daughter Lucinda own 200 shares of IBM in joint names. Elvin paid for them. They were reported as a gift for gift tax purposes when they were bought. All the shares are in Elvin's gross estate at his death, valued at that time. Only the $600,000 exemption that comes from the unified credit can prevent estate tax when Lucinda becomes sole owner at her dad's death. The previous gift will be counted in determining the estate tax, if it was greater than the $10,000/20,000 annual exclusion. If gift tax had been paid by Elvin, it will be subtracted from the total estate tax that is computed.

Example

Let us return to Jared and Robin, who owned securities in a brokerage account in joint names. Robin dies first.

Jared is not a U.S. citizen. All of the securities in the brokerage account will be in Robin's gross estate for estate tax
purposes unless it can be proven that Jared provided the
funds for them, or that he previously had owned them
alone before putting them in joint ownership with
Robin. Merely saying that Jared earned more than Robin,
or that she never worked is not enough. Real proof is
needed that Jared provided the money. Assuming there is
no such proof, so that all the joint holdings are part of
Robin's gross estate, there will be no marital deduction, as
Jared is not a U.S. citizen. Only the $600,000 exemption
can prevent estate tax on the shares that Jared inherits as
sole owner.

Our outline of the gift and estate tax rules that relate to joint
ownership indicates that the terrain is messy. Joint ownership
doesn't create tax benefits. On the contrary, it can produce tax
headaches. If an upper hand for tax purposes is being sought,
joint ownership is not the way.

Joint Ownership: Other Attributes

Why, then, should people use joint ownership? Well, for the
most part, they just shouldn't. Take notice of one of joint ownership's features. The entire property passes directly to the surviving joint owner, no matter what the deceased co-owner's
Will may say. That may collide with the deceased person's true
wishes.

Example

Wayne and Tanya are married and have three children.
Tanya is convinced that if she died first, Wayne would re-
marry within a week. She wants to protect her children so
that they will have an inheritance. Every major asset that
they have they own in joint ownership — condo, stocks,

bonds, real estate investments, and beach house. If Tanya dies first, full ownership of those assets will pass to Wayne, to do with as he pleases. His complete control of the assets will exist whether or not he is a U.S. citizen, for that fact does not bear on his ownership privileges.

Example

Noel and Cady also own every major asset in joint ownership. Cady has always deferred to Noel on money matters and financial decisions. Additionally, Cady spends heavily on clothes, jewelry, and gifts for friends. Noel's Will creates a QTIP trust for Cady, based on the idea that her inheritance should be managed by experienced trustees. On Noel's death, his objective will be totally frustrated, as full ownership of every major asset will pass directly to Cady, to do with as she pleases.

Even when there is a unified approach by husband and wife in their planning, joint ownership can upset everything. Assume the couple agree that, on the first spousal death, the $600,000 exemption should be exploited in that person's Will. Each spouse has made a Will that provides that that amount of assets should be left in trust for the lifetime benefit of the surviving spouse, to pass free from estate tax at his or her death to the couple's children. But if the major assets are in joint names, that objective cannot be reached. Full ownership of those assets will go directly to the surviving spouse, bypassing the Will and the trust provisions. Instead of the joint form of ownership, each spouse should have at least $600,000 in his or her individual name, so that the exemption can be exploited.

I am not a complete naysayer about joint ownership. There are special situations that can be served by joint ownership. If a couple has a vacation home in another state, and one of them dies, joint ownership of the place would give the surviving spouse full ownership of the place without having to go through probate court proceedings in the other state. Inheritance tax proceedings in that state may be necessary, however; that step may be unavoidable. If joint ownership is not used, both probate proceedings and inheritance tax proceedings in the other state would be necessary if the vacation house was owned by the spouse who had died. Of course, if the house had been owned by the remaining spouse, none of that would be necessary. In the latter case, however, no change in cost basis would occur at the other spouse's death.

Another situation that neatly fits with joint ownership relates to a person wanting to leave a remembrance to a special friend with a minimum of fuss and without provoking family members who might never have known of the friend's existence. Holding the asset in joint names with that special someone may be the best solution. Notice, however, that the joint ownership would have to be reported on the estate tax return. That may open the way for the family to discover the plot. Nevertheless, the special friend's inheritance is not likely to be vulnerable to attack, no matter what discovery is made. That is why using joint ownership is a safer path for the decedent to have used than making a provision for the friend in a Will or trust. Notice that if the $600,000 exemption from gift and estate tax is otherwise used up, there would be estate tax to pay on the jointly owned asset of which the special friend becomes complete owner. That cost may really rankle the family if it has to bear that tax burden.

More common than the special friend outside the family circle is the mischief that joint ownership can cause within the family itself. The usual setting is an older family member who is ill or handicapped and has a bank account or other assets in his or her name and also in the name of someone near and dear as joint owner. The arrangement may have been created as a convenience, enabling the other person to make deposits and withdrawals and so on, in the interest of the ill or handicapped person. But when death comes, the other person who had been so obliging and attentive may claim full ownership as the surviving registered joint owner. This scenario arises over and over within families.

Example

Inge, who is eighty-four and housebound, has her money market accounts in joint names with her son Craig. He has faithfully looked after her for years, ever since his father died. His two sisters are aware of the arrangement. Inge dies peacefully. Her Will leaves her estate to her three children in equal shares. After his mother's death, Craig claims the accounts, as surviving joint owner. His sisters, Marnie and Adela, assert that the joint ownership arrangement was only for their mother's convenience, so that Craig, who lived near their mother could get money for her when she needed it. The sisters argue that their mother was the "real" owner of the accounts, that she never intended that Craig should have full ownership at her death. Instead, the sisters assert, their mother's Will should control those accounts, with the result that the three children will share them equally.

Well, they're off to the litigation races, unless the fire can be doused very quickly. Each side will advance legal arguments coupled with emotional justification. There will be at least two lawyers involved, and maybe three. After angry opening shots are fired, a struggle in court may ensue. Even if a settlement occurs, the fight that has erupted may utterly destroy the relationship among the children. Even the two sisters may fall out with each other, for if Craig offers to settle for one-half, Marnie may go along while Adela stands her ground. Inge would have been better advised to keep ownership of the accounts in her name alone and give Craig a power of attorney. That would have enabled him to use the accounts for her during her lifetime. At her death, Craig's authority under the power of attorney would have ended, and all the accounts would have passed under her Will to be divided three ways among the children. By using the joint ownership arrangement, Inge unwittingly imposed two results on her family: a serious dispute among her children, and a fertile ground for lawyers to earn fees. Poor Inge!

Digging up the Estate Tax Money

Suppose that, despite all planning efforts, estate taxes have to be paid. Remember that not every estate will be in a position to conclude with no federal estate tax owing. The assets on hand may be greater than the $600,000 exemption. While some individuals may be able to devote the excess of their estates above the exemption to their spouses, other individuals will choose not to. They may favor leaving part or all of that excess to their children or other beneficiaries. And then there are individuals who are not married at the time of their deaths. Indeed, in many families, when the second parent dies, there is no surviving spouse, so that the marital deduction cannot be used to keep the government away from the assets. The chances are that, within a family, the day of reckoning will come at some point.

Under the tax law, responsibility for payment of the federal estate tax rests on the executor. But it is obvious that the executor is not going to dig into his or her personal pocket for the money. Otherwise, no one would ever serve as executor.

Generally, the law permits the Will maker to decide where to place the burden for paying the estate tax. In some states, every person who receives an asset that is subject to tax is responsible for contributing money to the tax fund to enable the estate taxes to be paid. But the law permits the Will maker to relieve a beneficiary of that responsibility and to place the burden elsewhere. The relief is provided by a direction in the Will that exonerates particular beneficiaries from paying tax.

Q: Are you telling me that if I leave a legacy to my son, he would have to pay the estate tax on it?

A: In some states, the answer is yes. For example, if you left a legacy of $50,000 to your son and said no more, and you lived in a state where each beneficiary has to contribute to the tax fund, your son would not collect the full $50,000. Instead, the executor would subtract from the $50,000 legacy your son's share of the estate taxes. If the average estate tax rate is 50 percent, your son would receive only $25,000, not $50,000.

Q: But that's an outrage! I want my son to receive the whole $50,000.

A: Then you must place the burden of paying the estate tax for your son's legacy somewhere else. You might place it on the beneficiary who receives the balance of your estate that remains after all cash legacies, bequests of particular property, debts, and expenses are taken care of. That balance is called the residuary estate. If the beneficiary of your residuary estate is your daughter, she may not be very happy about paying the estate taxes on your son's $50,000 legacy.

In some states, the law is different. The beneficiary who receives the residuary estate has the responsibility for paying the estate tax. But the state law is not impervious to the decedent's wishes. The Will maker can alter that rule and lay on each beneficiary of a legacy the responsibility for the tax on that person's inheritance. If you do not alter the responsibility that such a state law prescribes, when you specify a legacy of $50,000 for your son, he will receive it free and clear, and the residuary beneficiary is automatically stuck with the estate taxes on his legacy.

All of this means that the Will maker must carefully consider who is to bear the impact of paying the estate tax. Very often, the residuary estate is left to someone close to the heart of the Will maker. Thrusting all of the estate tax burden on that individual may be an unkindness. Further, the "estate" for which tax is due may include life insurance proceeds payable to a particular beneficiary, retirement benefits payable to a particular beneficiary, and assets that the decedent and someone else held in joint names. Those insurance proceeds or retirement benefits or jointly owned assets could well cause significant estate tax. Is the money to pay that tax also to come from the residuary estate?

The attitude of the residuary beneficiary could turn particularly sour if there are bequests of specific property, such as works of art or a house or jewelry, that turn out to be very valuable, so that the estate taxes could be considerable. That problem is compounded if the Will maker is unaware of how valuable the antiques or jewelry or other objects are. For example, if a Will maker leaves a collection of fifteenth century armor to a friend, and it turns out that the armor is worth $100,000, the friend may be delighted with the legacy. But if another person is required to pay the estate taxes, that other individual may have a different attitude entirely about the armor. Maybe the recipient of the armor should be called upon by the Will to produce the cash for the tax. If the armor is worth having, then the tax may be tolerable. He or she would be buying a valuable asset for the tax cost. And the recipient is free to sell the armor at any time, thereby recouping the cost and making a profit. If the legacy with the accompanying tax seems onerous to the friend, he or she could turn away from the legacy by disclaiming, and be rid not only of the clanging metal, but also of the tax obligation that overshadowed the bequest.

This subject of who pays the estate taxes is critical. The government will not go unpaid. The government has recourse to all the estate assets until the tax is paid. So the government is not at risk. It is the beneficiary who is given the responsibility for paying the estate tax by the plan of the bestower's Will who has all the risk. That responsibility must be handed out thoughtfully.

It also must be done clearly. If the effort is shrouded in ambiguity, or an opening exists for a would-be responsible person to duck and dodge the burden, arguments among the beneficiaries may ensue, and even litigation may result. Remember, big bucks may be at stake here. We started this tome by observing that taxes at death can be heavy, and by raising questions about this person's greed and that person's inclination to argue when an inheritance is at stake. Well, here is an issue to cause a giant blowup: who pays the estate tax? It is one more ingredient in the business of planning that requires full attention and clear decision.

Glossary

Accounting: judicial proceeding to review trustee's transactions

Actuarial tables: used by IRS to calculate present value of future interests

Annual gift tax exclusion: right to give $10,000 per person in any one year ($20,000 if your spouse agrees) without any gift tax liability

Antenuptial agreement: fancy name for premarital agreement

Basis: figure used as cost when calculating gain or loss on sale

Bequest: provision in will passing personal property

Bestower: person who makes gift or bequest or sets up trust

Bypass trust: trust to permit maximum use of unified credit by bypassing marital deduction

Charitable foundation: an entity that is created to benefit charitable purposes exclusively. The entity can be a corporation (usually called a not-for-profit corporation) or a trust. If things are done properly, no income or gains are subject to income tax, because they are devoted to charity. Gifts that individuals make to the entity are nontaxable gifts and are deductible for income tax purposes. The entity will be governed by the same rules as such public charities as the Red Cross, if requirements for widespread financial support from the public are met, or if the entity is devoted to making grants to particular public charities, like a hospital or museum. Otherwise, the entity is governed by rather strict rules relating to private charitable foundations. Most charitable foundations will be subject to those strict rules.

Charitable lead trust: a trust providing payments initially for charity, either during the life of some person or, more usually, for a period of years. When charity's right to payments ceases, the assets pass outright, or continue in trust, for individuals, who usually are the creator's descendants. Tax results: (1) a taxable gift is made of the right, determined actuarially in favor of the individuals, to enjoy the assets after charity's interest ceases. That gift is heavily discounted, because charity's right to payments, determined actuarially, is subtracted from the value of the assets initially placed in the trust. (2) In the overwhelming number of situations, there is no income tax deduction for the creator. An income tax deduction can be had in a very narrow situation, which usually will not be advantageous. If the trustee sells any trust assets at a gain, the gain is taxed to the trust. (3) There is no estate tax at the creator's death. (4) If grandchildren receive any benefits, the generation-skipping tax (GST) will apply.

Charitable remainder trust: a trust where one or more individuals receive payments, usually for life (or lives, if more than one individual). When the life (or lives) end the trust assets pass to charity. A common example: a person creates such a trust from which he or she will receive annuity payments for life, and at that creator's death the assets pass to charity. The creator transfers to the trust assets that have appreciated in value. At an appropriate time, the trustee sells the assets and invests the proceeds in investments that will yield sufficient dividends and interest to handle the annuity payments for the creator. Tax results: (1) no gift tax, as the individual's annuity is for him or her and not given away, and the interest of charity, while a gift, merits a gift tax charitable deduction. (2) At creation of the trust, the individual is entitled to an income tax charitable deduction for the value (determined actuarially) for charity's interest. But when appreciated assets are used by the creator to start the trust, the alternative minimum tax (AMT) will counteract that deduction. (3) The sale by the trustee of the appreciated assets, if not done precipitously after the trust is created, is not taxed to the creator or the trust. (4) At the creator's death, there will be no estate tax because the assets are passing to charity. While the tax results are favorable, and the creator will receive lifetime payments, bear in mind that at his or her death the assets will pass away from the family.

Classic marital deduction trust: surviving spouse is entitled to all income for life and has right to dispose of trust assets in favor of anyone

Common-law states: states not having community property regimes

Community property: a system of property rights that prevails for married couples in Louisiana, Texas, New Mexico, Arizona, California, Washington, Idaho, and Nevada. Spanish law is the historical forerunner, with some French influence, especially in Louisiana. The law varies among those eight states. Generally, husband and wife are partners in property acquired during marriage, except property obtained by gift or inheritance, which is the separate property of the recipient. Separate property also includes what each spouse owned when the marriage started. At death, a spouse can only dispose of his or her one-half share of the community property.

Contemplation-of-death rule: you must live three years after transferring insurance to keep it out of your estate

***Crummey* power:** ability of beneficiary of trust to withdraw annual exclusion amount in year in which gift to trust occurred (named after party to lawsuit that established power)

Decedent: person who has died

Deferral: delaying payment of tax until a later event

Deferred compensation: arrangements for deferred compensation can take many forms. For example, assume Julian makes a five-year employment contract with Blink Corp. under which he will serve as chief financial officer at an annual salary of $100,000. In addition, Julian will accumulate the right to receive, beginning at age sixty-five, payments from Blink Corp. of $35,000 for each year of his employment. Those payments will be made over three years. Julian has deferred until the future his right to $35,000 annually. He is not currently taxed on the $35,000, if the contract is properly written. If Blink Corp. does not actually put aside money for the payments, it is an unfunded plan. Either way, Julian pays income on the funds paid out at sixty-five and after, as and when he receives the money.

Defined-benefit pension plan: pays contractually set amount to retiree

Defined-contribution pension plan: pays whatever amount the contractually set contributions produce

Devise: provision in Will passing real property

Disclaiming: renouncing a legacy; a key part of what is known as postmortem estate planning

Discounts for minority interests: relates to valuation for gift tax and estate tax purposes. When a person owns less than a 50 percent interest in a corporation or partnership or investment, and majority control lies elsewhere, the issue is whether a markdown (discount) in valuing the person's interest is appropriate in valuing the interest for gift tax and estate tax purposes. The reasons are that the holder of the minority interest is not in a control position for managerial purposes when decisions are made about distributing profits and other benefits to the investors, and that anyone who would buy the minority interest will pay a price that reflects that powerless position. In contrast, the majority owner could probably obtain a premium in valuing his or her interest, and that premium will be added in when valuing the majority interest for gift and estate tax purposes. The IRS likes premiums and doesn't like discounts. Its dislike for discounts is greatest when the control of the corporation or partnership or investment lies with the family of which the minority holder is a member. The size of discounts and premiums is a negotiable item.

Donor: person who makes gift

Estate: everything that a person owns; most commonly refers to everything that a person died owning

Estate remainder trust: a form of trust that can be used for the marital deduction. This is the only marital deduction trust that does not require that the trust income be paid to the surviving spouse. During the spouse's life, either (1) income can be paid to the spouse or accumulated as the trustee decides, or (2) income is accumulated. At the spouse's death, the principal is disposed of as part of the surviving spouse's estate. So, if he or she leaves a Will, the principal will be disposed of as that Will directs, giving the surviving spouse full control. Under technical property law rules, that disposition of the principal differs from the classic marital trust where the surviving spouse (in addition to being entitled to all the income for life) has a power exercisable by his or her Will to dispose of the principal.

Family partnerships: these are partnerships in which at least one member of the family is active in management. Other family members, who also are partners may or may not be similarly active. For example, assume Delmore is a general partner of a partnership that owns and operates a floral business. Delmore's children, Joelle, age sixteen, and Katia, age fourteen, are limited partners. Their partnership interests were gifts by Delmore last year, and are held in custodian accounts under the Uniform Gifts to Minors Act in their state. Delmore draws a salary for running the business. The net profits are divided among the three partners: 60 percent for Delmore and 20 percent for each child. When Delmore transferred the partnership interests to his daughters, that was a gift for gift tax purposes. The income splitting will be respected by the government for income tax purposes if Delmore's salary is reasonable compensation for his services, and the income attributable to each daughter's capital in the business is not disproportionate in relation to their father's share of capital in the business.

Forced share: portion of estate of deceased spouse that must, under state law, be inherited by the surviving spouse

Freezing values: a strategy to prevent the value of an asset from getting larger, thereby increasing the person's prospective estate. An essential component of the strategy would be to channel the growth to younger members of the family. Classic example: Aleksa owned all the common stock of a corporation that operated dry-cleaning establishments. Ten years ago she restructured the corporation and exchanged her common stock for 100 shares of new common stock and 500 shares of preferred stock. The preferred stock called for a dividend of 6 percent if and when declared by the board of directors, and if a dividend was skipped for any year it would not be made up in a later year. The preferred stock would be entitled to a payout of $1,000 per share if the business were liquidated and the corporation wound up. The common stock could not have a dividend in a year unless the preferred stock first had one. On liquidation and winding up, the common stock would be entitled to what was left after the preferred stock was paid off.

After the restructuring, Aleksa gave the new common stock to a trust for her grandson Graham. Her accountant advised her that the corporation had a net worth of $500,000. As the liquidation value of the preferred stock was the same (500 shares x $1,000), Aleksa took the position that all the value of the corporation was represented by the preferred stock she kept and that the new common stock which she put in the trust had no value for gift tax purposes. The future growth of the corporation would accrue to the new common stock. Aleksa's interest in the corporation would be "frozen" at a top value of $500,000.

The tax law has been changed since Aleksa did those things. Today the freeze opportunity has been curtailed considerably. In addition, the generation-skipping tax has been added to the law, to apply to gifts and bequests to grandchildren.

Grantor: person who sets up trust

GRATs and GRUTs: these are tax-advantaged trusts. Example of a GRAT: Heather creates a trust from which an unchanging annuity (say $15,000 a year) is payable to her for a specified period (say twelve years). When that period is over, the trust assets pass to Heather's children. Result: Heather makes a gift at the outset of her children's right to the trust assets when the period ends. The gift is determined under actuarial principles, with the size of the annuity and the period of payment major factors. The longer the period for payment to Heather, the smaller will be the gift. But if Heather dies during the payment period, her estate for estate tax purposes would include part, and maybe all, of the trust, depending on how much of the trust assets are required after death to pay the annuity. So Heather should pick a period that is highly likely to end before her death. An alternative is for Heather to have an annual payment, which changes from year to year if the value of the trust assets changes. Heather's payment would be equal to a specified percentage (say 6 percent) of the value of the trust assets redetermined each year (this is a GRUT). So if the value of the trust assets is higher in the second year, the payment in the second year is larger.

Guaranty: in estate planning, an undertaking by one person to pay the debt of another (either a person or a corporation or partnership) if that other fails to satisfy the debt. Example: Omar wants to borrow money from a bank, but because his resources and credit rating are not strong, his mother Corinna undertakes to pay off the loan if he fails to. In planning, this is a way to enable someone, such as a child, to have access to money for some purpose, such as starting a business, without requiring the person who gives the guaranty to make a gift.

Incidents of ownership: tax jargon for rights of ownership in, say, an insurance policy

Income: in the context of trusts, income is the cash flow from traditional assets held by the trust (*see* Principal). Commonly, it includes dividends, interest, and rent. In the case of some trust assets, such as oil and gas interests and copyrights, the state law may allocate some of the cash flow to income and some to principal. For example, a trust holds a copyright on a book. That copyright will run out eventually, for, under the law, the copyright will expire. If all the receipts from sales of the book were to be considered income, the expiration of the copyright would leave a vacancy in principal. By allocating some of the cash flow to principal, the law prevents the vacancy from occurring.

Individual retirement accounts (IRAs): tax-favored accounts to which people may contribute limited amounts

Intrafamily sales and leases: transactions within a family group. Example: Lonny owns a two-story building on Chestnut Street where he conducts a retail business. The business is incorporated. Lonny sells all of the stock to his daughter Marcy, who will run the business hereafter. Lonny leases the property to Marcy's corporation, which pays rent to Lonny. The rent will provide Lonny with an income that he used to take out of the business before the sale to Marcy. If the stock was not sold at full value, or if the rent is not what a stranger would charge, there would be gift tax problems. Most likely, no gift tax return will be filed. The government may come across the situation either at Lonny's death, or via Lonny's income tax returns that report the sale of the stock and the rental payments. If no gift tax return was filed, there is no time limit (called the statute of limitations) within which the government must act.

Joint tenants with right of survivorship: a form of ownership that can be used for personal property (securities or bank accounts) or for real property. There can be two or more joint owners, but in practice generally only two. The owners have to agree on all matters while both are living. But an owner can sever the arrangement and demand his or her portion or force a sale and obtain the value of it in dollars (partition). The rights of creditors of each joint owner are governed by state law, but generally a creditor can only step into the shoes of the debtor-joint participant. If the co-owners are spouses and divorce occurs, the divorce court generally can award the property to a spouse or divide it between the spouses. If the joint ownership continues until one of the owners dies, ownership of that one's interest automatically passes to the other co-owner or owners without a Will or in spite of what the Will says.

Keogh plans: retirement plans for the self-employed and partners (usually professionals)

Legacy: personal property left to someone by Will

Marital deduction: mechanism by which all estate and gift taxation on transfers between spouses is eliminated

Marital property: this category becomes important for people who live in community property states (Louisiana, Texas, New Mexico, Arizona, California, Washington, Idaho, and Nevada) and, in case of divorce, for residents of many other states. Marital property generally consists of property accumulated by a married couple after marriage, except for gifts and inheritances.

Medical expense exclusion: must be paid directly to facility or person providing service

Million-dollar exemption: protects that amount per donor (or $2 million with spouse's consent) from generation-skipping transfer tax

Net gift: a gift made on the agreed condition that the recipient will pay the gift tax. Example: Belinda owns all the stock of a business corporation, which she wishes to give to her son Derek. The business is worth about $1 million. Belinda's other assets, which are her home and cash, are worth about $500,000. Belinda wishes to conserve those other assets as an inheritance for her daughter Charlene. Belinda gives the stock of the business to Derek on the condition that he pays the gift tax. Tax results: (1) the amount of the gift is reduced by Derek's obligation for gift tax, a result that is arrived at via a formula. (2) If the amount of gift tax Derek pays exceeds Belinda's basis for the stock of the business, Belinda will be deemed to receive taxable income.

Noncitizen spouse: subject to limitations on tax-free gifts that may be received and restrictions on marital deduction for estate tax

Optional settlements: installment payments of insurance proceeds

Personal residence GRIT: this is a tax-favored plan involving an individual's personal residence, whether it be main residence or vacation place. The owner places the residence in a trust, and reserves the use of the residence for a specified number of years. When that period ends, the original owner of the residence ceases to have any rights, and the trust assets, including the residence, pass to others, such as children. The owner makes a gift at the outset equal to the right of the others to have the trust assets in the future. That right is actuarially determined. The longer the period during which the owner keeps the use of the residence, the smaller is the gift. But if the original owner of the residence dies during the reserved period, the residence will be part of his or her estate for estate tax purposes, and no tax advantage is gained. So the reserved period that is chosen should be one that is expected to expire before the owner does. Before the law was changed, a GRIT could be used with all kinds of property. Now it is pretty much confined to a personal residence.

Per stirpes: a form of inheritance; see pages 226–27

Postmortem estate planning: reshaping a decedent's estate by disclaimers and other means to achieve a preferred economic or tax position

Pourover Will: at person's death, moves his or her assets into previously established trust

Premarital agreement: contract, binding in many states, that can affect inheritance rights and other conditions of the marital relationship

Present-value calculations: determining what money to be paid in the future is worth today

Principal: in the trust context, the bundle of assets that are placed in the trust; the proceeds from sale of those assets, including profits and gains; the new investments made with those proceeds; and additions to the fund via further gifts. Principal may comprise stocks, bonds, United States Treasuries, cash items like certificates of deposit and money market accounts, real estate holdings of all kinds, oil and gas holdings of all kinds, and business interests (such as shares of stock in a corporation and limited and general partnership interests). Less often, principal may also include works of art; copyrights to books, plays, and music; patents to inventions; and rights under contracts and agreements of all kinds (such as the right to collect money for something the bestower had done).

Private annuity: plan by which one person transfers property to another in return for the transferee's promise to make annual payments to the transferring person for his or her life. Example: Marla, who is sixty, transfers her stock in the family business, worth about $300,000, to her son Evan, in return for his promise to pay her $30,000 each year for her life. Some of Maria's annual payment will be subject to income tax. None of the payments by Evan are deductible for income tax purposes. There are also gift tax and estate tax issues to be resolved. The family's hope is that the stock will not be subject to estate tax at Marla's death. That is one of the open estate tax issues.

Remainder persons: once called remaindermen, these are the people who receive the principal of a trust after the income-paying stage is past

Rollover: moving lump-sum retirement payment into an IRA

S corporations: special entities under Internal Revenue Code (subpart S) that pass income and losses to shareholders without paying tax at corporate level

Separate property: becomes important for people who live in community property states (Louisiana, Texas, New Mexico, Arizona, California, Washington, Idaho, and Nevada) and, in case of divorce, for residents of many other states. Separate property generally consists of property that each spouse brought into the marriage, and gifts and inheritances received after the marriage.

Split-dollar life insurance: an arrangement to pay life insurance premiums at favorable gift tax cost. Example: Melody is employed by a corporation and is a minority shareholder. (For estate tax purposes it is important that she not be a majority shareholder.) A trust for her children takes out insurance on her life. The corporation advances money to pay the premiums. That is considered a gift by Melody to the extent of her "economic benefit," which is measured in alternative ways, each of them being far less than the amount of the premium. Melody also pays income tax on that economic benefit. When Melody dies, the corporation is reimbursed for its outlay, without interest, from the insurance proceeds. The trust collects the balance. From Melody's perspective, it is preferable if the corporation is an S corporation, not a C corporation, as that will avoid further taxable income for Melody. If the plan is handled correctly, the insurance will not be taxed at Melody's death.

Spray trust: one in which trustee has discretion to sprinkle benefits on beneficiaries

Sprinkling trust: same as spray trust

Stepped-up basis: assumption in an inflationary economy that the figure used as cost on inheritance will be higher than the cost of an asset when it was earlier purchased

Stock redemptions: a purchase by a corporation of stock owned by a shareholder. Example: Noreen and Jillian own all the stock of Blast, Inc. Under an agreement made by the women with each other and the corporation, when a shareholder dies the corporation will buy the stock of that person, leaving the survivor as the sole remaining shareholder. The purchase by Blast, Inc. of Noreen's stock at her death is a stock redemption.

Survivor annuities: arrangements for payments to a person after someone dies. Example: Dirk and Rick are business partners. They have an agreement that calls for payments from the business to either one's widow when one of the partners dies. The government will assert that the value of those payments is part of the dead partner's estate for estate tax purposes.

Tenancy by the entirety: exists in only some states. It is a form of combined ownership by spouses, and generally applies only to real estate. The owners have to agree on all matters while both are living. Neither one, acting alone, can sever his or her interest, so that without unanimity to end it, the co-ownership will continue throughout marriage until a spouse dies. In case of divorce, the court generally can direct division of the property or award it to one spouse. If the couple remains married, at a death the interest of the decedent will automatically pass to the surviving spouse, without a Will or in spite of what the decedent's Will may say.

Testator: person who draws Will

Time value of money: concept that a dollar today is worth more than, say, $1.05 a year from now; in this context, idea that money saved by deferring taxes can be invested until they're due

Transfer-for-value rule: relates to life insurance. The normal rule is that life insurance proceeds are collected by the beneficiary named in the policy free of income tax. But that is not always the case when ownership of the policy was transferred, before the insured died, for cash or something else of value. Example: Darryl is insured under a policy that is owned by his wife Geena. They are being divorced. As part of the divorce settlement, a trust for their children will buy the policy from Geena for an amount equal to the cash value of the policy. That transfer falls under the transfer-for-value rule. On Darryl's death, the trust's gross income will include the proceeds of the policy minus the cash paid to Geena plus the premiums paid by the trust after it bought the policy.

True objects of bounty: people who in so-called normal situations the bestower ordinarily would be concerned about and provide for. The group would include the bestower's spouse, children, grandchildren, and, if resources permitted, parents and siblings. If the primary members of the group, who are spouse and children, are not provided for significantly or at all, the bestower's Will plan may be open to attack by those bypassed persons. The plan may be particularly vulnerable if the plan is largely for the benefit of a girl friend or boy friend, or someone who seems to have been in position to influence or control the bestower. Whether the attack succeeds will depend on the facts and circumstances about the plan and how it come to be, including medical and psychiatric evidence about the bestower, the tenacity of the contestants, and the ability of each side to finance the contest.

Trust: splitting ownership of property into two parts (legal title and benefits of ownership) and vesting each part in a different person

Trustees: holders of the legal title to property in trust

Trust terminating at age twenty-one: alternative to permit putting annual exclusion amount in trust

Trust with window for termination at age twenty-one: alternative to permit putting annual exclusion amount in trust

Tuition exclusion: does not include room, board, books, and the like

Unified credit: reduction of $192,800 in the tax paid on gifts and the estate (equivalent to reducing taxable gifts and estate by $600,000)

Uniform Gifts to Minors Act (UGMA): widely adopted state legislation providing for custodianship and a vehicle akin to a trust to protect assets during minority

Uniform Transfers to Minors Act (UTMA): successor legislation, similar in content, to UGMA

Will: document executed with certain formalities to dispose of a person's estate upon his or her death

Index